The
Garland Library
of
War and Peace

The
Garland Library
of
War and Peace

Under the General Editorship of
Blanche Wiesen Cook, *John Jay College, C.U.N.Y.*
Sandi E. Cooper, *Richmond College, C.U.N.Y.*
Charles Chatfield, *Wittenberg University*

New Wars for Old

by
John Haynes Holmes

with a new introduction
for the Garland Edition by
Charles Chatfield

Garland Publishing, Inc., New York & London
1971

Library of Congress Cataloging in Publication Data

Holmes, John Haynes, 1879-1964.
    New wars for old.

    (The Garland library of war and peace)
    Reprint of the 1916 ed.
    1. War. 2. Peace. 3. Evil, Non-resistance to.
I. Title. II. Series.
JX1952.H7 1972   327'.172   71-147623
ISBN 0-8240-0398-5

Introduction

John Haynes Holmes appeared in many roles throughout his life (1879-1964): as pastor of the Community Church of New York (until 1919 the Church of the Messiah, Unitarian) from 1907 to 1949; as an apostle of the social gospel tradition and of ecumenicism; as an advocate in the cause of civil liberties through the American Civil Liberties Union (of which he was a charter member and chairman of the board from 1939 to 1949); as a founder and long an officer of the N.A.A.C.P.; and as an exponent of pacifism. In New Wars for Old Holmes defined pacifism in relation to the opening phase of World War I. He delivered the sermons and addresses from which the book was drawn when many Americans were choosing sides in the European conflict. Peace organizations were riven and individual peace advocates were torn by difficult questions.

"Is it ethically possible to stand against war once one's nation is fighting for survival?" they asked. Numerous pacifists in England thought so, and they banded together in groups such as the Union for Democratic Control, the No-Conscription Fellowship, and the religious Fellowship of Reconciliation. Some of them became catalysts for the formation of an American Fellowship of Reconciliation ten days after

INTRODUCTION

Holmes signed the preface to this book. Within a month he had joined the small new group. Most of its members had been active in social work or progressive reform or were clericals in the social gospel tradition. As the nation supported the war with mounting intensity, the companionship of men and women whose social passion was arrayed against it became ever more important to Holmes.

"Should the United States stand aside once England and France were threatened with defeat, and should it abrogate its own privileges?" peace advocates asked. Many of them thought not and began their swing toward the defense of this specific war effort. Others urged the Wilson administration to exert vigorous national leadership and even plied their private influence for a neutral commission to mediate between the belligerents. This became the major program of the Woman's Peace Party in 1915-16. Meanwhile, a succession of organizations culminating in the American Union Against Militarism (A.U.A.M.) was building resistance to preparedness policy, arguing that the United States should not create a military capacity with which it might presume to sway the European power struggle. John Haynes Holmes was active in the A.U.A.M., associating there with social workers, professionals, and reformers whom he counted as friends.

The peace movement in America was in the process of realigning over these two related questions when Holmes wrote New Wars for Old. *In the book he*

6

sought terms upon which absolute pacifism might be fused with progressive reform. His effort was timely, and the book went through thirteen editions and reprints in as many months, according to his later recollection.[1]

The war, certainly American participation in it, simply was not justifiable, he insisted, and Allied victory would neither preserve peace nor advance civilization. In this respect he identified himself with an "international mind," a dissenting minority of sensitive men and women opposed to the war from various nations — Karl Liebknecht of Germany, for example, Romain Rolland of France, Rosika Schwimmer of Hungary, Norman Angell and Bertrand Russell of England, Jane Addams and Emily Balch, Rufus Jones and Walter Rauschenbusch, Norman Thomas and Eugene V. Debs, among others in the United States.

These men and women distributed the responsibility for the war among all the nations embroiled in it. Also, they distinguished between the motives of the governments and those of the peoples universally fighting in the spirit of idealism. Self-sacrifice and devotion, no less that national aggrandizement, were entrenched on both sides. Those who shared the "international mind" were not neutral in the struggle for human dignity and justice. They were passionate humanitarians. But they denied that the essential

[1] *Holmes, I Speak for Myself (New York: Harper & Bros., 1959), pp. 115, 166.*

causes of mankind were defined by the blood-stained boundaries drawn across Europe. The New York pastor's contribution to their literature was to re-assess the traditional doctrine of non-resistance in the light of modern war, and to link it to the case for American neutrality.

Holmes argued that because of war's ironic and tragic nature peace and liberty would be drawn into the undertow of violence. The irony of war as a social phenomenon was that "through its very effectiveness, it propagates itself." The more noble war seems the more it fastens itself on honorable men: "Just because we have fought to end war, we will in spite of ourselves have consecrated and thus perpetuated the traditions of fighting."² That was true enough, no doubt, but Holmes's assertion had the ring of a debater's case in which the opponent's strongest point is simply inverted. Holmes had proven himself to be an expert debater. But he was a minister too, and in his sermons and writings this logical irony of war was subordinated to its real tragedy, the fallacy to which he referred in New Wars for Old: the most idealistic reliance on force invariably creates opposing force and ends in violence. The logic of force is that it can defend and liberate men, but the fallacy of force is that it actually brings conflict and is the concomitant of tyranny, Holmes declared. As long as war is present in its latent, legitimized form it will period-*

²*Holmes,* The Spiritual Conditions of an Enduring Peace *(New York: Church of the Messiah (n.d. [1918-1919]), p. 10.*

8

ically flood the lands.

The first condition of lasting peace is, therefore, not military victory but, rather, "the total abolition of war ... war in preparation as well as in explosion."[3] The martial trappings and symbols must go. Foreign policy based on fear must be replaced. The notion that war may be a good and justifiable thing must be dispelled. Men must learn that the means determines the end. They must find alternatives to fighting.

A minister of the social gospel, predominantly socialistic in his thought, John Haynes Holmes insisted that men are obligated to resist social injustice. That was the steadfast message that fired many with whom he associated in and outside of the church throughout his life. He had been instrumental in creating the Unitarian Fellowship for Social Justice in 1908, and four years later he interpreted the cause of social justice as The Revolutionary Function of the Modern Church. *The coming of war forced him to wrestle with the problem of dealing with injustice and aggression without resorting to violence, and Holmes re-evaluated non-resistance in this light.*

The term "non-resistance" plainly troubled him because of its negative, passive connotations. He could find no historical substitute for it, however. He identified its principal components as passive resistance (example), love, and rational persuasion, and he

[3] *Holmes,* The Price of Peace: Are We Willing to Pay It? *(New York: Church of the Messiah (n.d. [1919]), p. 11.*

argued for the social effectiveness of each. He distrusted any form of coercion, any manipulation of power. But he invited precisely those considerations of relative political power by his attention to the utility (as well as the ultimate truth) of historical non-resistance. In a measure he prepared the way for the modern idiom of nonviolent action by stretching the traditional label to fit new categories of value, particularly social utility in the service of brotherhood and democracy.

He argued the case for non-resistance logically, on the grounds that the means determine the ends of action; but he advanced it historically also, surveying the tradition established by some modern Socialists, by Quakers, Waldenses, Franciscans, early Christians, and others in order to show the long continuity of a minority dissenting from war. That these groups were in the minority was reason enough for Holmes to be attracted to them: "I seemed to know where I belonged, and always this seemed to be with the minority," he reflected toward the end of his life.[4] But it was even more important that in some cases the determined spirit or persuasive voice of the minority had prevailed, that they had practiced the political ethics of non-resistance, that their examples so often had made a mockery of the ethical claims of superior powers. Those historic examples of people without power asserting their political rights and spiritual tenets fired Holmes with hope in 1915 and

[4] I Speak for Myself, *p. 31.*

formed the transition from sectarian ideals to national policy in his book.

He wrote, in effect, that the United States had the opportunity to maintain an island of brotherhood and democracy in a sea of hate and arbitrary power. The promise of American life was to fulfill the role of the prophetic minority in the world and to conquer Europe, when war should have reduced it to helplessness, with the power of ideals and political system, brotherhood and democracy. The United States in the flush of a progressive era might substitute new crusades against disease and natural catastrophe, against injustice and inequality, for the old wars of man against man.

It was a euphoric vision. It lifted the fondest hopes of progressivism to an international plane. The title itself was an extension of William James's exploratory essay, "The Moral Equivalent of War."[5] Holmes's book mirrored the progressive's confidence in an open-ended universe and his apprehension that the United States might be plunged into the closed system represented by war. It reflected the attempt of a minister of the social gospel to reconcile the absolute claims of love and peace with the contingencies and brute conflicts of history. It carried the force of the modern rejection of the authority of tradition, together with the frustrating search for reliable principles of experience. In these respects

[5] *James's essay was published in* McClure's Magazine, XXXV *(August, 1910), pp. 463-68, and has been widely reprinted.*

11

INTRODUCTION

New Wars for Old *was a statement of faith rather than a solution of dilemma, and it was a period piece.*

It was also a portent of the future. In clear, forceful language Holmes dispelled many then prevalent arguments for the efficacy of warfare. He anticipated the requirement of pacifism in the modern world for a form of non-resistance that would be socially redemptive. He wrote something of a prescription for Gandhi, and when he learned of the Indian leader soon afterwards he became an American disciple, and president of the All World Gandhi Fellowship. Holmes remained active in the Fellowship of Reconciliation; it played in some respects the role of an organized church in his life. It was his denomination at least figuratively. It provided companionship again in World War II when Holmes kept his original faith despite the anguish of being isolated once more from the path taken by most men of good will.

This book represented an essentially personal experience. Here John Haynes Holmes came to terms with himself on the war question. That, in turn, was the critical test of the social pilosophy which had flowered in his generation, and so New Wars for Old *is a useful document in our social history as well as an important event in the development of modern pacifism and in the life of its author.*

When, in April, 1917, Holmes sought solitude in which to frame his response to American intervention, he went to Cambridge with the arguments settled in his mind. He did not debate the merits of the case as he sat alone or paced the length of his room. He waited for some inner assurance of courage and for clarity of mind. On the very eve of national commitment he returned to his New York lectern and laid before his congregation the concerns that leadened his heart. "The pew is always entitled to the full confession of the pulpit," he said, "but never so urgently as at the time when such confession touches the deep issues of life and death."[6]

The minister briefly reviewed his position, developed at length in his book, that war is never justifiable, that in its hate and death and destruction it is the antithesis of Christian living. The impending crusade was especially wrong, he judged:

> *Our participation in the war, . . . like the war itself, is political and economic, not ethical, in its character. Any honor, dignity, or beauty which there may be in our impending action, is to be found in the impulses, pure and undefiled, which are actuating many patriotic hearts to-day, and not at all in the real facts of the situation. The war itself is wrong. Its prosecution will be a crime. . . . I question the sincerity of no man who supports this war — I salute the devotion of every man who proposes to sustain it with his money or his blood. But I say to you that when, years hence, the whole of this story has been told, it will be found that we have been tragically deceived, and all our sacrifices have been*

[6] *Holmes*, A Statement to My People on the Eve of War *(New York: Church of the Messiah, 1917), p. 4.*

13

made in vain.[7]

The God-appointed task of America, he said, had been to "discover terms of reconciliation, to work out methods of cooperation, to soften hate and dispell suspicion, to spread abroad sweet influences of confidence and healing — this is a task as beneficent as it is prodigious."[8] But his country seemed to him to have cast aside her historic trust. Against the clash of arms her pacific ideals would scarcely be heard even within her own borders. Outraged, he declined to abandon her. His duty was to defend the national ideals which war would debase, those very things which men were fighting abroad to preserve — democracy, brotherhood, and international concord.

He wished to continue in his pastorate, to bless and honor the men who would go to war as well as those who would not, and like them all to "have obeyed his conscience and thus performed his whole duty as a man."[9] He did not ask the members of his congregation to disavow their nation's part in arms. But he earnestly hoped that they would preserve in their church a sanctuary from the conflict.

Holmes kept his ministry throughout the war. He labored for the preservation of civil liberties, and at the battle's end his voice was heard urging the nations to pay the price in self-denial demanded for lasting

[7] Ibid., p. 9.

[8] Ibid., p. 15.

[9] Ibid., p. 11.

INTRODUCTION

peace. He stamped his book with the force of personal example and in this way strengthened the conception of moral alternatives to war which would enlist the services of men and women disillusioned with the Great Crusade.

Charles Chatfield
Department of History
Wittenberg University

NEW WARS FOR OLD

NEW WARS FOR OLD

Being a Statement of Radical Pacifism in terms of Force
versus Non-Resistance, with special reference to
the Facts and Problems of the Great War

BY

JOHN HAYNES HOLMES

NEW YORK
DODD, MEAD AND COMPANY
1916

TO

STEPHEN S. WISE

AND

FRANK OLIVER HALL

The one a Rabbi who perpetuates the prophetic
tradition of Israel

The other a Minister who perpetuates the apostolic
tradition of Christianity

Both wise teachers and brave exemplars of the
religion of Brotherhood

This Book is humbly Dedicated

PREFACE

I

WHEN the Great War burst upon the world in August 1914, it was natural that affrighted and outraged men should regard this disaster as a final demonstration of the failure of Judaism, Christianity, the organised peace propaganda, and international socialism. The tradition of Israel reaches back to a period antedating the advent of Christianity by more than seven centuries; the gospel of love, associated with the name of Jesus, has been known to humanity for nearly two thousand years; the peace movement, led by able and distinguished men, backed by abundant resources, well-organised and persistently aggressive, has had three generations to impress its doctrines upon the modern mind; and during the last half-century or so, we have seen a massing of the forces of labour, in all countries, under the banner of socialism, which seemed to constitute a sure protection against war. And yet, when the crisis came, no one of these great forces proved of any avail. The tide of conflict swept across Europe, Asia, Africa, and the seven seas as swiftly and terribly as though no bulwarks had ever been raised against it. What wonder that men in their disappointment and fear, declared religion a failure, the peace movement a farce, and socialism an arrant sham!

That this indictment is rightly to be levelled against Jews and Christians, pacifists and socialists, is to my mind undeniable. Never has humanity been called upon to witness a more tragic spectacle than that of the millions of Germans, Austrians, French, Russians, English — all of them pledged in one way or another to the cause of peace — marching away to the battlefront, at the first sound of alarm, not only without protest, but with enthusiasm. There were some Jews and Christians, we may well believe, who revolted inwardly, if not outwardly, against the call to arms; there were some peace advocates, we know, who were distraught and ashamed; the attempt of the socialists, before the declarations of war were made, to stay the flood of madness then threatening the race, stands out as one of the few glorious episodes of the dreadful days of July and August, 1914. But that, when the actual moment of dread decision came, these millions of religionists, pacifists, internationalists, abandoned their spiritual professions and clung to patriotism as the one sure passion of their souls, is a sober fact. Everywhere they gave way at the very moment when, if ever, they should have stood fast, and thus failed!

That this failure of individuals, however, involves any failure of the various churches or movements, to which these individuals had pledged allegiance, is, to my mind, the unfairest of charges. Judaism, Christianity, the peace propaganda, socialism, a failure? When, let me

ask, has the world ever put into practical effect, in the
form of laws and social institutions, the moral principles
of Judaism or the spiritual ideals of Christianity?
Where is there a government which has heeded even the
simplest of the recommendations of the modern peace
movement, and placed any genuine pacifist in a position of political responsibility? To what extent has society, in any of its many fields of activity, ordered its relations upon the basis of out-and-out socialism?
Christianity, pacifism, socialism — when and where and
how have these had any chance? All have been professed, but not one has been practised. Lip-service is
the uttermost of reverence which ever has been paid to
them. Other forces, of a wholly different character,
have controlled the movements and fashioned the organisations of society — and these forces it is which have
led us to the horror of the present cataclysm of universal disaster. Monarchical governments, founded
upon superstitions of divine right, secret diplomacies
which make falsehood a virtue and identify statesmanship with deceit, balances of power determined by
immoral rivalries for world empire and dominion, an
economic system based upon exploitation of labour at
home and consumers abroad, vast armaments of war
reared on the specious pretence of maintaining peace,
the barbaric idea of force as the safeguard of security —

> " The heathen heart that puts its trust
> In reeking tube and iron shard,
> All valiant dust that builds on dust,
> And guarding calls not Thee to guard "—

these have failed! But not those great movements of brotherhood, goodwill, co-operation, which have preached their message to ears that would not hear, and knocked for admittance at portals that would not open. This hour marks perhaps the hour of darkest failure in all of human history. But it is the failure not of Christianity but of civilised barbarism, not of Christ but of Cæsar, not of love but of blood and iron!

II

And yet it is in this hour of universal ruin, that the gospel of force is being preached with a vigour which has never been known before! On every side we are being told that, in the world of men as in the world of beasts, there is no security save " in tooth and claw." Books and pamphlets are pouring from the presses in an endless flood, to warn us of the perils of " defenselessness," by which is meant a reliance upon international goodwill which scorns the mailed fist and the clashing sword, and the need of " preparation," by which is meant arming ourselves to the teeth against our neighbours. We have even been called upon to witness, during the last few months, the spectacle of a group of men, gathered self-consciously in Independence Hall, in the brave attempt to organise a movement for the establishment of *peace by force!* Obsessed with the idea that the security of the world is threatened by one nation, namely Germany, and that peace can be secured by the destruction of one militaristic machine, namely the German army, we forget that militarism, in

its various political and economic aspects, is inwrought
in the very fibre of our entire western civilisation, and
finds embodiment not merely in one army of one nation,
but in all those vast armaments on land and sea which
characterise every great power of the modern world.
Nay worse — we forget that, in attempting to destroy
Germany and to protect ourselves by force against
the menace that Germany represents, we are ourselves
taking up her weapons, reproducing her system, doing
her work.   So that humanity actually finds itself face
to face with the very excellent probability that German
arms, in due course, will be destroyed, but that, by
the very process of victory, the German spirit will find
itself triumphant in France, England, Russia, America.
Kluck, Hindenberg, Mackensen, destroyed — but Nietzsche, Treitschke, Bernhardi, world-conquerors!

It is this situation which makes imperative an unfaltering reaffirmation of the true gospel of peace,
which is none other than the gospel of righteousness
preached by Isaiah, the gospel of love proclaimed by
Jesus, the gospel of goodwill maintained by all the pacifists of the ages, the gospel of democracy and co-operation set forth by socialists everywhere — in one word,
the gospel of non-resistance!   In the *sturm und drang*
of these terrific days, it is difficult for any one mind
to state this gospel with the poise and power which
should characterise its utterance.   The very haste made
necessary by the threatening aspects of the time, pre-
vents that careful and reverent treatment which the
theme rightfully demands.   But to get the word spoken

with some degree of clearness and persuasion at once, is the challenge of the hour to those who are convinced that "they that take the sword shall perish with the sword." My humble and yet passionate desire to do my part in meeting this challenge must be accepted as the explanation of this book. In preparing its pages, I have tried to do something more than produce one more discussion of the issue presented by the Great War. This conflict is, of course, the occasion, and very largely the determining condition, of all that I have tried to say. But my primary purpose has been to penetrate to the very heart of the dilemma suggested by my title, and open up, therefore, from the deepest moral and spiritual viewpoint, the basic questions of peace, security, and the law of life itself. This line of thought has made it necessary for me to discuss, in the course of my main argument, relations between individuals even more than relations between groups of individuals or nations. But the human problem is the same in both cases, and leads therefore to the same conclusion. That my attitude toward the present crisis may be unmistakable, however, and especially that my thesis may receive the startling illumination provided by the European conflagration, I have interpersed my discussion throughout with references to the Great War; and in my concluding chapters have considered such immediate questions as " Is War Ever Justifiable? " " Is Permanent and Universal Peace to be Desired? " and " The Duty and Opportunity of America To-day."

III

It is important, if the argument presented in this book is to be read with sympathy, or even understood, that certain facts should be particularly noted in this place.

(1) First of all, let me give due warning against the unfortunate suggestions contained in the word, non-resistance. I have adopted this word, as the *motif* of my argument, so to speak, with the greatest reluctance, and only because, in spite of diligent search, I have been able to find no word in our English language which was not even more inadequate and inaccurate than this very misleading term. Let me state at once, however, and with all possible emphasis, that, in using the word, non-resistance, I accept none of those unfortunate and immoral implications of acquiescence, cowardice, feebleness, which the word seems inevitably to suggest. Non-resistance, as I have set forth at great length in my chapters on "What Non-Resistance Means" and "Exemplars of Non-Resistance," means to me an essentially positive and indeed aggressive state of mind and attitude. The true non-resistant is militant — but he lifts his militancy from the plane of physical, to the plane of moral and spiritual force. This point I regard as so important to a true understanding of my argument, that I am almost tempted to advise that Chapters IV, V, and VI be read before any of the rest of the book is approached. This much at least I will venture to ask — that no reader reject the book until these chapters have been perused.

(2) Secondly, I would point out that my argument is, from beginning to end, almost wholly one of expediency. I have thus couched my lance, if I may so express it, not because I am indifferent to the idealism involved in my plea. On the contrary, I believe that the law of love should be obeyed even though it lea always to death, as it did in the case of Jesus. I tal. it for granted, however, that this idealistic part of m argument needs no advocacy. Everybody agrees tha the counsel of the spirit is right, but the question remains, Will it work? Men balk because they are certain that this gospel will not stand the pragmatic test. Just here, in this matter of workableness, is the " rub "; and just here, therefore, have I focussed my discussion. From this point of view, my thesis may be said to stand or fall, according as the arguments in Chapters III and VII prove convincing or unconvincing.

(3) Lastly, I would point out that I have made no attempt to discuss the economic aspects of the problem of war. As a member of the Society for Eliminating the Economic Causes of War, and as one who is predominantly socialistic in his thought, I am convinced that war can never be abolished until the capitalistic system of domestic and foreign competitive exploitation is first abolished. But as a student of human history and of human nature, I am also convinced that war can never be abolished, even under a socialistic régime, until mankind is fronted right morally. These two questions are of equal importance. They can be discussed separately or together. For my purpose in this

book, I have chosen to separate them, and have deliberately chosen the latter for my discussion.   Economic
students, more competent than I, have discussed, and
will continue to discuss, the former.

IV

The material in this book has been used many times
during the past year, in sermons and addresses.   Three
of the chapters — namely, the eighth, ninth, and tenth
— have previously appeared as separate pamphlets, but
have here been corrected, revised, and amplified.   The
sections in Chapter V on Isaiah and Jesus have been
published as separate essays in " The Christian Regis-
ter " and " The North American Review " respectively.
The rest of the volume is published here for the first
time.

In closing, I beg to make acknowledgment of the
services of my Secretary, Miss Mary C. Baker, whose
patience, fidelity, and efficiency have been indispensable
in the writing of this book.

JOHN HAYNES HOLMES

Church of the Messiah,
New York City,
November 1, 1915.

TABLE OF CONTENTS

"War and peace resolve themselves into a mercury of the state of cultivation. At a certain stage of his progress, the man fights, if he be of a sound body and mind. At a certain higher stage, he makes no offensive demonstration, but is alert to repel injury, and of an unconquerable heart. At a still higher stage, he comes into the region of holiness; passion has passed from him; his warlike nature is all converted into an active medicinal principle; he sacrifices himself, and accepts with alacrity wearisome tasks of denial and charity; but being attacked, he bears it and turns the other cheek, as one engaged, throughout his being, no longer to the service of an individual, but to the common soul of all men."

Ralph Waldo Emerson, in *Lecture on War.*

CHAPTER I

INTRODUCTION
A STATEMENT OF THE PROBLEM

"The modern prophet, employing the methods of science, may again proclaim that the kingdom of heaven is at hand. . . . And what is this message of the modern prophet but pure Christianity? — not the mass of theological doctrine ingeniously piled up by Athanasius and Augustine, but the real and essential Christianity which came from the very lips of Jesus, 'Blessed are the meek, for they shall inherit the earth.' In the cruel strife of centuries has it not often seemed as if the earth were to be rather the prize of the hardest heart and the strongest fist? To many men these words of Christ have been as foolishness and as a stumbling-block, and the ethics of the Sermon on the Mount have been openly derided as too good for this world. . . . The Master knew full well that the time was not yet ripe. . . . But he preached nevertheless that gospel which is by and by to be realised by toiling Humanity, and he announced ethical principles fit for the time that is coming. The great originality of his teaching, and the feature that has chiefly given it power in the world, lay in the distinctness with which he conceived a state of society from which every vestige of strife, and the modes of behaviour adapted to ages of strife, shall be utterly and forever swept away. . . . The future is lighted for us with the radiant colours of hope. . . ‡ Strife and sorrow shall disappear. Peace and love shall reign supreme."— John Fiske, in *The Destiny of Man.*

CHAPTER I

I

THAT the present age constitutes the most fateful period of time " the world has seen since the records of mankind began to be kept," was asserted by a competent student of public affairs as long ago as August, 1914. To many of us this assertion seemed exaggerated, even though the week which saw Germany's declaration of war against Russia, France's declaration of war against Germany, and at last, after days of heartbreaking suspense, England's launching of great ships into the storm of conflict, was the most thrilling and terrible that we had ever experienced. As the dreadful struggle has gone on, however, from month to month, dragging in nation after nation, extending to every one of the six continents and seven seas of the globe, and piling up such a toll of shattered cities, wasted fields, exhausted wealth, pain, death, misery, as baffles computation, it has become evident enough that humanity has never in all its history beheld such a spectacle or faced such a crisis. There have been universal wars before this. The decline and fall of the Roman Empire in the fourth and fifth centuries, the great struggles for imperial dominion in the Middle Ages, the campaigns of

3

Napoleon in the twenty years following the Revolution — all these were cataclysms which engulfed mankind in ruin and despair. But no one of them is in any way comparable to our own War of the Nations. Never before have so many highly organised peoples been involved in life-and-death struggle — never before have whole nations been martialled in arms for combat — never before have the lines of battle been so extended, and the number of soldiers engaged so prodigious — never before have such mighty weapons been at the disposal of contending armies — never before have such stupendous forces been let loose upon the world. Already there has been a refinement of efficiency, a thoroughness of destruction, a ruthlessness of attack, a frightfulness of slaughter which has staggered the race. And we are as yet only in the early stages of a combat which must witness prodigies of horror, hitherto unimagined as well as unknown, before the end of the ghastly business is reached! What this end will be, no man at the present moment can dare even so much as to surmise. That it will involve the fall of dynasties, the exhaustion of nations, the wastage of vast stretches of territory, the indefinite enslavement of future generations to debts of incalculable proportions, the permanent reversion of great peoples in wealth, activity, ambition, physical strength, moral standards, is reasonably certain. That it will mean the tumbling of our entire economic system, the extinction of whole areas of modern civilisation, the return of Europe to the condition of Germany in the years following the Thirty Years' War,

when bands of brigands roved unmolested through silent
wastes once crowded with fair cities and waving fields,
even the sweeping destruction of the modern world by
the terrific power of the engines of its own creation, as
Mr. H. G. Wells has not hesitated to suggest,[1] seems
not impossible. For the first time since the pyramids
were builded in the Egyptian deserts, men find themselves living in an age, and looking upon a situation,
wherein the forces of human life have passed beyond the
control of those who have madly created them and as
madly set them free! For the first time, perhaps, in
history, anything may happen!

II

Not yet, however, in speaking of battles and campaigns, wasted wealth and slaughtered men, have we
reached the heart of the situation which constitutes this
war the supreme crisis of the ages. Nor can this be
done by considering such isolated and comparatively
unimportant matters as the various military, political
and industrial phases of the struggle. In order to see
and understand in all its seriousness the exact nature of
the present crisis, we must pass beyond the particular
aspects of the phenomenon and come to the phenomenon
itself — or rather we must gather together all these
different aspects into a single synthesis, and thus discover what is the single great problem which is involved.
And this process will hardly be begun, before it will
become evident that the present problem in its essence

[1] See his *Social Forces in England and America,* page 383.

is none other than that most fundamental of all problems — the nature of human existence, the law of human life, the rule of human conduct.

For generations, indeed centuries, in the past, man has been moving forward slowly but surely to the great goal of a permanent civilisation, based upon the ideas of reason, righteousness, and good will. Again and again has progress toward this end been halted by accident, retarded by fear, turned aside or thrown back by ignorance, stupidity, and sin. Sooner or later, however, the pathway has been rediscovered, the momentum of advance resumed, and the line of progress therefore continued. Especially in recent times has this progress, to all appearances at least, been rapid and permanent. The mind of the world in the opening years of the twentieth century was most emphatically an optimistic mind. It beheld serious obstacles being overcome, knotty problems being solved, remote ideals being realised. It seemed to see humanity, after centuries of wandering in the wilderness, now nearing the borders of the promised land. Long a barbarian, man had spoken as a barbarian, thought as a barbarian, understood as a barbarian; but now, if the signs were valid, man was becoming civilised, and lo, with his attainment to civilisation, he was resolutely putting away barbarous things.

Even in what had long seemed to be the most discouraging of all fields — that of international and interracial relationships — was sure progress apparently being made at this time. To an almost astonishing degree were the long-sought ideas of reason, righteousness and goodwill taking form in definite institutions of order and fraternity. Two Hague Conferences had consummated the great achievement of assembling " all the world in one room," as Dr. Frederick Lynch has vividly expressed it.[1] The Hague Court had been successfully established as a kind of supreme court among the nations. Numerous treaties of arbitration between great states had been signed, thus blazing a pathway through the tangled wilderness of barbarism to " the pleasant places " of understanding, sympathy and co-operation. International societies of every possible description had been organised, and were year by year bringing into ever closer personal communication and fellowship the best minds of every country. Great international movements, such as socialism, woman suffrage, universal religion, and the peace propaganda itself, were more and more tending to obliterate the artificial boundaries of nations, and thus to unite people upon a basis not of geographical accident, but of those sublime interests of human good which from their very nature transcend all distinctions of language, creed, nationality and race. In spite of blind and selfish statesmanship, which still remained faithful to ancient precedent in fostering national pride, in serving so-called national interests in various quarters of the world, in organising immoral alliances and ententes and balances of power which had no higher object than that of placing one group of nations in unfriendly array

[1] See his *The Peace Problem,* page 15.

against another, and especially in building stupendous armaments on the specious plea that such preparations for war are the only guarantee of peace — in spite of these facts, most forward-looking persons had come to believe that, so numerous and powerful were the forces making for peace, the old perpetual menace of international conflict had at last passed by forever. For the first time in the history of the world, it seemed as though we were beginning to realise outwardly the inward truth of St. Paul's great dictum —" God hath made of one blood all nations of men, for to dwell together on the face of the earth." For the first time, it seemed as though Jesus's definition of love as the law of life were going to be vindicated.

And then, in the space of a single night, as it were, came the crash of ruin! Without warning of any kind, the whole fair structure of our hopes and dreams came tumbling to the ground. Confident that we were at last civilised, we awakened, as in the clutch of an earthquake, to discover that we were still barbarians. Believing that, after two thousand years of effort, Christianity was at last imposing its divine law of brotherhood upon the human heart, we were made to behold that we were still, like any tiger of the jungle, " red in tooth and claw with ravin." Trusting in the conserving influences of education, industry, religion, and the modern movements of international association, we found ourselves hurled back into the early horror of sheer brute struggle for survival. In an instant, the realm of dreams was gone, and we were face to face

with the hard, cold, bitter facts of a world which we
thought had been conquered and subdued. In one fell
moment, hope was shattered, faith destroyed, courage
lost. A hundred ancient doubts rose up to plague us.
A thousand primitive questions challenged us anew.
The original and basic problems of life, solved as we
had thought forever, were again before us for consideration. It was as though unnumbered æons of time
were instantaneously wiped out, and we were back in
the days of primeval chaos when " the earth was without form and void, and darkness was upon the face of
the deep," with no hope but that of a new day of creation, in some far distant time, when " the spirit of God
(would once again) move upon the face of the waters,"
light be again divided from darkness, and the dry ground
of unfolding life again appear from out the waters of
desolation.

III

Just here, now, in this reversion to first moral principles — in this sudden conjuring up, in more terrible
form than ever before, of problems which we thought
had been laid once for all — do we find the supreme
crisis, and tragedy as well, of this present hour. In
essence, these problems present but a single issue. Is
the flesh supreme, or may we still place reliance upon
the spirit? Must we put our trust in " chariots because they are many and horsemen because they are
strong," or may we still, with Isaiah, have confidence in
God alone? Is Bernhardi's doctrine, that " feeble-

ness is the unpardonable sin against the Holy Ghost "
established, or may we still believe, with Jesus, that
" the meek shall inherit the earth "?   In form, however, these problems are as various as the various relationships and activities of men.   Three at least are
of prime importance to us at this moment in our discussion of the general question of pacifism.

First of all, there is the perennial problem of the establishment of international peace.   The idea of a
permanent condition of concord among the different
peoples of the earth, is as old certainly as the annals of
recorded history, and may safely be thought to be as
old, perhaps, as humankind itself.   It appears in the
teachings of Confucius and Lao-Tse, which are among
the most ancient which have been preserved to the
modern world.   It flames in lines of fire from the writings of Isaiah and the sayings of Buddha.   It adorns
the pages of Thucydides as he tells the tale of ancient
Greece, and of Livy as he recounts the similar narrative
of Rome.   It is the inspiration of many of the noblest
passages in the *Annals* of Tacitus and the *Meditations*
of Marcus Aurelius.   It constitutes the warp and woof
of the fabric of Jesus's gospel; and marks predominantly the teaching and practice of all the early Christians from St. Paul to the last of the line of the so-
called Church Fathers.   It glorifies the Middle Ages
in such a phenomenon as the Truce of God, and in such
a person as the sainted Francis of Assisi.   It is a vital
part of the Reformation, as witness the steadfast testimony of Erasmus, the early and as yet uncorrupted

doctrines of Luther and Calvin, and especially the
radiant visions of George Fox. Taught in the seventeenth century in the name of a revealed religion, in
the eighteenth century in the name of an abstract humanity, in the nineteenth century in the name of a very
practical science, industry and commerce, this idea of
peace had become in our time the predominant ideal of
the hour.

It is interesting, as well as pathetic, to recall, in this
moment of dissolutionment, the extent to which this ideal
of international harmony and goodwill had seized upon
the imagination of the modern world. Only a few
months ago, and everybody was cherishing the hope that
this vision of peace, which had so long been so far removed upon the horizon of the future, was at last in
process of actual realisation. Militarists, with a few
exceptions like Lord Roberts, were pointing to the great
armaments of modern times and declaring that such
preparations for war were the surest guarantee of
peace. Scientists like the great Russian, Bloch, were
telling us that the armaments, with which all the great
nations of the world were so amply provided, had been
developed to a degree of such terrible efficiency, that
warfare between contending forces on land and sea had
been made to all intents and purposes impossible.
Economists like Norman Angell, were showing us, in
terms of trade, investments and finance generally, that
war in our age was as ruinous to the victor as to the
vanquished and was therefore already become an
anachronism to which kings and premiers could no

longer make resort. Jurists and statesmen of all
countries were rejoicing in the Hague Conferences, willingly referring matters of dispute to the Hague Court,
and competing with one another in the signing of
treaties of arbitration. Scholars were taking comfort
in the great international societies of learning, working-
men in the international labour movement, Christians in
the growing international consciousness and co-operation of the churches of many lands, peace lovers everywhere in the sweeping progress of the organised peace
propaganda. All the forces of the time — military,
political, commercial, educational, industrial, religious
— seemed to be moving straight toward the fulfilment
of the long-cherished dream of the prophets and seers.
The will to peace was already at hand — the way was
very rapidly being found. Then, as we have seen,
came the war which, from the first day of hostilities,
was fought on a scale and with a fury never known before. And instantly the problem of peace was reduced
to its simplest terms, as though we were living once
again in the days of Cain. Is there any such thing as
peace? Is not man a fighting animal and war therefore
a permanent contingency of man's existence? Did not
Frederick the Great state the final truth of the matter
when he said, in one of his numerous letters to his friend,
Voltaire, " I study the pages of history, and see that
wars have always broken out at a period of every ten
years. I believe that there will be some abating of this
fever of conflict, but I also believe that this conflict
will never cease."

A second problem raised up anew by the outbreak of
the Great War, is that of security — security for the
individual, for the nation, and for the great organised
body of society at large. This problem has its roots,
of course, in nothing less fundamental than that most
primitive and potent of all human passions, the instinct
of self-preservation. Every organism, from the lowest
form of animal to the highest type of man, yearns to
possess life and to pass on this life to succeeding generations. Nor is this yearning in any way confined to the
individual as such. On the contrary, it is as much a
sensation of the herd, so to speak, as of the isolated
organism — so that groups of men, such as nations, for
example, are just as instinct with the desire to live as
any single member of the group. It is this which ex-
plains the passion for security, as we call it, which has
played so large a part in the military history of mankind. If any careful study of the wars of the world,
from the most ancient time down to our own day, should
be made from the standpoint of causes and results, I am
certain that it would be found that more wars had been
fought for the sake of security against barbarians,
heathens, enemies feared and hated for one reason or another, than for all other purposes of revenge, conquest,
dynastic pride, or what not, put together. If men
have leaped eagerly into war in the past, it is very
largely because they desired to gain that supremacy in
arms which could alone guarantee them national security. If men have clung to war in our age, it is because they feared that there might appear at any time

some crisis of last resort in which an appeal to arms could alone protect them from destruction. If men have ever consented to peace, it is because they have felt, for some good reason or other, secure. And if they have dreamed to-day of peace as a permanent condition of good, it is because they have felt that the establishment of such a condition would bring to them just that perfect assurance of security which has been so eagerly desired, and never yet attained.

Now just exactly as the world had come to the point of thinking, a few years or even a few months ago, that the reign of peace was about to appear upon the earth, so also, for the same reasons, had it come to the point of thinking that security was about to be realised for each and every nation in the concert of nations. It made little difference whether the observer was a pacifist or a militarist, he was in either case reasonably assured of a world organised, or very nearly organised, for security as well as peace. The pacifist saw the rapidly multiplying influences of international goodwill, and the mechanism created and operated by these influences, to which we have already made abundant reference. The militarist looked upon a very different scene, but saw indirectly the same result. The great nations of Europe were building and maintaining armaments so terrible that no one of them would dare to lift its sword against another. These nations were arrayed in alliances or ententes, which formed a balance of power and therefore an equilibrium of forces which made a cataclysm impossible. Smaller nations of Europe, like Belgium, for example, which were unable to protect themselves by force of arms, were guaranteed security by treaties of neutrality, which protected their territory from invasion by their more powerful neighbours.   Still others of these smaller nations were protected by treaties of alliance or secret agreements with the larger and more powerful states, as Portugal with England, and Serbia with Russia. In some way or other, all the European nations were parts of a great diplomatic or militarist organisation, the strength and completeness of which were the guarantee to each of safety.   Every now and then, to be sure, on the occasion of an Italian war in Tripoli, or an outbreak in the Balkans, a dreadful fear would seize the peoples of Europe, and for a moment the whole organisation, built up with such infinite pains and held together at such enormous expense, would seem on the verge of collapse.   But the crisis would pass almost as suddenly as it had appeared, and confidence would be restored.

Then, as we have already seen, came the Great War, and with it the discovery that, in the matter of security as in the matter of peace, we were all of us living in the land of dreams.   The pacifist, to his consternation, saw his bulwarks against war swept away as the swollen Mississippi, in flood time, sweeps away its levees.   The militarist, to his equal consternation, beheld his armaments make war certain rather than impossible, his treaties of neutrality torn up as so many " scraps of paper," and his nicely adjusted balances of

power the perfect preparation and the potent guarantee not of security for any nation or group of nations,
but of universal disaster for all.   In other words, the
whole promise of security was nullified everywhere and
at once, and the whole problem raised anew for settlement.   Every nation in the war to-day is fighting first
to protect itself against extinction at the hands of its
enemies, and secondly to assure to itself, when the battle
is done, such a new order of affairs as shall render it
forever safe from future attack.   And every nation
outside of the war to-day, from little Switzerland in the
very heart of the ring of flame to great America three
thousand or more miles away, is considering as the first
and foremost duty of the hour the question of how to
secure itself from all possibility of suffering such disaster as has engulfed its combatant neighbours.

The third problem precipitated by the Great War is
more serious and significant than either of the two just
mentioned.   Indeed, it is a problem occasioned and
presented by these two, and therefore as much more
important as the end is more important than the means.
For peace and security are certainly nothing in themselves.   A man, or a nation, does not want peace for
the sake of peace, nor security for the sake of security.
The oyster, for example, enclosed within the granite-
like walls of its shell and buried away in the mud at the
bottom of the bay, undoubtedly is at peace with itself
and the world, and may be regarded as reasonably secure.   The African lion, pacing his cage in the zoo-
logical garden, is at peace when his meal has been de-

voured, and is at all times perfectly secure behind his
bars.   The convict in his cell lives in a condition of
peace so undisturbed as to tempt him to insanity or
revolt, and enjoys a degree of security which is his day-
and-night despair.   In such conditions as these, peace
and security are easy enough to attain, undoubtedly.
But what do they amount to when so attained?   Who
of us desires them as ends in and for themselves?   The
oyster, for all its peace and security, offers to us no
temptations.   The lion, mere brute creature that he is,
would gladly rove the jungle, and battle in danger for
the necessities of life, if he could only escape the calm
security of his cage.   And what convict does not break
his dungeon walls, when opportunity offers, in hungry
quest of that life which the peace and security of the
prison cell deny?

Peace and security, in other words, have no value,
nor even meaning, in themselves.   They attain value
and meaning only as they lead to a higher, richer, more
abundant type of life.   Life is the great thing — the
essential thing.   Hence the third problem, of which
peace and security alike, as I have said, are the mere
conditions!   What is life?   What is the goal of existence toward which the individual and the nation
should alike direct their powers?   What is the ideal
plan of vital action in which peace and security should
be incorporated as means to ends?   This is the final
question to-day, as in every day of the world's history.
And a few years — nay, a few months — ago, there
were few of us who would not have been ready to declare

that we were beginning to understand this question and
approximate an answer thereto. We believed, with perfect assurance, that the gospel of life had been spoken,
in part if not in whole, by certain of the great prophets
of old, and that little by little, this gospel was beginning to be accepted and practised by men. Our age,
we would have said, was pre-eminent in its endeavour to
fulfil the law of life long since laid down by those who
have lived the life of love. But now, forsooth, under
the stress and strain of an unforeseen international
struggle, we discover that this problem, like the others
of which I have spoken, is not yet settled. The gospel
of love is challenged by the gospel of power, the law of
service by the law of necessity, the religion of the heart
by the religion of the will. The whole issue of what
life is and how it is to be used, in other words, we find
to be no longer an incentive to action but a proposition
for debate. Existence is thrown back upon itself.
The whole order of human relationships is cast into the
melting pot of war. After centuries of development
and struggle, we are face to face to-day with exactly
the same question that baffled the hairy cave-man as he
gnawed his bone and plotted evil against his neighbour.
Not merely how to establish peace, nor yet how to gain
security, but how to live — this is our question. With
the return of the world to chaos, as I have said, life be-
gins anew!

IV

Here, now, are the more important of the problems
which have been raised by the outbreak of the War of

the Nations.   And here, by the mere statement of these
problems, do we find ourselves taken into the very
heart of the question which we are proposing for discussion.   For whatever may be the various answers
which are offered to our problems, these are all to be
classified, in the last analysis, under two separate heads.
In other words, our attempts to settle the issues raised
by the stupendous spectacle of a world in arms bring us
at once face to face with two perfectly distinct and
mutually exclusive doctrines of life.

On the one hand, we find the doctrine which I shall
call, for our purposes of discussion in this book, the
doctrine of force.   This doctrine finds its ultimate
justification, as we shall see at some length further on,
in an interpretation of all forms of activity in terms
of the great phenomenon of the struggle for existence.
All life, say the supporters of this doctrine, is a process
of struggle.   The grass blades in the pasture struggle
against one another for the ray of sunshine and the
drop of rain.   The insects flitting about in the open
air of the harvest field, battle for the means of sub-
sistence which can be enjoyed by but a few.   The wild
creatures of the jungle rend and tear in one long, bloody
and powerful contest not merely for dominance but for
survival.   And what is true of leaf and fly and animal is
true also of man, in both his savage and civilised stages
of existence.

But the doctrine of force bases itself not only on this
great and undeniable fact of struggle, but also on
what it regards as the further fact that this struggle is

always pursued on the level of physical energy. Whether it be the plant or the insect, the animal or the human which is battling, it is always the physical weapon which is used; always the organism which can gather up within itself the largest amount of sheer material strength and direct this strength most effectively against the enemy, that is the one which wins out in the contest for survival. Exemplars of this struggle run all the way from the hawk and the wolf to an Alexander, Napoleon, and von Hindenberg. The weapons of the fray begin with the tooth of the tiger and the fang of the serpent, and end, for the present at least, with the submarine, the Zeppelin, and the 42-centimetre siege gun of the Germans. Interpretations of the battle take forms as various as the half-articulate cry of the savage shouting vengeance against his foe, and the carefully wrought philosophy of Nietzsche or history of Treitschke. " All are but parts of one stupendous whole," however — a doctrine of supreme reliance upon the efficacy of physical force, in a struggle which means life or death to the combatants involved!

But the defenders of this gospel, if we may call it such, do not end with pointing out facts which they believe cannot be contradicted and therefore must be accepted. They go on and point out the interesting circumstance that these phenomena of struggle and survival on the basis of physical energy are not only real, but " true and righteous altogether." They are justified, that is, pragmatically, and thus raised at once beyond the level of the merely physical to the infinitely

higher level of the moral and spiritual.   The struggle,
in other words, is something more than a mere contest
of strength.   It is, at bottom, a testing of soul — a
divine process for the selection of the fit from the unfit, the strong from the weak, the worthy from the unworthy, the heroic from the cowardly.   The struggle
of organism with organism is no mere lustful fight for
food, or water, or propagation of the species.   Rather
is it a battle of good against bad, of health against disease, of growth against decay, of life against death.
Here in these mighty struggles do we see the creative
process.   It is this, continued through many ages, by
beasts unnumbered, that has at last brought man upon
the scene.   And it is this, continued again through
many ages by man himself, which is developing step by
step the super-man who is some day destined to appear
as the final achievement of the divine handiwork.
Battle, bloodshed, slaughter, destruction — these are
but the methods of severing sheep from goats.   Look
upon marching armies, flaming cities, devastated fields,
sinking ships, ravished women, frightened children, and
you look only upon what happens when God, as Julia
Ward Howe has put it in her hymn,

" . . . is sifting out the hearts of men before his
judgment seat."

Such is the doctrine of force, as it has been exemplified
in all ages and taught more or less openly in some.
Easy is it to deduce, from this statement of its general
content, the specific answers which it gives to the prob-

lems stirred up anew. as we have seen, by the Great
War.

In regard to the problem of peace among the nations,
the champions of this doctrine take attitudes of varying
degrees of thoroughness. Some declare, without
apology of any kind, that war is not bad but good, and
that a permanent state of peace, therefore, is to be
deprecated rather than welcomed. Such an advocate
is General Bernhardi, and, if we can judge correctly,
the entire militaristic group of the German Empire.
Others there are, like John Ruskin [1] and Professor
Cramb,[2] of Cambridge, who recognise the hideous character of war and deplore its occurrence, but believe that
war has certain virtues which are unique to itself, and
to this extent, therefore, is to be accepted as necessary
and beneficent. Then again, there are men, numerous
in our country as in others, who are convinced that
war is wholly dreadful and should be done away with
immediately and forever, but who believe that this end
can never be accomplished save by the development and
maintenance of weapons of force on so stupendous a
scale that no one nation shall dare to venture its existence upon such a hazard as that of declaring hostilities. The variety of these opinions is evident. But
behind them all is the one idea, so central to the doctrine

---

[1] One side of his attitude only. For a description of John Ruskin's views see below, Chapter IX, page 303. His ideas were of
course hopelessly inconsistent with one another, as he himself
readily admitted. His feeling of utter detestation of war was
sound; his thought of war's contribution to civilisation a perfect
illustration of pseudo-knowledge.

[2] See his book, *Germany and England.*

of force, that our ultimate reliance, in this as in other problems of life, must be upon the sword. One nation may desire war as a blessing; another may seek steadfastly to avoid war as the worst of curses. But both nations alike must arm themselves to the teeth, and use identically the same weapons for the attainment of their so widely different ends.

As regards the problem of security, the advocates of force are somewhat more closely agreed. There is no security possible in this world, they assert, except that which is won and held by main strength. We sleep in our homes at night with a feeling of reasonable security, first because our doors are locked and barred, and secondly because there paces in the street before our dwelling an armed representative of the law. Were our doors for any reason thrown open, or the policeman for any reason withdrawn from his post, we would feel instantly alarmed for the safety of both property and life. And as with individuals, so with nations! We may talk until doomsday about guaranteeing national security by treaties of neutrality, alliance, or arbitration, or by practising righteousness and goodwill in international relations. Treaties of any kind, as Mr. Roosevelt is never tired of pointing out, are not worth the paper they are written on unless backed by the mailed fist and the drawn sword. The tragedy of Belgium, terrible as it was, seemed almost worth while to a man of Mr. Roosevelt's views as an immortal demonstration of this thesis. And as for friendship, goodwill, righteousness — these may be all right in the private relations of individual citizens, but they can avail absolutely nothing in relations between jealous, suspicious, and hostile states. Force can alone save us from destruction. "Speak softly and carry a big stick" is the only maxim of prudence.

It is only when we get to our third problem, that of life itself, however, that we meet the perfect expression of the gospel of force. Here do we find this doctrine raised to the dignity of a new code of morals, a new revelation of religion. Power now becomes the great possession, struggle for mastery the great activity, success or victory the great end. The good man is described not as the one who is meek, gentle, kindly, sympathetic, but as the one who is strong, self-assertive, brave, ruthless in his pursuit of ends. The bad man is pictured not as the one who is mean, deceitful, cruel, selfish, but as the one simply who is weak. Virtue here becomes synonymous with valour — sin synonymous with humility. Nietzsche sums it all up in one of his most familiar passages —" What is good? — all that increases the feeling of power, the will for power, power itself in man. What is bad? — all that proceeds from weakness. What is happiness? — the feeling that power increases and that resistance is overcome. Not contentedness but power — not peace but war — not virtue but capacity — this is the rule of life. The weak shall perish, and people shall help them to do so — this is the first principle of charity. What is the worst of crimes? — sympathy for the weak and unfortunate — Christianity!"

V

Opposed now, in every sense of the word, to the doctrine of force, and presenting in its entirety the other side, so to speak, of the theory of life, is what I shall call, for lack of a better name, the doctrine of non-resistance. This word, as we shall see,[1] is hopelessly inaccurate, but it has long since assumed, by reason of historic usage, a distinct if not adequate connotation, and therefore must be employed.

At bottom, the doctrine of non-resistance, exactly like the doctrine of force, is a summons to battle. It agrees that the life-process is an uninterrupted struggle for survival between contending organisms. It agrees as well that this struggle began upon the plane of physical energy, and that the weapons of the flesh have ever played a potent part in the determination of victory. It denies, however, that the battle for existence was ever at any time limited to the physical plane, insists that it has again and again been lifted to higher levels, and points out that other weapons than those of the flesh have long since proven their superiority. Nothing is more impressive, for example, in the modern study of evolution, than the gradual supplanting of the struggle for self-preservation by what Drummond terms " the struggle for the life of others." The more widely we extend our observation of the biological process of development, and the higher we climb in the scale of animal life, the more frequently we encounter

[1] See Chapter IV, " What Non-Resistance Means."

"mutual aid" as the determining factor of survival.
Not the claw of the tiger but the love of the tigress
for her cubs, not the mammoth strength of the ele-
phant but his disciplined membership in the herd —
these are the things that really make for the preservation of the species. "The strength of the wolf is the
pack," says Rudyard Kipling in his *Jungle Book*, "and
the strength of the pack is the wolf." So true is this,
indeed, that a long-range survey of the line of evolution shows conclusively that the weaker animals, which,
because of their inadequate strength, have learned the
lesson of co-operation, are the ones which are winning
out in the battle for life, and the savage animals, on
the other hand, like the lion and the bear, which rove
the jungle alone in the proud glory of unconquerable
power, are the very ones which are losing and thus
gradually disappearing. Physical force, in other
words, is for some reason or other showing itself to be
a failure in the struggle for survival.

And what is merely suggested here in the animal
realm, is triumphantly indicated in the life of man.
For man, whatever his physical relationship to the brute
creatures from which he sprang, must be described, in
the last analysis, not as a physical but rather as a
spiritual being. With his appearance upon the earth,
life at once moves to a loftier plane and seeks to adapt
itself to a nobler standard of activity. If the law of
existence for the animal is the law of force, then, as
Huxley declared in his famous *Romanes Lecture*, this
law is overthrown by man in favour of a law of his own

discovery or creation — the law of love. Or, if this higher law, as John Fiske and others have declared, has already appeared in the field of animal existence and has there competed for supremacy with the law of sheer brute strength, then this higher law is deliberately chosen by man for the practice of his life to the total exclusion of the other, and spirit is forthwith pitted in a death grapple with flesh for the mastery of the human soul. The whole story of humanity, from this point of view, becomes an exciting romance of the persistent endeavour of the race to rid itself of force and possess itself of love, as the one all-sufficient weapon of advance. And history, if it teaches us anything with precision, certainly teaches that man strengthens his hold on life, rises in the scale of existence, wins peace, security and happiness for his reward, just to the extent that he succeeds in this one supreme endeavour of the soul.

It is this fact which is set forth with such compelling power by the prophets of all ages, both ancient and modern, who have discerned with clear vision the truths of the spirit and have formulated these truths into a wondrous gospel of love, service, sacrifice and goodwill. From no great teacher of ethics and religion have these things been hidden; by every great teacher have they been translated into noble gospels of human brotherhood. But supreme among all these seers of " things invisible " must be counted Jesus, the brave carpenter of Nazareth, who, in a time which rang with the crash of arms and among a people who had long been trodden into the dust under the iron heel of conquest, dared to lift his voice on behalf of the most consistent, thoroughgoing and uncompromising gospel of non-resistance that the world has ever seen. " They that take the sword shall perish with the sword — resist not evil, but whosoever shall smite thee on thy right cheek, turn to him the other also — ye have heard that it hath been said, Thou shalt love thy neighbour and hate thine enemy. But I say unto you, Love your enemies, bless them that curse you, do good to them that hate you, and pray for them that despitefully use you and persecute you — all things whatsoever ye would that men should do to you, do you even so unto them — he that findeth his life shall lose it, but he that loseth his life for my sake shall find it "— these are the words he spoke in eternal challenge of every doctrine of life which would place reliance, for any purpose, under any conditions, upon the use of violence, force or aggression of any kind. Jesus saw clearly enough that life was a struggle. He himself followed no easy path, and at last went down in defeat before his enemies. But he insisted in his preaching, and demonstrated in his practice, that this struggle, for man at least, was a struggle not for physical survival but for spiritual fulfilment; and urged, therefore, upon all those who would truly live, the one great end of love.

Such in meagrest outline is the doctrine of non-resistance! That it is the exact antithesis in every particular of the doctrine of force must be evident even from such a summary interpretation as this which is set down in the above paragraphs. We need not be

surprised, therefore, to discover that, in its answers to
the problems of the Great War, which we have more
than once considered, it challenges the doctrine of force
on each and every issue.

Thus, as regards the question of peace, the non-resistant asserts, without qualification or equivocation of
any kind, that war is the sum of all villainies and peace
the sum of all blessings.   He believes that war may
have its benefits, as peace may have its ills; but that
benefits and ills are incidental to the main factors in
the situation, which, in the case of war, are wholly bad,
and, in the case of peace, are wholly good.   Peace has
never brought harm to any individual or group of individuals; war, on the other hand, has never brought anything else.   The highest ideal of organised humanity,
therefore, must be the establishment of " peace on
earth, good will toward men."   So long as war continues under any form, or for any purpose, the race
must fall far short of the fulfilment of its " one true
aim."

But the non-resistant does not stop with this unqualified endorsement of peace as a permanent condition
of human good.   On the contrary, he goes on to point
out, with great definiteness, the method for attaining
his ideal.   This is none other than that of preparing
for peace, by putting one side forever the weapons of
war and building diligently and seriously the social
mechanism expressive of ordered knowledge, sound
reason, and truthful friendship.   To seek peace by preparing for war, says the non-resistant, is the rankest

absurdity, demonstrated by the failure of any people in any period of history to find the peace thus sought. There has been the peace attained by Rome — the *Pax Romanum* — which is the obedience dictated to a helpless world by the iron rod of conquest. There has been the peace pictured so vividly by Tacitus, when he described the legionaries of the Imperial City as " making a desolation and calling it peace." There has been the peace, dictated by treaties and assured by balances of power, which is an armed truce between the close of one war and the opening of another. But the true peace, described by Isaiah as a time when " nation shall not lift up sword against nation, neither shall they learn war any more," has never come for the simple reason that men have never had the wisdom nor the courage to adopt the one true method to this end — that of " beating their swords into ploughshares and their spears into pruning hooks."

To the problem of security, the non-resistant gives much the same answer that he gives to the problem of peace. Man desires security as he desires peace; but he fails to attain the one, just as he fails to attain the other, for the reason that he seeks security by the methods that create insecurity, just as he seeks peace by the methods that create war. The bolted door and the armed policeman, you say, are the evidences of security! On the contrary, they are the evidences of insecurity. No man feels himself safe behind such barriers. Bolts and bars are indefinitely multiplied, the city police are supplemented by private watchmen, loaded revolvers are kept in bureau drawers and under pillows, intricate systems of automatic alarm are installed at great expense — with the result that security is as far away as ever. And what is true of the individual is equally true also of the nation! The vast armaments of our time are evidences not of security but of fear. Ship is added to ship, fortress to fortress, army corps to army corps — and still the fear grows, until at last in a very madness of mutual apprehension, the Great War bursts upon the world. If the colossal armaments of this age could not win and hold security for any one of the great peoples involved, what armaments, pray, can be huge and terrible enough to attain this end?

The fact of the matter is, of course, as the non-resistant has all along pointed out, that the appeal to force is the cause and not the cure of fear, the occasion and not the end of insecurity. Security, at the best precarious in this uncertain world, can be won, if at all, in only one way. Let the individual be patient, forbearing, sympathetic, kind to his neighbours — let the nation practise justice, righteousness, goodwill in its relations with all foreign peoples — and all the security that the world can give will thereby be attained. To arm is to raise up arms against you — to be suspicious is to generate suspicion — to prepare for contingencies is to create those same contingencies. To disarm yourself, however, is to disarm your neighbour — to trust is to be trusted — to be peaceful is to win peace. " As ye sow, so shall ye reap." And if perchance, by accident or crime, peril sweeps down upon you, then, for individual and nation alike, it is always possible to die. No one of us is under any obligation to live. Indeed, it is the crowning belief of the non-resistant that to live by breaking the highest laws of life is infinitely worse than death.

This lofty assertion of idealism brings us at once to the non-resistant's answer to the whole great question of life itself. Physical survival, so important, as we have seen, to the champion of force, here becomes of insignificance. The passion for self-preservation is historically the most primitive, and ethically the lowest, of all vital instincts. Long since has the law of survival, in every system of individual morality, been superseded by the law of sacrifice. Not to live but to love, not to save ourselves but to save others, not to survive at any cost but to die for any cause — this is the standard by which we gauge our conduct. Calvary still stands as the noblest symbol of the soul. And what is true of the individual, is true also of the nation. No more here than anywhere else can there be tolerated a double standard of morals. The martyr nation is as sublime, and may be as necessary, as the martyr hero. Jesus's message was to nations as well as to men, when he laid down the laws of blessedness —" Blessed are the poor in spirit, for theirs is the kingdom of heaven . . . Blessed are the meek, for they shall inherit the earth. Blessed are they which do hunger and thirst after righteousness, for they shall be filled. Blessed are the merciful for they shall obtain mercy. . . . Blessed are

the peacemakers, for they shall be called the children of
God."

Here, now, is a survey of the whole problem of pacifism which is presented to us for discussion. What is
outlined in this chapter I propose to amplify at length
in the chapters which follow. My purpose is to state
the case for pacifism in terms of force versus non-resistance. I shall try to say all that can be said for this
sublime and much-maligned ideal, as fairly and yet as
fully as possible. My mind is by no means closed upon
the subject. I am conscious of no over-weening ambition to force this interpretation of life upon unwilling
minds. I certainly am not eager to be dubbed a
pacifist or a non-resistant, as either title is a hopeless travesty. In a time, however, when reliance upon
the methods and the ideals of brute force has involved
the world in the most frightful disaster of history, and
men, all unmindful of the lesson, are still urging us to
push on faster and farther in the same old way to the
same old end, I feel that there is need for a statement,
however feeble, of the other side of the case.

In offering this statement, in the uncompromising
form here adopted, I am perfectly well aware of the
fact that I am exposing myself to the charge of folly.
" You are only wasting your time and strength," is the
word which has already come to me, " for it must be as
evident to you as to anybody else that there is not one
man in a million who takes any stock in the principle of

non-resistance, and not one chance in a million that this idea will ever be accepted by the majority of men in the future. Why not turn aside from conceptions which, however ideal in themselves, are futile, and do what you can to discover and commend to men those things which may be useful right here and now for ' the healing of the nations '? "

To such a charge as this, I beg to offer two replies.

The first is the reply dictated by the unchanged and unchangeable idealism of the human heart. It is the reply which Ralph Waldo Emerson gave to this very charge in his non-resistant *Lecture on War*, when he said, " We never take much account of objections which merely respect the actual state of the world, but which admit the permanent excellence of the project. What is the best must be the true, and what is true must at last prevail over all obstruction and opposition." It is the reply to the same charge, expressed in more general terms, by John Morley, in his *Essay on Compromise*, where he says, " In the formation of an opinion as to the truth or falsehood or right significance of a proposition, we have nothing to do with the circumstance that it is not practicable. We must have the best opinion, even if we know that this opinion has an infinitely small chance of being speedily or ever accepted by the majority, or by anybody but ourselves." It is the great reply given by Leo Tolstoi, in his *Confessions*, when he tells about his experience of witnessing the execution of a criminal in Paris. " When I saw the head divided from the body," says the great Russian, " and heard the sound with which it fell separately into the box, I understood that no theory of the wisdom of all established things, nor of progress, could justify such an act; and that if all the men in the world from the day of creation, by whatever theory, had found this thing necessary, I knew that it was not necessary, that it was a bad thing; and that therefore I must judge of what was right and necessary, not by what men said and did, not by progress, but by what I felt to be true in my heart."

This may well be considered in itself an all-sufficient reply to any charge of futility against the advocacy of idealism.   But there is a second reply, dictated in this particular case by the conditions of the times.   The counsel of non-resistance has hitherto fallen upon the ears of a heedless world.   But is it certain that this must ever be its fate?   For centuries the gospel of force has been practised with unremitting fidelity, and the result is one long uninterrupted record of devastation, bloodshed, misery, and death.   It has been estimated that fourteen hundred billions of human beings have been killed in war since history began — enough mortals to populate eighteen planets like the earth on the present basis of population.   How much wealth has been destroyed by the same process is probably beyond all bounds of calculation.   How many kingdoms have risen only to fall, how many peoples have prospered only to be destroyed, how many civilisations have flourished only to be swept away, by this same fell method of life, the pages of history only too impressively record.

And now, behold, in this latest period of human progress, a more widely-extended, more destructive, and more cruel war, than mankind has ever known before! Is it not possible, that, under the stress of such an agony of woe as weighs upon men's hearts to-day, their minds may at last be prepared for the hearing, if not the immediate practice, of the gospel of non-resistance? Having found the way of force to be the path " that leadeth to destruction," may not men be ready at least to consider the alternative way of love? Defeated, baffled, wasted, face to face with death, may they not heed the prophet voices, and mayhap try a plan of action which, at the worst, cannot bring a greater tide of woe upon the world than has already come?

Such at least is my hope, as I prepare this new statement of an ancient gospel. The failure of modern civilisation in our time has sobered us, shocked us, set us to thinking on new lines. We are ready, as perhaps never before, to see a new vision of truth, to try a new way of life. Hence the wisdom of appealing once again to the mighty words of old —" Behold, I will save my people by the Lord their God. I will not save them by the bow nor by the sword nor by battle, by horses nor by horsemen. . . . But I will make war to cease. I will break the bow, and cut the spear in sunder ; and burn the chariots in the fire. . . . I will speak peace unto the nations."

CHAPTER II
THE LOGIC OF FORCE

" Error has its logic as well as truth. Once you reject the political action of the working class, you are fatally driven . . . to
accept the tactics of the Vaillants and the Henrys." [1]— George
Plechanoff, in *Anarchism and Socialism.*

[1] August Vaillant was the terrorist who attempted in 1892 to
blow up with dynamite the French Chamber of Deputies. Émile
Henry was the terrorist who avenged Vaillant by blowing up the
café of the Hotel Terminus in Paris.

CHAPTER II

I

At first sight it may seem as though the whole weight of the argument on this question of non-resistance were on the side of the opponents of the doctrine. The burden of proof, as it is called, is assuredly on the shoulders of the man who would contend that the problems of life can be met and solved without resort to force of any kind. If there is any presumption in the case at all, it is against him rather than for him.

A closer examination of the problem, however, is certain, I believe, to upset this original impression. Not the advocate of non-resistance but the advocate of force, is the one who is on the defensive at the start, and the one therefore who is laden with the burden of proving his case. Ask the average man if he believes in the use of force for the settlement of practical difficulties, and see how eagerly he will repudiate such an idea. Confront the average man with an outbreak of violence and bloodshed, and see how quickly he will denounce it and call for its suppression. A fight between two neighbours, a brawl between gangs of hoodlums in the slums, a beating up of a burglar by a policeman, a lynching of a Negro criminal in the South, a riot between strikers and strike-breakers, a civil war

39

in Mexico, an international war in Europe — all these
episodes of violence are at once denounced by public
opinion as wrong on the face of things. There may
have been a time when the use of force in such ways as
these was regarded as right on general principles, but
to-day such use, by either an individual or a nation,
must be shown to be justified by very definite and unusual conditions, if it is not to be condemned as an unpardonable offence against the social order.

When we turn to the ideal set forth by the non-resistants, however, we find the situation exactly re-
versed. The great majority of persons agree, without argument of any kind, that the works of gentleness,
mercy, goodwill, are wholly beneficent. Nobody seeks
justification, by appeal to special circumstances and
conditions, for the use of reason in the settlement of
difficulties, and the employment of love in the allaying
of violence. These things justify themselves. They
need no explanation and call for no defence. To love
one's neighbour, to serve him in his need, to forgive him
in his wrath, to pity him in his sin, is the natural, the
normal, the human way of living. To hate, despise,
injure, kill one's neighbour, is the unnatural, abnormal,
inhuman way of living. Significant is it to note that,
when St. Paul names " the fruit of the spirit," which
is " love, joy, peace, longsuffering, gentleness, goodness, faith, meekness, temperance," in contrast with
" the works of the flesh," which are " adultery . . .
idolatry . . . hatred, variance, emulations, wrath,
strife, seditions, envyings, murders . . . and such

like," he takes particular pains to point out that against the former " there is no law." By which he very plainly means to infer that the works of the flesh are under condemnation unless acquitted by special trial of law, whereas the fruits of the spirit stand of themselves, " honest, just, pure, lovely, and of good report."

It is evident, therefore, that the burden of proof in this contention is upon those who would use force under any circumstances and not upon those who would try, under all circumstances, to use the gentler methods of sweet reasonableness and goodwill. Force, in other words, is a principle so dangerous in operation and so destructive in result that men have long since come to agree together that its employment must be restricted within the narrowest possible limitations. It is like poison, which can be used only by physicians for certain very specific medicinal purposes. It is like fire-arms which can be carried only by persons who have been duly licensed by the city for special reasons. It is like dynamite, which can be transported through the streets only in certain quantities, at certain times, in certain ways, and for certain ends. Anybody who desires to use poison, carry fire-arms, or handle dynamite is at once on the defensive. He must show cause for his desire, and justify this cause beyond all manner of doubt, before he can be permitted to proceed. And so also with the use of force! This is universally regarded as so perilous in all cases, and so wrong in most cases, that it is forbidden in general terms both

by the statutes of the state and the precepts of religion. "Against such there is (the) law!" It is
commonly agreed that there may very likely appear
from time to time certain particular conditions, such
as the burglary of a house or the invasion of a nation,
which make resort to force unavoidable, and the law
therefore of none effect. But the presumption is always against such conditions; and they must be established beyond question before a verdict of acquittal
can be rendered.

The question as to whether the use of force can ever
be regarded as unavoidable and as a consequence justifiable, raises at once, of course, the whole issue of non-
resistance, and will therefore be discussed at great
length as our argument proceeds. Assuming for the
moment that there may exist conditions which seem to
make necessary the lifting of the ban against physical
violence, I desire at this point to ask if such violence,
once let loose, can be kept within the limits of these
conditions? Granting, for the sake of argument, that
there may be a certain restricted area within which
force may justifiably be employed, I want to inquire if
such force, when liberated in this area, can by any possibility be prevented from leaping the barriers imposed,
and working unforeseeable havoc in remoter areas
where it does not belong and where it should never be
allowed to enter? Do we realise, in other words, how
perilous the use of force really is, and how easily, therefore, even under the most carefully guarded conditions,
it may sweep beyond control?

An experience of my boyhood, which remains as vividly impressed upon my mind to-day as though it took place yesterday, may be offered here, perhaps, as an interpretation in parable form of the idea which I am trying to suggest. One day, early in the spring of my ninth or tenth year, I was playing with some lads of my acquaintance in an open field, which was covered by a heavy growth of long, dry grass. One of us suggested, in a moment of idleness, that it would be " great fun " to set fire to the stubble, and have a conflagration. How it happened that such heedless youngsters had any thought of danger in such a proceeding I cannot imagine, but as a matter of history it is necessary to record that some one of us suggested that such a fire might get away from us and that it would be well therefore to make some endeavour to keep our blaze within bounds. In the most serious way in the world, therefore, we boys set vigorously to work with spades, shovels, sticks and other implements to dig a series of trenches, which should enclose in a rough square some two or three hundred square feet of ground. Here, now, was our prairie, which was to be devoured in flames, and here were our rivers which were to stop the blaze. Nothing could be better, and in a few moments a match was lit and the dry grass was burning. But alas! how little we understood the peril of fire, and the folly of expecting to keep it within the bounds which we had so carefully imposed! For the grass was long and dry, the trenches were narrow and poorly dug, a good breeze was blowing from the east and before we could so much as snatch a coat to beat out the flames, the blaze was sweeping on through the field, straight toward a large wooden stable, filled with horses, and a little group of frame houses just beyond. Frightened boys, shouts, screams, running men, buckets of water, an alarm of fire, engines, firemen, hose — these were the rapid succession of events in our playground. And to this day, I imagine, there are a dozen or more grown men who cherish, as I do, the unextinguishable grievance against the world, that the careful and laborious endeavours which these boys had made to keep their prairie fire within bounds were never praised or even acknowledged!

Here, now, as I have said, is a kind of parable on the unforeseen results of appeal to arms on any question. There is a power in physical force, as in fire, which, when once liberated, sweeps away all the restrictions which may be raised against it. There is a logic in force, a kind of fatalism, if you will, which makes the descent into Avernus not only easy, but inevitable. Once agree that the use of force is necessary and therefore can be justified under certain conditions, and lo, before you realise it, you are moving steadily on from step to step, from stage to stage, and at last are justifying the use of force under all conditions. Not non-resistance, as is so commonly asserted, but force, however narrowly restricted, is the straight road to anarchy!

II

In order to understand just what this logic of force really means, it will be necessary to consider, first of all, what are the special conditions which are generally accepted to-day as justifying the use of force. These conditions, when all extraneous and unwarranted excuses for violence are eliminated, are two in number.

The first condition is laid down with great clearness in a statement by Prof. Rauschenbusch in his remarkable book entitled *Christianising the Social Order.* Discussing the industrial troubles of our time, and especially the violence which is constantly breaking out in the strife between capital and labour, Prof. Rauschenbusch asserts, " I do not hold that the use of force against oppression can always be condemned as wrong. The test of brute strength is the *ultima ratio* when all higher arguments have proved vain. The great Roman historian, Livy, expressed the general conviction, ' War is just for those for whom it is necessary, and arms are holy for those to whom no hope is left except in arms.' "

A study of this defence of force, as a weapon of progress, shows at once that it involves two definite propositions. In the first place, it is declared that force is justified when men are suffering from oppression. This oppression may be oppression of the body, as in the case of chattel slavery. It may be oppression .of the mind, as in the case of the denial of free thought and free speech. It may be oppression of the soul, as in the case of religious persecution. It may be general social oppression, as in the case of political and military tyranny. But whatever the particular kind of oppression, it is equally intolerable; and wherever it is found to exist, all men, especially those suffering from its burdens, are justified in using force to destroy it. It is this doctrine, is it not, which is laid down in the American Declaration of Independence? Here it is announced, in immortal phrase, that all men are entitled to " certain inalienable rights," that among these are " life, liberty, and the pursuit of happiness," and that when these are denied to, or alienated from, men, these men are justified in taking up arms on behalf of freedom. " Prudence will dictate," says the Declaration, " that governments long established should not be changed for light causes — and accordingly all experience hath shown that mankind is more disposed to suffer, while evils are sufferable, than to right themselves by abolishing the forms to which they are accustomed. But when a long train of abuses and usurpations evinces a design to reduce them under absolute despotism, it is their right to throw off such government and provide new guards for their future security."

But there is a second proposition laid down in Prof. Rauschenbusch's statement. Not only must a state of oppression be known to exist, if force is to be justly used, but all other ways and means of securing liberation must be tried before resort is made to arms. Men suffering under oppression must appeal to their op-

pressors for emancipation; they must define their
grievances and specify their desires; they must petition,
protest, agitate; they must plead, persuade, pray.
But when they have done everything that can be done
— when their petitions have been denied, their prayers
flouted, and their agitations suppressed — when they
have endured, suffered and died to no effect — then
at last may they appeal to the arbitrament of arms.
"Patience, . . . smiling at grief" is a noble monu-
ment " for the dead, but it is an impossible model for
the living. If men would live in joy and not die in
shame, they must again and again strike their tyrants
to the dust with that one weapon of revolt which these
tyrants can alone understand. "When all higher arguments have proved vain," then may " the test of brute
strength " take its rightful place as " the *ultima ratio.*"
By such doctrine have the liberties of the race been
won; by such doctrine are these liberties now maintained.

An illustration of this apparent justification of force
is seen in the American Revolution, which reveals with
perfect clearness both the propositions here involved.
There can be no question, of course, as to the conditions of oppression which existed in the thirteen colonies in 1775. The Declaration of Independence makes
no less than twenty-seven specifications of " injuries,
usurpations and oppressions," as they are termed.
For eight years, from the close of the French and Indian Wars to the outbreak of the Revolution itself, the
American colonists suffered under the tyrannical ex-

actions of the government of George III, and here in the Declaration do we find a dictated statement of just what these exactions were.   Surely, if ever there was a condition of intolerable political oppression, it was here.

And the second condition of Prof. Rauschenbusch's defence of force is equally well illustrated by the Revolution.   Not only did oppression exist, but every reasonable endeavor had been tried by the colonists to secure release from these oppressions.   They had sent petitions to the Commons; they had despatched appeals to the sovereign and his ministers; they had sent ambassadors to speak on their behalf on English soil. And it was only when petitions had been refused, their appeals ignored, and their embassies dismissed from the royal throne, that the colonists took up arms for independence.   Patrick Henry stated the whole case, in his oration before the Virginia House of Burgesses, on March 23, 1775 —"Let us not deceive ourselves longer," he said.   "We have done everything that could be done to avert the storm which is now coming on.   We have petitioned; we have remonstrated; we have supplicated; we have prostrated ourselves before the throne.   Our petitions have been slighted; our remonstrances have produced additional violence and insult; our supplications have been disregarded; and we have been spurned in contempt from the foot of the throne.   In vain, after these things, may we indulge the fond hope of peace and reconciliation.   There is no longer any room for hope.   If we wish to be free, we

must fight! I repeat it, sir, we must fight. An appeal
to arms, and to the God of hosts, is all that is left us."

The soundness of this whole contention, especially as
embodied in the American Revolution, seemed to me incontestable until about two years ago, when I chanced,
one fateful evening, in Carnegie Hall, to hear a notable
address by Mrs. Pankhurst. In the opening passages
of her speech, this famous leader of the English Militants professed the most naïve amazement that any true
American should be opposed to the methods which she
and her associates were practising on behalf of the
woman suffrage movement in England. "Why," she
said, "citizens of this country, which had its birth in
violent revolution, come to us every day and deprecate
the revolution in which I am engaged in my country. I
have heard opposition expressed in Newport, where in
the year 1774 the patriots of America destroyed the
homes of two men who were officers of the crown under
the Stamp Act. I have met with doubts and question-
ings in Providence, where in 1775 the British schooner,
Gaspeé, was burned to the water's edge by the outraged
colonists. I have even encountered sceptics in Boston,
where, before the Revolution, the house of Andrew
Oliver, a stamp officer, was burned by a rioting mob, the
contents of the residence of Chief Justice Hutchinson
were seized and destroyed, and three hundred and forty
chests of tea, belonging to British merchants who were
guiltless of any offence against America, were thrown
into the sea."

The logic of Mrs. Pankhurst's speech on this occasion

troubled me, but did not convince me. Recognition that her parallel was just came only with the reading of Mrs. Pankhurst's more detailed defence of her policy, in the book which she published some months ago under the title of *My Own Story.* Here, in the course of a full account of the operations of the Militants from their more or less innocent beginnings to their sudden ending on the occasion of the European cataclysm, do we find a two-fold justification of the movement.

In the first place, says Mrs. Pankhurst, the women of England are the victims of outrageous and intolerable oppression. The democracy of England is a democracy for men, and not for women. In spite of political and social liberties such as the world has seen in no previous period of history, more than one half of the population of the Kingdom suffer under disabilities of the most serious description. Women are denied the right of suffrage. They are denied, under many circumstances, the control of their property. In the marital relation, they are denied the possession of their bodies. In escape from the marital relation, they are denied equal privileges of divorce with their husbands. In the field of industry, they are forced to live and work under intolerable conditions, from which there is no release save through the charity of men. Sentence by sentence, paragraph by paragraph, page by page, Mrs. Pankhurst specifies their disabilities, as the Declaration of Independence specifies the disabilities of the American colonists under British rule. From such iniquities, or others no worse, she points out that men have long since

delivered themselves, by argument when possible, by
force when necessary. Women, now come at last to
self-consciousness, are proceeding to " profit by their
example " !

Having established, as she believes, that the women of
England are oppressed, Mrs. Pankhurst offers a second
justification for her militant movement — namely, that
the women have tried every other method of redress in
vain, and are now resorting to violence only as a last
resort. For more than a generation, she asserts, English women have pointed out their disabilities and petitioned for redress. For twenty years they have had a
majority of the members of the House of Commons
ready to vote in favour of enfranchisement, and the ministers of both parties have refused to introduce a bill.
Argument, organisation, agitation, have all been in vain.
Only open war is left, and this war, says Mrs. Pankhurst, we have now declared. And then she proceeds to
quote the very speech of Patrick Henry to which I have
referred above, and offer this as the final and perfect
justification of all that she and her associates have done
in their campaign of violence. " I ask my readers,"
says this great leader, " to put themselves in the place
of those women who for years have given their lives un-
stintingly to the work of securing political freedom for
women. I ask you to consider that we had used, in our
agitation, only peaceful means until we saw clearly that
peaceful means were absolutely of no avail. Now we
lighted the torch, and we did it with the absolute conviction that no other course was open to us. We had

tried every other measure, and failed." Then, quoting the speech of Henry, she continues, " If it is right for men to fight for freedom, then it is right for women to fight for freedom and the freedom of the children they bear. On this declaration of faith the militant women of England rest their case."

Here, now, in this perfect parallel between the motives behind the American Revolution and those behind the English Militant Suffrage movement, do we have a striking illustration of what I have called the logic of force. Once admit that force can be used to secure deliverance from oppression under certain very definite and perhaps narrow conditions, and instantly these conditions are extended to vindicate violence of the most outrageous description. Once agree that one man was justified in taking up arms against tyranny, and sooner or later another man, under what seem to be very different circumstances, will declare himself a victim of tyranny and forthwith proceed to draw the sword and kindle the torch. For oppression, we must remember, is a condition existing not in the outer world of affairs but in the inner world of the mind. It is not the fact but the thought about the fact that is really important. Millions of men have lived in chains and fetters all their days, and been conscious of no outrage whatsoever. Other millions have enjoyed a fair degree of liberty, perhaps, but have seen visions and dreamed dreams, which have borne their souls into new worlds of the spirit, and thus made their comparative freedom an intolerable bondage. Oppression, in other words, is at

bottom, a psychological and not a sociological phenomenon.   A man is enslaved when he thinks he is enslaved;
a man is free when he thinks he is free.   You and I believe that the women of England are victims of no very
great degree of injustice; but so undoubtedly thought
Lord North and his ministers of the rebelling American
colonists in the great days of the Revolution.   What
you think, and I think, about the conditions of the life
of a certain man or group of men, after all, does not
greatly matter.   The one thing that is vitally important
is what the man himself, or the group of men, think
about this condition.   If they regard this condition as
one of oppression, find that the world will not accept
their interpretation or accede to their appeals for redress of grievances, and then learn from their forebears,
as Mrs. Pankhurst learned from Patrick Henry, that
force under these circumstances is justifiable — what is
to restrain them from taking action?   Who is to judge,
not to-morrow, or next year, or next century, but here
and now to-day, as to whether violence is right?   Where
is there any judge in such cases but the parties themselves concerned?   What does Livy's declaration that
" war is just for those for whom it is necessary," mean,
if not " that war is just for those " who find it necessary, or think it necessary, in their own particular case?
And if, as this same historian tells us, " arms are holy
for those to whom no hope is left except in arms," why
are they not holy for all who have tried every hope
they know, and find nothing left them but rebellion or
despair?

The logic of force, so far as this defence of its employment is concerned at least, is plainly nothing short of universal anarchy. Long ago was it discovered in England that the logic of Mrs. Pankhurst's movement was that every man or woman in the Kingdom who had a grievance against the Cabinet, should forthwith proceed to break windows, destroy mail, burn houses, assault ministers, and precipitate riots. It is time now that we saw that this is the logic not only of Militancy but of the American Revolution, and of every other outbreak of violence that the world has ever seen. Justify the employment of force against oppression anywhere, and you justify it everywhere. Justify it against real oppression, and inevitably you justify it against imagingary oppression. Justify it against oppression which can be righted apparently in no other way, and you justify it against oppression which can be righted easily in many other ways. Justify the American Revolution, and you justify the Militants who break windows, the redskins who go upon the war-path, the anarchists who shoot kings and presidents, the McNamaras who blow up bridges and newspaper offices. Nay, you not only justify violence yesterday, but you encourage new violence to-day or to-morrow. If " the test of brute strength is the *ultima ratio* when all higher arguments have proved vain," why should not the Negroes of the South, who are oppressed by a thousand disabilities and are denied resort to any of the saving outlets of democracy, prepare a revolution ; why should not the millions of men and women, who are exploited in mines, factories,

and sweatshops and have cried in vain these many years
for liberation, take up arms and smite the lords who
hold them captive; why should not the unemployed, who
walk our city streets by night in hunger and nakedness,
and lift their idle hands by day for work which never
comes, break into our churches, houses, and storehouses,
and use them for their own? It is easy to praise revolt
that succeeds, but what about revolt that fails? It is
easy to justify the use of force which has brought
benefits to men, but what about the use of force which
has brought calamity? It is easy to commend the violence sanctified by a century or two of glorious tradition, but what about the violence which breaks, raw and
crude and bloody, upon your own defenceless head
to-day? Is not force, after all, force, as logic is logic?
If we justify it in one place and at one time, must we
not justify it in all places and at all times? If conditions are granted once at the behest of one group of
men, why must they not be granted again at the behest
of another group of men? Our trenches are deep, but
is it well, after all, to light the fire?

III

But there is a second condition under which the use of
force has been justified by men in the past and is still
justified to-day. I refer to the familiar plea of self-
defence. We may always have resort to force with perfect propriety, so it is argued, when our property, life,
and honour, or the property, life, and honour of those
committed to our care, are in peril of injury or destruc-

tion. To fight with any weapon that may be handy in defence of your own is justifiable from every point of view.

In seeking an illustration of this second principle, which shall be as unimpeachable as that of the American Revolution under our first principle, I find myself thinking of the instance of Marcus Aurelius, Emperor of Rome, in the closing years of the second century of the Christian era. This great man is without question " the noblest Roman of them all." Nay, more than this, he is safely to be numbered among the few almost perfect characters of history. With the single exception of Jesus and perhaps Socrates, it is probable that this wise ruler and saintly man holds a place second to none in the affection and reverence of humanity. " Marcus Aurelius," says Mr. Lecky, in his *History of European Morals,* " was the purest and gentlest spirit of all the pagan world, the last and most perfect representative of Roman Stoicism — as nearly a perfectly virtuous man as has ever appeared upon our world."

Now if we turn from the observation of the personality and character of Aurelius to a study of the events of his career as Emperor of Rome, we discover two very remarkable things. In the first place, we find that this man, who was all his life a lover of peace and a hater of war, and who dreamed as few men have ever dreamed of the coming of a day when peace would everywhere be established among men, spent the larger part of his reign in waging some of the bloodiest wars in all the history of the Empire. During fourteen of the nineteen years that he held the Roman sceptre, Marcus Aurelius wore the armour of a Roman soldier, lived in the camp of the Roman legionaries, and led his troops in battle and campaign against the barbarians of Germany, Asia, and the country north and east of the Danube River.   We wonder how this extraordinary fact could for a moment be possible — how this peace-loving author of the *Meditations* could be one of the most persistent, courageous, and at times ruthless warriors that Rome produced.   And when we turn to the records to find an explanation, we discover that this Stoic philosopher was driven to take up arms in order to defend the Empire committed to his care from hostile incursions from across its borders.   For it was in the reign of his father, Antoninus Pius, who was second only to his illustrious son in the virtue of his life, the exaltation of his thought, and the wisdom of his rule, that there began those threatening invasions of the barbaric hosts from the territories beyond the Rhine, the Danube, and the Euphrates, which finally overthrew the Empire which had subdued the world.   By the time that Marcus Aurelius had come to the throne, these invasions had become persistent and dangerous.   Hurled back beyond the frontiers at one place, they promptly broke out at another.   And thus for fourteen of his nineteen years as Emperor, as I have said, this brave and patient ruler, this lover of peace and dreamer of dreams, kept himself at the head of his armies.   And so far as I have been able to discover, all historians unite in praising Aurelius for fighting this long succession of wars, and in declaring that through his great feats of arms, the doom of Rome was postponed for at least one hundred and fifty years.

Here, now, is an excellent example of what is meant by the use of force for purposes of defence. Aurelius never took up arms as a conqueror. In all his years of fighting, he added not a single square mile to the territory over which he held domain. Had the Empire not been invaded, his nineteen years of rule would have been years of uninterrupted tranquillity. But when the incursions came from over the frontiers east, north, and west, there was nothing for him to do but act. Just because he was the best of men as well as the most faithful of rulers, he drew the sword and defended by the sword the Empire which had been committed to his hand.

But there is a second feature of Marcus Aurelius's reign which is even more remarkable than the first. I refer not only to the fact that this lover of peace was a successful warrior, but to the still more paradoxical fact that this man, whose virtue is surpassed only by that of Jesus and whose love for humanity constitutes one of the most cherished memories of the race, proved himself to be, with the possible exception of Diocletian, the most persistent and ruthless persecutor of Christianity that Rome ever produced. John Stuart Mill declares, in his *Essay on Liberty*, that the persecution of the Christians by a man like Marcus Aurelius is " one of the most tragical facts in the history of the world." Terrible beyond words were the deeds which were done under the sign and seal of this gentle, kindly, and wholly right-

minded monarch. The persecutions in Smyrna, which
" far exceeded in atrocity," says Lecky, " any that
Christianity had endured since Nero," were authorised
at this time. The fearful story of the persecutions in
Lyons, which Lecky describes as " one of the most atro-
cious in the whole compass of ecclesiastical history," is
a part of the record of his reign. Polycarp and Justin
Martyr, two of the noblest of the church fathers, fell
victims to the sword of this beneficent Emperor. Men
and women burned to death, children slaughtered like
sheep, old men placed in torture, maidens outraged by
ferocious soldiery — these were the horrors committed
at the direction and under the authority of him whose
precepts have been the guide of life and whose life the
type of sainthood, for seventeen hundred years. Search
the pages of history from end to end and no stranger
anomaly than this can anywhere be found.

Attempts to explain this anomaly have of course been
many. It is impossible, of course, to attribute such
deeds to any natural ferocity in Marcus Aurelius's character, for every circumstance sustains the theory that
he was gentle, pure, and generous beyond all previous
example. Equally impossible is it to attribute the persecutions to any occasional or momentary outbreak of
religious fanaticism, for the *Meditations* are an immortal witness to the fact that he was among the calmest
and most broad-minded of men, absolutely tolerant of
all forms of religion, Christianity excepted. Neither is
.it possible to believe that Marcus Aurelius cherished any
particular hatred for Christians as Christians. In the

first place, he was most decidedly a man immune to personal hatreds of any kind; and in the second place, the *Meditations* give the clearest indications that he knew nothing about the Christians, and had no interest in their teachings or practices. The only explanation of the phenomenon which has ever found acceptance by historians is that laid down in most satisfactory form in the *Encyclopedia Britannica.* " The Christians," says the writer of the article on Aurelius, " had assumed a much bolder attitude than they had hitherto done. Not content with bare toleration in the Empire, they declared war against all heathen rites, and, at least indirectly, against the government which permitted them to exist. In the eyes of Marcus Aurelius they were foes of that social order which he considered the first of a citizen's duties to maintain; although the most amiable of men and of rulers, he considered it his duty to sanction measures for the extermination of such wretches."

In this statement we have what may be regarded as a true explanation of the extraordinary paradox of Aurelius's persecutions. And it is an explanation which preserves unimpaired the flawless character of the man, even if it fails to justify the acts which he committed. Exactly the same motive, in other words, which led Marcus Aurelius, the sincere lover of peace, to wage relentless war against the barbarians across the frontier, led this same Marcus Aurelius, the sincere lover of his kind, to conduct persecutions of terrible ferocity against the Christians within the realm. The Emperor lifted the sword in the one case on exactly the same principle that he lifted it in the other. In both cases, he was engaged in the splendid business of protecting his Empire against wanton and threatening attacks of its enemies. In both cases, he was appealing to arms on the high ground of self-defence. And I have no doubt that, if he had been made to choose between destroying the enemies beyond the borders and the enemies within the Christian church, he would have unhesitatingly selected the latter, as by all means the more dangerous of the two.

Here, now, in the instance of so radiantly beautiful a character as that of Marcus Aurelius, do we find a perfect illustration of the tragic lengths to which the logic of force will conduct us if once we yield to the appeal of self-defence. Any form of violence can be justified on this ground. Pope Alexander VI was justified in all that he did against the Florentine priest, Savonarola, for the latter had declared war upon the church and was doing all he could to weaken and discredit it. The citizens of Athens were justified in condemning Socrates to drink the hemlock, for this philosopher was the unrelenting foe of the institutions that these citizens held dear. Caiaphas was justified in nailing Jesus to the cross of Calvary, for the Nazarene had threatened more than once to destroy Jerusalem and overthrow the temple. George III was justified in making war upon America, in defence of the integrity of his Kingdom. The South was justified in firing upon Sumter, in de-

fence of slavery. Germany was justified in marching
through Belgium and France, in defence of the liberties
of the Empire. Go through all the history of the world
— study all the persecutions, outrages, slaughters,
martyrdoms, wars — search out the motives that determined these tragedies of blood and iron. And I venture to prophesy that, in every case, it will be found
that the injury was wrought because some man, or institution, or country, felt it necessary to defend something
which was assailed and in danger therefore of destruction.

What indeed is defence, after all, but aggression from
the other point of view? The wars of Marcus Aurelius
were all of them defensive wars, as we have seen. But
again and again he invaded the countries of his foes,
ravaged their fields, burned their cities, and slaughtered
their inhabitants, on the perfectly sound military principle that offensive action of this kind was the best
means of preserving the frontiers of the Empire intact.
The persecutions of Marcus Aurelius were all of them in
defence of the government against the attacks of the
Christian, as we have also seen. But the officers of the
Empire hunted out the Christians in their homes and
churches, drove them from street to street and city to
city, and put them to the sword or the torch wherever
found. Efficient defence always means efficient assault.
It is ridiculous, said a distinguished American statesman in my hearing not long ago, to talk about building
up a navy for coast defence. There is no such thing,
he continued, as a coast defence. The only navy worth

anything is a navy which is ready to attack the enemy
upon any one of the seven seas and put his ship and men
altogether out of business.

The present war in Europe is the supreme example of
this great truth.   Never in any previous war of history
has fighting been so persistently aggressive.   And yet
every one of the nations involved, from Germany on the
one hand to Montenegro on the other hand, is fighting
on the defence.   Austria precipitated the whole conflict
in order that she might defend herself against Serbia —
and in the process has nearly wiped Serbia from the map
of Europe.   Russia mobilised her troops and entered
upon the war in order to defend the interests of the Slav
against Austria — and for months after the fight began
her troops were fighting in Galicia and Bukowina.
Germany took up arms against Russia — and her
armies have destroyed Belgium, conquered northern
France, and are far advanced in Russian Poland.   Offence, immediate and terrible, as Germany is teaching
the world with awful impressiveness, is the only sure
defence.   To hit the first blow, and hit so hard that the
enemy is forthwith put out of action, is the whole programme of protective battle.   From the standpoint of
force, Germany was perfectly right to sweep Belgium,
and invade France and Poland, in order to defend herself against Russia.   This was defence in the best sense
of the word — it was defence which really defended !

To resort to force, therefore, from motives of self-
defence is as perilous as to resort to force from motives
of liberation.   In this case as in the other the fire leaps

the trenches and kindles the conflagration. It is doubtful if defence, even when successfully kept within bounds, is ever itself defensible. Nothing hinders progress more lamentably than the defence of the things which ought not to be defended. There is no falsehood so gross, no superstition so hideous, no prejudice so base, no institution so hoary and decayed, that millions will not rush to its defence and wildly take up arms on its behalf. If a thing cannot be its own defence, on the ground of reason and beneficence, but must appeal to arms that it may live, then it is time, high time, that it should die. The sword is the weapon of death, wielded by death to do the work of death. For this reason, if for no other, is it never the friend of life, and never therefore to be safely lifted to do life's work.

IV

Such is the logic of force! Justify violence on either of the two grounds which I have specified, and immediately you kindle the flame which devours the world. Is it right to use force as the *ultima ratio* in the battle against oppression? — then may anybody take up arms who thinks himself to be oppressed and helpless otherwise to gain freedom! Is it right to use force in self-defence? — then may any man, nation or religion, sweep the world with ravage that security may be assured by world dominion. The logic of force is in the one case anarchy, and in the other case, murder, persecution, and universal war. It is the old lesson of violence breeding violence, hate breeding hate, war breeding war. The present situation is the perfect illustration — a world founded upon force as the ultimate principle of life, tumbling to ruin before the assaults of the weapons itself has builded for liberation and defence!

A few months ago, shortly after the outbreak of the Great War, there died a man who was ranked during his life as one of the supreme intellectual leaders of his time, and who had a larger influence, perhaps, in the movement for great armaments of the last twenty or thirty years than any other one person. I refer to Admiral Mahan, the discoverer, or creator, of the modern theory of sea-power. A few weeks after his death, there appeared in one of our great religious journals, a tribute written by a friend who had known Mahan intimately through many years, and had shared, even to the last moments of his life, his innermost thoughts. And this is what he said —"Admiral Mahan, though by profession a man of war, was at heart a man of peace. He advocated preparedness for war and readiness to strike, only as the best means he was yet aware of, to further peace in the end. But now it appears that . . . in extolling England's sea-power, Mahan had been spurring on the present autocracies of Europe to use his lessons against England and all that the Anglo-Saxon mind stands for in the world. Here was an unexpectedly *logical application* of his thesis — and we need not be surprised to learn that it gave him pause."

CHAPTER III
THE FALLACIES OF FORCE

" Force is no remedy."— John Bright, in *Speech on the Irish Troubles* (1880).

CHAPTER III

THE danger that is involved in the use of violence for purposes however closely restricted, must now be clear. Once liberate force, under any conditions, and you set in motion consequences which are beyond all calculation and control. The doctrine of force, however hedged about with qualifications, leads straight in the end to the anarchic principle that force may be freely used by anybody who has an end to gain or an interest to guard. The logic of force, in the last analysis, is nothing more nor less than the definite establishment of the barbaric faith that strength may be synonymous with good. We are returned, in other words, to the ancient maxim, Might makes Right!

I

Not yet, however, have we demonstrated that the use of force should be dispensed with altogether. For the fact that a certain weapon or agent is dangerous is no conclusive argument for its abolition. Nothing is more terrible in its possibilities, for example, than fire, as the parable in the last chapter indicated with great clearness. But nobody would argue, on the basis of this parable, that man should try to live without making use of this essential element. Dangerous as it is, fire is still

69

indispensable to life. Its discovery undoubtedly marks
the beginning of civilisation, and its progressive utilisation in processes of heating, lighting, transportation,
and manufacture, the development of civilisation.   Its
dangers are admitted; but these imply not abandonment
but control.

So also with dynamite, lyddite, and other instantane-
ous explosives. Nothing more perilous is known to
man than these terrifying agencies of destruction. And
yet they are manufactured in vast quantities in every
land, transported regularly on lines of public travel,
stored in great centres of population, and used as commonly in certain industrial operations as sand or cement.
These explosives, in other words, are necessary agencies
of social life. They accomplish certain things which
cannot be accomplished in any other way. Therefore is
their use, under certain rigid restrictions of inspection
and precaution, not only permitted but encouraged.

Poisons of various kinds furnish another illustration
of exactly the same kind. Only a few months ago, for
example, recurring deaths from the accidental use of
bichloride of mercury started a vigorous agitation
against this particular drug. Great stress was laid
upon its perils; but nobody, so far as I know, advocated
its out-and-out suppression. Like all poisons, it was
fatal to human life, but like all poisons also, it fulfilled
indispensably certain needs. Therefore was it argued
that its use should be not prohibited but regulated.
And laws restricting its sale to certain licensed agencies,
its use to certain authorised persons, and its manufac-

tured form to tablets of a certain shape and bottles of a certain size, were speedily passed in many states.

Now what is true here of such elements as fire, explosives and poisons, would seem to be true also of physical force as an agency of human action. It is true that the use of force is attended by dangers of the most serious description. Leaping the barriers of control, it works havoc far and wide. Adopted with reluctance by an unselfish man for unselfish ends, it is straightway adopted with eagerness by a selfish man for selfish ends. Taken as a last resort to save the race, it is seized as a first resort to destroy the race. And yet, in spite of the perils involved in its employment, it cannot be dispensed with altogether. Again and again there appear contingencies in human life when the use of force becomes absolutely necessary. On every side there exist problems of human relationships which cannot be solved save as resort is made ultimately to the " *arma virumque*," of which Virgil proudly sang. Peace, for example, between men and nations alike, can never be maintained except by the action of authority backed by force. Security both for the individual and for the state, can be guaranteed by nothing short of the clenched fist and the loaded gun. Life itself can fulfil its uttermost capacity and reach its farthest goal only as its will to power is given free exercise and scope. There are certain fundamental points of view, in other words, from which the use of force is seen to be indispensable to the maintenance and development of life. The peril of its use is as nothing to the peril of its disuse. Magnify its dangers

as much as you please, and still you have demonstrated
nothing but the wisdom of caution and the unwisdom
of precipitancy. You have shown us not that we must
stop, but only that we must be sure that we are right
before we go ahead!

II

Now it is just this basic idea of the efficacy of force
in certain contingencies — the necessity of force for
the solution of certain problems and the achievement of
certain ends — that I propose to consider in this chapter. And let me state with all possible emphasis, at the
very outset of my discussion, that I believe that this
idea is utterly and pre-eminently fallacious. It is a
superstition inherited from past ages of barbarism and
savagery, which knew no weapon but that of force and
no aim but that of conquest. It is a delusion carried
over from the primitive time when man struggled single-
handed against the ravin of wild beasts and the raging
of the elements. Like the vermiform appendix, it is a
survival of man's animal organism and experience, which
should long since have fallen into disuse. Force is
efficacious to no end — it is necessary for no purpose.
It brings not peace, but war. It guarantees not security but insecurity. It accompanies the lowest and
not the highest type of human existence. From the
very beginning of the world it has been tried, and from
the very beginning of the world it has proved itself a
failure. Life has survived in any form only as it has
escaped the destructive influences of force. Life has

climbed from one form to another in the slow process of
evolution, only as it has discarded the downward
tendencies of force. Life is to-day expanding, mounting, attaining — finding after long centuries of disappointment, some promise at least of ultimate peace,
security and joy — only as it is resolutely putting away
the works of the flesh, and seeking, however haltingly
and fearfully, the things of the spirit. Of all the
fallacies of history, the fallacy of force is the most
prodigious and the most fatal. " If there be any
virtue and if there be any praise " in the monstrous
horrors of the Great War now raging through the
world, they are to be found in the fact that at last,
through an unexampled cataclysm, this fallacy of fallacies has been blasted forevermore.

III

If we follow the lead of those who believe in the gospel
of force most thoroughly and teach it most consistently,
we shall find ourselves carried straight back to the basic
principles of life as these are revealed in the earliest
forms of organic existence upon this planet. The
ultimate justification of force is a biological justification, reflected first in the struggle for existence, and
secondly in the survival in this struggle of those creatures which are the strongest and as a consequence the
fittest. The law of nature is the law of struggle —
and the goal of nature is the goal of survival. To
struggle, fight, contend, is to share in the world-process
— and to succeed is to share in the triumph of this

process.   He who appeals to arms, therefore, is making
an ultimate appeal.   He has the universe on his side.
He is one with tides and winds, storms and seasons,
rolling suns and marching stars.   He who refuses to
make use of force, on the other hand, is outlawing himself from nature, interfering with the cosmic process,
defying the will of God.   To live by the law of force in
human relationships is simply to provide that, with man
as with the plants and animals, the fittest and therefore
the worthiest shall survive.   To ignore or repudiate this
law of force in human relationships, on the other hand,
is to betray the fit to the unfit, and thus expose mankind
to degeneration, decay and ultimate death.   Force,
therefore, and life are interchangeable terms.   The one
is not possible without the other.

General Bernhardi, in the second chapter of his book
on *Germany and the Next War*, has given as clear an
exposition of this point of view as could be desired.
" The aspiration toward the abolition of force," he says,
in one place, " is directly antagonistic to the great universal laws which rule the development of life.   The use
of force is a biological necessity of the first importance.
At the basis of all healthy development, nay of existence
itself, is the struggle for existence.   This struggle is
regulated and restrained by the unconscious surviving
of biological forms.   Everywhere the law of the
stronger holds good.   Those forms survive which are
able to procure for themselves the most favourable conditions of life, and to assert themselves in the universal
economy of nature.   The weaker on the other hand

succumb. To supplant or to be supplanted is the essence of life, and the strong life gains the upper hand."

A return, now, to the early ages of biological history would seem to indicate that General Bernhardi is perfectly right in laying down this interpretation of life in terms of physical energy and prowess. Certainly, in these more primitive epochs of the world's development, force seems to have been not so much the dominant as the sole principle of action. To all appearances nature had discovered but one method of evolution, the battle for physical supremacy, and with marvellous thoroughness proceeded to prepare her contending creatures for the fray. She built her armaments, manufactured her weapons, stored up her munitions of war — and straightway the world was filled with monsters of almost unimaginable size and strength, who battled in the ooze and slime for the mastery of creation. "Equipped from her arsenal with her varied arms and armour," says Dr. J. C. Kimball, in his *Studies in Evolution*, "nature sent forth her myriad creatures into their great life-battle."

It may be interesting to pause here, for a moment, and survey some of these mighty warriors of the antediluvian age, that we may appreciate with what completeness the law of force was tested at this time. Here, for example, was the Dinichthys, a Devonian ganoid fish, which was thirty feet long, and was protected about its head with a suit of massive articulated armour. Here were some monster reptiles, the Megalosaur, the Mosasaur, the Dinosaur, etc., which varied in length from fifty, sixty, to one hundred feet, were plated over with thick scales for defence, and armed for attack with claws hooked back like sickles. The Mastodon, with his huge bulk, thick hairy hide, and tusks twelve and fourteen feet long, has been made known to us by deposits in Siberian fields and Arctic wastes. Less familiar is the Glyptodon, which carried on his back a solidified bony armour, nine feet across and weighing four thousand pounds. Then there is the Megatherium, which had clawed feet which were a full yard in length. And no less terrible was the Machairodus, or sabre-toothed tiger, whose open mouth was an arsenal set with four rows of long, sharp, glistening, sword-like teeth.

Here are only a few of the frightful monsters, armed like modern dreadnaughts for attack upon and defence against their enemies, which swam the seas and rivers, walked the earth, and battled ceaselessly for existence, in these early prehistoric times. Surely if force ever did its perfect work, it did it in the persons of such magnificently equipped creatures as these. If living organisms were ever fitted to battle and survive, these were the ones. And yet when we look abroad over the world to-day to find these monsters and congratulate them, we search for them from pole to pole in vain. Nowhere are they to be found. They have vanished, every one. Yea, vanished so long ago and so completely, that, were it not for an occasional bone uncovered from some remote deposit in the earth, and a few degenerate survivors like the shark and the alligator, still lingering in our own time, we should never even know that such creatures once walked the earth and boasted, as they battled for existence, that to meet force with force is the basic condition of security, happiness and peace. Something would certainly seem to be wrong with General Bernhardi's interpretation of life. Force has here had its chance to demonstrate its central place in the law of life, and yet, if survival is any evidence of efficacy, it has failed, and failed completely. What is the explanation?

A very clear suggestion as to what is involved in this matter is indicated by the character of the animals which occupy the world in greatest numbers at the present time, and thus may be regarded as having successfully withstood the test of survival. Horses, cows, dogs, sheep, goats, wolves, monkeys, etc.; plants, birds, insects, fishes — these are no new-comers upon the scene. All species of this type can be traced back to origins as remote as those of the huge giants whose battles must have shaken sky and sea. At the very time, that is, that these " monsters of the prime " were bestriding the earth like so many colossi, other creatures, diminutive in size, puny in strength, unarmed in any way for either attack or defence, were struggling here for life; and, *mirabile dictu*, these are the creatures which have survived! Not the Megalosaur but the horse, not the Glyptodon but the dog, not the Megatherium but the deer, have endured into this later age. The small have outlived the great, the weak defeated the strong, the gentle overcome the savage. Scythe-like claws, sabre-like teeth, tusks, bony armour, iron scales — all these

have availed nothing.   Something else has been at work
here in the great process of evolution — something as
silent, and yet as potent, as the attraction of the
spheres.   Nor is it difficult to discern what the secret is!

At the basis of the development of the great monsters
of the early days were the very factors of which General
Bernhardi has spoken so emphatically — first struggle,
and secondly force as the weapon of survival in this
struggle.   The outward expression of this type of life
is seen in the huge armaments of attack and defence
with which these mighty creatures were equipped.
These armaments were provided, of course, with the distinct idea, if we may so express it, of protecting the animals which wielded them from injury and destruction.
But strangely enough, as experience slowly but surely
demonstrated, they worked just the other way.   Each
monster, armed literally to the teeth, was a foe to every
other.   Battle and death were the order of the day,
with extermination sooner or later the inevitable result.
Had the work of propagation been maintained in equal
ratio with the work of destruction, this fate of extinction might have been prevented or at least indefinitely
delayed.   But the combativeness of these monsters, developed, by the armaments which they carried, to a
point of blood-thirstiness never paralleled in all creation
since, kept them moving in isolation.   The bulk of their
armour and the effectiveness of their offensive weapons
seriously interfered with the process of breeding.   And,
worst of all, these armaments were so costly from the
standpoint of mere maintainance, that all the vital en-

ergies were utilised for this one end, to the practical exclusion of everything else.   These mighty monsters were their own worst enemies.   In this case as in every other, force proved itself to be an instrument of death, and not of life.

How different is the spectacle, however, when we come to the other type of animal, of which I have spoken. Provided with no weapons to kill their foes, covered with no armour to protect them from attack, these feeble creatures had no course open to them but to congregate in flocks and herds and packs, and seek strength in the mere fact of numbers.   Association rather than isolation, was their way of life; co-operation rather than conflict, was their programme of action; self-sacrifice rather than self-assertion, was their spirit of endeavour. Held together by sheer necessities of defence against their mightier competitors, and impeded by few rivalries. or hatreds among themselves, these animals found the: process of breeding easy and rapid.   Cumbered by no, elaborate armour, they were able to divert vast stores: of energy into the channels of propagation, care for the young, and mutual aid.   In spite of disasters to individuals and occasional disasters to entire groups of individuals, flocks developed into herds, herds into multitudes of herds, multitudes of herds into countless myriads.   Everything here was directed to the increase of strength, the multiplication of energy, the conserving of life.   And while thus, by association, co-operation, friendship, sympathy, love, and self-sacrifice, these forms of life survived all invasions and calamities, the

mighty monsters busied themselves with mutual slaughter, and thus little by little left the world to the weak-
lings which they despised.

What is really involved in this miracle of survival
through love, as contrasted with extinction by force, has
been interpreted again and again by our modern students of evolution.   Charles Darwin himself pointed the
way in his *Origin of Species* and *Descent of Man*.   Herbert Spencer developed the theme in a hundred passages
in his *Principles of Biology, Principles of Ethics*, and
Principles of Sociology.   Prince Kropotkin produced
a special study of the subject in his *Mutual Aid as a
Factor in Evolution*.   John Fiske answered Huxley's
doubts upon the question in his Phi Beta Kappa address
on *The Cosmic Roots of Love and Self-Sacrifice*.
Henry Drummond retold the story with ample authority
and surpassing beauty of phrase in his *Ascent of Man.*
And all pointed to the same great fact that, from the
beginning of earthly life, two forces and not one have
been at work.   On the one side is the physical force of
sheer brute strength, as exemplified by the lonely
monsters of swamp and field.   On the other side is the
spiritual force of mutual aid, co-operation, love, as exemplified in the insects, the birds, and the herding
animals.   These two forces have never of course been
thus absolutely divided.   The tiger nursing her cubs
shows the entrance of love into the most savage life.
The stags battling for the doe show ferocity invading
the realm of association.   But just because of this
mingling of the two tendencies or passions in every

organism, are we enabled to see the more clearly the nature of the real battle which is being fought. Here is no struggle of claw against claw, and fang against fang. Bernhardi is all wrong when he thus describes the evolutionary process. What has really been going on, in the breast of each individual animal as well as in the whole world of organic life, is the struggle of the monster against the herd, of brute force against mutual aid, of fierce aggression against co-operation, of blasting hate against protecting love. Not two armed giants battling for outward survival, but two great principles of action battling for inward supremacy — this is the tale of evolution. And its lesson is read aright only when force is seen to be a failure, leading to extinction all who use its weapons, and love is seen to be a success, leading to eternal life all who bow to its commands.

Of the validity of this conclusion, man is of course the perfect demonstration. From the purely physical standpoint, man is the feeblest of all creatures. He cannot run like the deer, fly like the eagle, swim like the fish, fight like the lion. He has not so much even as a coat of fur to cover his body from the cold, or a tooth or claw or fang to strike his enemy a blow. Defenceless as he is, he has been driven by the sheer necessities of the situation to protect himself by the clever exercise of his wits and the ready sympathy of his comrade. And by these weapons, which seem to be no weapons at all, he has to his own surprise gained the mastery of the physical world. Never was there a clearer demonstration of the futility of force. "From the dawn of life,"

says Drummond, summing up the whole matter in his
Ascent of Man, " two forces have acted together (in the
evolutionary process), one continually separating and
destroying, the other continually uniting and cherishing.
Both are great in nature, but the greatest of these is
love! "

IV

With this crumbling of the foundations of the Bernhardi doctrine, the entire philosophy of force comes
tumbling to the ground.   Upon this the whole case has
been rested, and with this the whole case disappears.
An understanding of the completeness of the wreckage
cannot be had, however, unless we push on from the
field of biology to the field of history, and show from
the study of man as a social agent rather than as an
evolutionary product, how absolute is the fallacy of
force.   And right here I would anticipate, without
further delay, the objection, which must already have
become apparent, to my description of man as a physi-
cally defenceless animal.   Man, you say, defenceless!
Man the feeblest of all creatures!   Man, the master of
nature through the operation of intellectual and spiritual forces!   Is there anything which could be more
ridiculous than this?   Why, man is the most combative
of all animals.   And his battles have been just as much
on the physical plane as those of any of the lower animals.   He has used his reason, to be sure — but for
what purpose so exclusively as that of producing
weapons of offence more terrible than any which

nature herself has ever been able to evolve? He
has used his associative instincts, no doubt — but to
what end more effectively than that of amassing great
multitudes of his fellows for the work of death on so
vast a scale that nothing in nature short of flood, fire
or famine has been able to match it. What man has
lacked in his own body, he has long since supplied by
inventions and manufactures. He cannot run like the
deer — but he has the automobile. He cannot fly like
the eagle — but he has the aeroplane. He cannot swim
like the fish — but he has the submarine. He cannot
fight like the lion — but he has swords and spears and
guns. He has no actual protection for his body — but
look at his trenches and battleships and forts. He has
neither teeth, fangs, nor claws — but he has dreadnaughts, 42-centimetre guns, and Zeppelin airships.
Man, an illustration of the triumph of love over force!
Is not just the opposite the case? Is not man the supreme illustration of force as the determining factor of
survival?

So it would seem, especially in this age which marks
the culmination in society of the power of destructive
force. And yet I believe that, if we look a little closer
at this problem, we shall find that the phenomena of
human history present exactly the same story of
struggle between physical and moral force as the phenomena of natural evolution, and point to exactly the
same conclusion of the failure of force as a conserving
principle. What, indeed, is the story of human progress but the story of the discovery, in every field of

human relationship, of the fallacy of force, and of its gradual displacement in favour of love?

Take, for example, the domestic relation! In the early days of social development, a man obtained a wife in exactly the same way that he obtained his dinner. He went out and captured her — took her home by force, held her by force, and used her by force. In oriental countries we find this practice still typified in the institution of the harem, where women are held as in a prison behind barred windows and locked doors, and under the constant guard of eunuchs. In the beginning, that is, the relationship between husband and wife was a relationship joined by force and maintained by force; and if anybody had dared to assert that husband and wife could be held together in peace and harmony by any other method, he would have been held to be as crazy as the man who to-day contends that peace between the nations can be secured by any other means than competitive armaments, balances of power, and secret treaties of alliance. Nevertheless, the change has come in our day, because force has proved itself a failure. Bolts are not strong enough, bars stout enough, eunuchs watchful enough, to hold an unwilling wife to an eager husband. The only thing that can hold her is the surrender of her own will, and this is to be won not by compulsion but by love. To-day a man does not capture his wife, but woos her. He does not hold her to him by chains, but binds her to him by affection. Long since has he learned that, in the domestic relation at least, there is no compulsion that is so potent and so permanent as the passion of the heart.   Therefore, to the extent that he would keep his wife fast to his own heart, he puts no bonds on her but those of his own reverent devotion.   He loves her, serves her, cares for her, worships her — and lo, she is his forever!

Analogous to this is the problem of the treatment of children.   Time was when it was implicitly believed that the only way to control and care for children was through the use of force.   In Rome, as in other ancient countries, the father was given power of life and death over his own offspring.   And such a grant of extreme authority was justified on the ground that in no other way could the growing boy or girl be made obedient to the parent, and the home therefore be held together. All such barbarity as this, of course, has long since passed away.   And little by little is disappearing as well, from home and school and college, the twin barbarity of corporal punishment.   For experience is teaching us that, in the case of the child as in the case of the wife, the use of force always fails of its appointed purpose.   If the child is to be saved, he must be led by love and not driven by blows.   There must be laid upon him the compulsion not of passionate violence, but of patient example, wise instruction, affectionate care. To strike the child is to stir his anger and arouse his fear.   To love the child is to win his confidence, challenge his faith, hold his allegiance.   Even with the incorrigible, the juvenile delinquent, the out-and-out degenerate, the method of force is doomed to utter failure. For love alone can hold, and alone therefore can save.

Another illustration of the same truth comes to us from the field of industry. In the early relationship between employer and employé, as in the early relationship between husband and wife and between parent and child, force was again regarded as indispensable. That a man could be held to his labour by any other means than that of physical compulsion, was believed to be impossible — and therefore we had in primitive times the universal institution of slavery, with its chains, its whips and its auction-blocks. Later epochs brought us serfdom, feudalism, peonage, and in our own time the wage system. But all of these have gone, or are rapidly going, for each and every one of these relationships, just to the extent that it has been founded upon outward force for its continuance, has proved itself a failure and a fraud. Force has not worked here any more than it has worked in the home or in the school. If there has been constant trouble in the labour world from the slave rebellion of Moses to the trade rebellions of 'Gene Debs and Tom Mann, it is because force and not goodwill has been the bond of union. If there is trouble and turmoil in the labour world at this late hour, it is because compulsion, dependence, subordination, inequality, slavery, still survive in one form or another. And if peace, security, and happiness have anywhere been won in the labour world in the past or in the present, it has been by the application of the age-old ideals of liberty, equality, fraternity between man and man.   One thing is becoming clear in our time in the tangled problems of industry, even if everything else is still doubtful.   I refer to the sweeping fact that these problems are never going to be solved by strikes, lockouts, police clubs, militia bayonets, court injunctions, McNamara broils and Ludlow massacres, but by co-operation, democracy, elimination of master and servant, abolition of wages and profits, the union of all workers in all work upon a single level of comradely association.   When force is gone, and " one equal temper of heroic hearts " is come — our labour problem will no longer be a problem.

Identical in its lesson is the melancholy history of prisons and prisoners.   Up to within comparatively modern times, and still very largely in our more enlightened days, force of the most rigorous description has been the one weapon universally commended and used for the control of criminals.   Hundreds of offences, running all the way from the murder of a man to the theft of a pig, have been punished in all countries at various periods in the past, with death.   Less than a hundred years ago, in England, it was possible to hang a thief upon the gallows.   Along with this extreme example of force, have gone all manner of less terrible examples, typified by such instruments of torture as the rack, the thumb-screw, the wheel, the stocks, the whipping-post, the ducking stool, chains, subterranean dungeons, filthy prisons, etc., etc.   One shudders when one recalls how men have for ages been

broken, whipped, strung up, fettered, starved, buried
alive, in the sacred name of law and order; and one
shudders still more when one recollects that this kind of
brutal treatment is still visited upon most of our prisoners in most of our prisons at the present moment.
One only has to think of our modern death-houses, cell-
blocks, "coolers," chain-gangs, bull-rings and even
whipping-posts, to realise how exclusively we are still
depending upon the use of force for the control and reform of criminals.   And yet, from the beginning of ordered society down to this very moment, such methods
have never been anything but colossal failures.   They
have never done anything that they were supposed to do.
Capital punishment has never stayed the hand of a
single murderer.   Chains, bars, armed guards and
rigid discipline, so far from controlling men, have only
driven them to madness and rebellion.   The whole system of relentless force, so far from redeeming or reforming men, has only brutalised them into confirmed crimi-
nality.   Visit any prison conducted on the old lines of
violent repression, and see how its record is one unvarying story of outbreak, assaults, bloodshed, and insanity,
and its inmates one unvarying line of fourth and fifth
offenders.   In this case, as in all others, force is a failure.   And in this case, as in all others, the opposite of
force, namely reason and goodwill, is alone a success.
Go to the notorious Sing Sing prison in Ossining, where
are confined some sixteen hundred of the vilest criminals in New York State, and see the success of Warden
Osborne and his ideals of mutual welfare.   Armed

guards withdrawn and the men placed in charge of convict officers in the cell-blocks and convict foremen in the
factories, freedom of intercourse and association guaranteed and fostered, rules and regulations formulated
by the prisoners and their violation punished by a court
of their own choosing, athletics encouraged, honour systems instituted, recreation and school facilities provided
— with the immediate result that rebellions have ended,
sickness and insanity are steadily diminishing, and control is as easy as formerly it was difficult! Go to Oregon, and see the prisoners taken from behind their iron
bars and granite walls, placed at work on roads, in forests, and on the farms, and held in bonds not by state
guards but by convict leaders! Go to Colorado and see
prisoners despatched hither and yon as free men,
charged with the tasks of state, and maintaining in
strictest honour the imposed limits of their freedom!
Strike a man, and he strikes back — confine him, and he
breaks away — brutalise him, and he becomes a brute.
But trust a man, help him, love him, serve him, and no
matter what his record of crime, he responds in kind.

Political relationships provide still another illustration of the same universal truth. For centuries men
believed that government rested upon force. Kings and
parliaments looked to Janissaries, Swiss Guards, Black
Hundreds, for their support, with the result that revolutions were ever the order of the day. Now, with the
slow advancement of democracy, we are venturing to
rest our government not upon the force of armed soldiery, but upon the consent of free citizens — with the

result that revolutions are no longer a part of history.
Peace comes to a community when the cossack is withdrawn, and the court of law is established in his place.
Security is held by every citizen, when revolvers and
knives are snatched from his belt, and opportunity
granted for the settlement of differences on an equal
basis of reason and goodwill. Life develops, flourishes,
blossoms in fragrance and beauty, when tyranny is overthrown and freedom won. Contrast Turkey and America, the army of the Sultan and the Supreme Court of
the United States — and we have an all-convincing example of the failure of the sword and the success of the
spirit in the task of government.

A special application of this truth is seen in the matter of colonial administration, more particularly as
exemplified by the experience of Great Britain. In the
eighteenth century, England, like every other colonising
power of that day, regarded the inhabitants of its colonies as subject peoples, and its territories across the
seas as crown lands. In the case of *émigré* or transported Englishmen, of course, certain liberties were
granted or permitted which were withheld in the case of
native populations. But even upon these former no
final governmental authority was bestowed, and the exercise of force was regarded in the last analysis as the
guarantee of loyalty. The futility of this doctrine was
clearly demonstrated by the successful revolt of the
Americans in 1775; and England was wise enough to
see and learn the lesson taught by this experience.
From that time on, the British people founded their

colonial policies on principles of liberty and not of authority, of goodwill and not of force, with the result
that they have builded during the last one hundred years
an empire of unexampled stability and power. The supreme test of the abnegation of force as a definite policy of colonial administration came with the outbreak of
the Great War in Europe. Canada, New Zealand, Australia, these were to all intents and purposes independent principalities. They were not even bound to England by the tie of economic self-interest. They had no
concern in the European quarrel, so far as the problem
of their own particular welfare was concerned. There
was no power in the hands of the mother-country which
could force them to enter the struggle against Germany,
if they chose not to do so. All such power had long
since been surrendered. And yet, at the instant that
England and Germany clashed in mortal combat, the
free colonies of the Empire leaped into the fray, and
from that day to this have been pouring a steady tide
of men, munitions and money into the area of conflict.
Even the South African Republic, so lately conquered
and overthrown, and so hazardously granted the privilege of self-government by the Asquith Ministry, re-
sponded to the call. Only Egypt and India stood, and
still stand, in any doubtful attitude of allegiance to
King George — and these, be it noted, are the very
colonies from which the hand of force has not yet been
lifted. Just to the extent, in other words, that absolute power has been withdrawn and free relationships
of goodwill substituted, just to that extent loyalty has

been quickened, security established, and happiness fostered.   In this field, as in all other fields of human activity, force is a failure, and love a demonstrated success!

And what is true in all these various relations of the master, is true also of his victim.   Driven to despair by the bondage imposed upon him, goaded to desperation by nameless cruelties, robbed of every weapon of revolt save the *ultima ratio* of sheer brute strength, the imprisoned wife, the beaten child, the exploited working-man, the tortured convict, the political outlaw or religious heretic, have again and again striven for release by pitting force against force, madness against madness. Especially in the field of politics, as in the revolutions of '48, and in the field of industry, as in the labour struggles of the first three quarters of the nineteenth century, has violence been resorted to as the way to emancipation. And in the action of the rebel, exactly as in the action of the tyrant, has this resort been accompanied by almost uninterrupted failure.   Sometimes, by some miracle of chance, as in the American Revolution or the Italian War of Liberation, the strength of the revolutionist has overcome the strength of the ruling power. Sometimes, by dint of long previous preparation, as in the Civil War, resort to arms has been the last act in a struggle already determined by educational, political and economic processes.   But in the vast majority of cases, appeal to force has resulted either in immediate disaster, or, if momentarily successful, as in the case of the French Revolution, has but led, through storm, to the darkness of reaction. Nothing in history is more pitiful than the oft-told tale of the helpless multitudes madly beating themselves to pieces against the unyielding walls of tyranny. Slave rebellions, peasants' revolts, Chartist riots, Bomba horrors, Communes, Homestead massacres, Ludlow shambles — the story runs in an unbroken and bloody stream from Spartacus to John Lawson; and everywhere there is the same fatal outcome. For one time that force has brought life, liberty and happiness to the outraged masses, a thousand times it has brought death, bondage, and misery. Force is a failure no less for the rebelling slave than for the repressing master. Nay, for the slave it is more often a failure, for in the battle of strength against strength, might, not right, must win. Inevitably does the master, with his legions as in Rome, his soldiers as in France and Italy, his private guards and state militia as in America — in one word, the whole organised power of society — on his side, prove the stronger of the two. It was realisation of this fact, undoubtedly, which led Shelley, an anarchist of the anarchists, to counsel the

> "Men of England, heirs of glory,
> Heroes of unwritten story,
> Nurslings of one mighty Mother,"

on the occasion of the massacre at Manchester, to seek vengeance and liberation by methods peaceable and not violent. Thus, in his *Mask of Anarchy*, did he write

> "Let a great Assembly be
> Of the fearless and the free

On some spot of English ground
Where the plains stretch wide around.

" From the corners uttermost
Of the bounds of English coast;
From every hut, village, and town
Where those who live and suffer moan
For others' misery or their own,

" From the workhouse and the prison
Where pale as corpses newly risen,
Women, children, young and old
Groan for pain, and weep for cold —

" From the haunts of daily life
Where is waged the daily strife
With common wants and common cares
Which sows the human heart with tares —

" Let a vast assembly be,
And with great solemnity
Declare with measured words that ye
Are, as God has made ye, free—

" Be your strong and simple words
Keen to wound as sharpened swords,
And wide as targes let them be
With their shade to cover ye.

" Let the tyrants pour around
With a quick and startling sound,
Like the loosening of a sea,
Troops of armed emblazonry.

" Let the charged artillery drive
Till the dead air seems alive
With the clash of clanging wheels,
And the tramp of horses' heels.

"Let the fixèd bayonet
Gleam with sharp desire to wet
Its bright point in English blood
Looking keen as one for food.

"Let the horsemen's scimitars
Wheel and flash, like sphereless stars
Thirsting to eclipse their burning
In a sea of death and mourning.

"Stand ye calm and resolute,
Like a forest close and mute,
With folded arms and looks which are
Weapons of unvanquished war."

Similar realisation it is also, which has created in
our time, under the inspiration of Marx and Engels,
and under the guidance of Bebel, Liebknecht and Jaures,
the great movement of international socialism, which
seeks the mastery of the modern world not through the
old methods of violent revolt, but through the new and
nicer " methods of education, organisation, and political
action . . . the weapons of civilisation," as Robert
Hunter calls them in his *Violence and the Labour Movement.* Nothing in all history is more wonderful, to my
mind, than the story of the winning of the labour movement in all countries to the cause of pacifism. Never
were any people under a heavier burden of oppression,
and therefore under a greater temptation to armed rebellion, than the labouring multitudes of our own day.
Never was the sword of hate and revenge held out to
their hands more persuasively than by Bakounin and
his terrorist disciples. More than once, as in the Char-

tist days and on many occasions of revolt in Italy,
Spain and France, did the " physical forcists " seem
triumphant over the " moral forcists." Especially in
1872, when the International was virtually disbanded,
did the wise leadership of Marx away from terrorism to
pacifism seem utterly vain. But after sore struggle
the victory for order as against violence was won. And
to-day we have the stupendous spectacle of a vast international body, 12,000,000 in numbers, organised for
the conquest of the wealth and dominion of the world,
putting force as a weapon of combat altogether aside,
and deliberately choosing the counter weapons of the
pen, the platform and the ballot. " They have refused
to hurry," says Mr. Hunter. " They have declined all
short cuts. They have spurned violence." Never was
there such a spectacle! And in it we must see, not the
triumph of any fanatical idealism, but the calm, reas-
oned conviction of the fallacy of force as a " power of
deliverance."

And so we might go on, multiplying the illustrations
of this thesis almost without limit. But why continue?
All tell exactly the same story, and point to exactly the
same conclusion. Every relationship of human life had
its beginning on the animal plane of physical control.
The mighty principle of love was never altogether ab-
sent even in the struggles of the forest beasts, as we
have seen. But force as the law of life was everywhere
in the ascendent. And man, like his animal progenitors, gave this principle of life every conceivable chance
to prove its efficacy. But the more thorough the trial,

the more convincing its failure. Not because love was
known to succeed, but because force was known to fail,
has man little by little turned to the one and away from
the other. And to-day he is solving his problems and
reaching his goal just to the extent that he is having
the courage and wisdom to put his perfect trust in love.
Force avails nothing, achieves nothing, secures nothing. It is the instrument of destruction, and not of
conservation — the agent of retreat and not of advance
— the minister of death and not of life. With man, as
with the animal, two forms have contended for mastery,
" one continually separating and destroying, the other
continually uniting and cherishing." And if man is
to-day something more than an animal in character, his
superiority may perhaps be more truly attributed to
the fact that he has little by little subdued the flesh to
the spirit, mastered force in favour of love, than any
other one thing. The story of man's climb from brute-
hood to potential sainthood is the story of his climb
from the claw to the brain, from the fang to the heart.
In the home, the school, the church, the state, the mart,
he has scourged force from him as a traitor, and drawn
love to him as a friend. In every field of action, he
has tried more and more to lead rather than to drive,
to woo rather than to subdue, to serve rather than to
master, and his perpetual reward has been peace, security and mounting life.

v

In every field of action — save only one! In the international field, little or no progress has been made.

Still to-day, as in the ancient days of Persian satraps
and Roman consuls, relations between states are founded
upon force. And yet where, in any department of
human life, has the futility of force been more completely demonstrated than in the department of internationalism? Consider for a moment those particular
problems of the modern world which were raised all
anew by the outbreak of the Great War.

First of all, there is the question of peace — the question of the method by which peace between rival states
may be most surely and easily maintained. The answer
that has been given to this problem, ever since the day
when Æsop met the boar in the forest sharpening his
tusks against a tree, has uniformly been the affirmation
that the best way, indeed the only way, for nations to
insure peace is to make ready for war. George Washington gave a crystal clear statement of this position,
when, in his address to the two houses of Congress in
1790, at the time when all Europe was bursting into the
conflagration kindled by the French Revolution, he declared that " to be prepared for war is one of the most
efficient means of preserving peace."

That there is a certain superficial persuasiveness
about this dictum is obvious enough. And yet it may
be well doubted if any other theory of the human intellect has ever offered quite so arrant a challenge to
experience and so impudent a defiance of reason as this
hoary doctrine of preparedness. For what have the nations of the world been doing, since the beginning of

time, but preparing for war; and when in any age has
this business of preparation ever brought anything but
war, war, war? The Sargons, Sennacheribs and
Tiglath-Pilesers of old Assyria, with the possible exception of the rival Pharaohs of Egypt, made the mightiest war preparations of their time, but it would be
difficult to find a year when they were not waging war
against the Pharaohs or the Pharaohs against them.
Sparta was pre-eminent among all the cities of the
Grecian world for her sacrifice of every human interest
to the things of war, and she also was pre-eminent for
the number and savagery of the wars which she fought.
Rome was the greatest military power that mankind has
ever seen — and the doors of the Temple of Janus,
which were opened in times of war and closed in times
of peace, were closed but twice, and both times but momentarily, in a period of six hundred years. Every
country of the Middle Ages was organised on the basis
of the feudal system, which was a system constructed
for the express purpose of enabling an entire people to
be prepared for war — and every country of the Middle
Ages was fighting an almost continual battle against its
neighbours. The last half of the nineteenth century
was a period remarkable for the completeness and
efficacy of its preparations for war — but the Crimean
War of 1855, the Danish War of 1864, the Austrian
War of 1866, the Franco-Prussian War of 1870, the
Italian Wars of Liberation, ending in 1870, the Russio-
Turkish War of 1877, the more recent Spanish-Ameri-

can, Boer, Turco-Grecian, and Russio-Japanese Wars,
and the continual struggles in the Balkans, are a part
of the record of this period.

It would seem preposterous that any further demonstration of the futility of this principle of preparedness could be needed, after the uninterrupted testimony
of something like three thousand years of fighting. But
whether needed or not, a final demonstration came with
a vengeance in August, 1914. Here for forty years
have the nations of Europe been building up such armaments as eye hath not seen, nor ear heard, nor the heart
of man conceived, in any previous age of human history. Never have there been such armies as those of
Germany, Austria, Russia and France. Never has there
been such a navy as that of England. Never have there
been such fortresses as those lining the frontiers and
shores of all these states. Never, in other words, has
preparedness been so complete. Every citizen was a
soldier in active service or reserve. Every ship was po-
tentially a war-vessel or transport. Railroads were
constructed on strategic rather than commercial lines.
Passenger-cars and freight-cars were measured in terms
not of the passengers and freight they could carry in
time of peace, but of the soldiers and munitions they
could transport in time of war. Schools and hotels
were built with an eye to the possibility of their instant
transformation into barracks and hospitals. If anything in the way of preparation for war was left undone
during these years, the world has yet to find it out.
And now, as the end of it all, we behold not peace at all,

but the greatest and most terrible war in the history of
mankind! The very presence of armaments so complete
and so ready for instant use made war not impossible
nor even uncertain, but inevitable. Not one of the nations, on those fateful days of July and August, 1914,
dared to wait, even twenty-four hours, for negotiations.
The risk of waiting was too great. The advantage of
the first blow was too vital. And prepared to strike,
they all struck — and war in a night was the result.
The Serbian ultimatum was like a spark in a dynamite
factory. Explosion was immediate and universal.

Thousands of years of unvarying experience, crowned
in one day by the most stupendous calamity of the ages,
have destroyed at last forever the old idea that preparation for war is a guarantee of peace. Never again can
any man who is sane argue for battleships and armies on
the plea that these mechanical horrors are needed to preserve the peace. At last we see what Charles Sumner
saw, as long ago as 1837, when he said, in his famous
oration on *The True Grandeur of Nations*, " This maxim
is transmitted to us from distant ages, when brute force
was the general law. It belongs to the dogmas of barbarism. It is the child of suspicion and the forerunner
of violence. It is a mere prejudice, sustained by vulgar
example and not by enlightened truth. It is a mis-
chievous fallacy, the most costly the world has witnessed, dooming nations to annual tribute in comparison
with which the extortions of conquest are as the widow's
mite." And if, while seeing the fact, we do not quite
understand the reasons for the fact, we have only to

turn to the unanswerable statement of John Quincy
Adams, then Ambassador to England, in his letter to
the English premier on behalf of President Monroe's
suggestion for disarmament on the border line between
England and Canada: "The increase of naval armaments on one side upon the Lakes, during peace, will
necessitate the like increase on the other, and besides
causing an aggravation of useless expense to both parties, must operate as a continual stimulus of suspicion
and ill-will upon the inhabitants and local authorities
of the borders against those of their neighbours. The
moral and political tendency of such a system must be
to war and not to peace."

If the Great War has shattered the idea that force
can make for peace, it has on the other hand strengthened immeasurably the old-time doctrine of force as applied to our second problem — that of security. Men
the world around are looking upon stricken Belgium,
ravaged France, wasted Galicia, Poland and Bukowina,
and with one accord they are declaring that armaments
must be built and maintained on a scale never known before, if only to protect the nations from such a dire
fate as has been met by these unhappy people. So
long as war is liable to come, protection must be had
against its incursion, and where can such protection be
found except in arms? Peace, as we now see, cannot
be assured, even by the method of preparation. But
preparation, for this very reason, is more essential than
ever before in order that we may be secure when trouble
comes. Safety we must have; and in the world as it is

now constituted at least, this can be guaranteed only
by resort to force.

It may well be doubted, however, by those who have
any knowledge of human experience, if this argument
for security is any sounder than the similar argument
for peace, which we have just seen to be so fallacious.
For where, in all the history of ancient and modern
times, is there a single nation that has ever found permanent security in arms? Assyria, Babylonia, Egypt,
Sparta, Rome — these, like the mighty monsters of
early biological times, were effectively protected against
all possibility of military disaster. Surely these peoples, with their swords and spears, their chariots and
horsemen, their phalanxes and legions, were secure forever. And yet, just like these monsters with the bony
armour, the scythe-like talons and the sabre-like teeth,
they have every one disappeared. Assyria is but a
mound in the desert, Egypt but a melancholy wreck of
empty shrines and rifled tombs, Sparta a plain without
so much as one stone standing upon another, and Rome
but a legend " to point a moral and adorn a tale." In
spite of their armaments, or shall we say, because of
their armaments — all of them gone, all of them fallen
upon insecurity, and perished!

Later ages tell identically the same story, in only
slightly different terms. Charlemagne, Charles V,
Philip II, Charles XII, Peter the Great, Frederick the
Great, Napoleon — behold the geniuses who have sought
not merely glory but security in arms. And all of
them failed ignominiously in their quest. And in our

day, the same story is being repeated still again. For why are not men wise enough, in these dreadful hours of world disaster, to read aright the lesson that is being taught? Force, you say, must be relied upon for security? When, I answer you, was force ever so implicitly relied upon for security as it was yesterday, and when has it ever brought disaster so complete? Belgium was not unarmed, that she was swept away to ruin! On the contrary, she had an army proportionally only slightly smaller than that of Germany; she had a frontier lined with cannon, troops and forts; and in Antwerp she had the best protected city in Europe. Galicia was not defenceless, and therefore a prey to Russia! On the contrary, her cities were fortresses, her railroads military highways, her mountain-barriers citadels, and all her men armed soldiers. Russia was completely armed — but disasters immeasurable are sweeping down upon her. France was strained to the breaking-point in support of her fleet and armies — and the fairest and richest sections of her territory are to-day in the hands of the enemy. England's fleet surpassed and still surpasses anything ever seen upon the seven seas — but her empire is trembling to its foundations with the shock of war. Germany, with the greatest military machine at her disposal the world has ever known, is already doomed to such cataclysmic ruin as has come upon no people since the fall of Spain.

Force, you say, the guarantee of security? On the contrary, force is the guarantee of nothing but disaster. For force breeds force, and the work of force is death. Build a battleship, and you arouse the suspicion of your neighbour, who matches your one battleship with two. Construct a fort, and you stir fear across the border, and your fort is straightway fronted by two forts. Raise an army of a million men, and all the nations, disturbed and apprehensive, raise armies of other millions — and all the world is fixed in arms. France totters and falls to-day, because her army shouted *Revanché* across the Alsatian border. England gasps in a struggle which bleeds her white, because she challenged with dreadnaughts the freedom of the seas. Germany is doomed to certain extinction, because she built a military machine so terrible that all of Europe lifts up arms against her.

> " Lo, all our pomp of yesterday,
> Is one with Nineveh and Tyre,"

because it is built upon the same explosive foundations. He who seeks defence in force, brings force down upon him. He who sows the dragon's teeth, reaps ere long the crop of armed men. " They that take the sword shall perish with the sword," said Jesus when he bade Peter to put up his weapon, and make no resistance to his arrest. If there is any security in this world of chance and change, ignorance and hate, it is not by force that it can come. Security, like peace, is the fruit of love. It comes not from violence but from goodwill. It is maintained not by the hand, but by the heart. Norman Angell sums up the whole question in his *Arms and Industry* when he speaks of the remarka-

ble one hundred years of peace between England and
America, and referring to the lapse of any attempt of
either nation to seek security against the other by resort to arms, says, " We have secured ourselves by the
only means that will ever give permanent national
safety — a better understanding of the real character
of the relationship between nations."

And what about the last of these three recrudescent
problems — that of the true character of life? What
of Bernhardi's dictum that there can be no high and
noble life save that which is based on the utilisation of
force? What of Ruskin's idea that no great literature
and art have ever been produced save as a consequence
of war and the war-spirit? What of Professor Cramb's
suggestion that war provides an exaltation of spirit so
essential to life at its best that mankind will not be willing to dispense with it utterly? Do such propositions
as these constitute a final vindication of the gospel of
arms, or are they, on the contrary, a final demonstration
of the fallacy of this gospel?

History once more has its conclusive answer, for
those at least who have ears to hear its voice. For
what is left to us by these nations which have lived by
the law of force most faithfully and developed the war-
spirit therefore most consistently? Chaldea gives us
a few statues, reliefs and hieroglyphic inscriptions;
Egypt some glorious temples, mighty pyramids and
mysterious sphinxes; Tyre, Sidon, Phœnicia, mere
names. Out of all the ancient East, as a supreme expression of human genius, and a priceless treasure of

human achievement, comes only the religion of the Jews, who for centuries cowered beneath the iron heels of conquerors, and only twice, for momentary periods in the great days of David and the Maccabees, lifted the sword of victory on the field of battle.   Impressive is it to remember that Isaiah looked upon the fall of Samaria, watched the invasions of Sennacherib, and shared in the humiliations of Ahaz and Hezekiah — that Jeremiah flourished in the days which witnessed the fall of Jerusalem and the captivity of Israel — that Deutero-Isaiah, the greatest spiritual genius of the Jewish race before Jesus, lived amid the supreme sorrows of the Exile — and that Jesus himself came at a time when the darkness of Roman conquest and dominion was over all the land of Palestine.

Identical is the story of the classic world.   Four names are here supreme from the standpoint of militarism — Sparta, Macedonia, Carthage and Rome. But wherein, with the exception of the last, have these names significance to-day?   Sparta is the warrior-state *par excellence* — but she left nothing to posterity but a few doubtful legends of martial heroism and endurance. Macedonia produced Philip, Alexander and the matchless phalanxes which followed these conquerors to war — and perished of exhaustion.   Carthage dyed sea and land with blood, but is now remembered only as the occasion of Cato's cry for vengeance and the scene of Scipio's meditation on the futility of arms.   As for Rome, she gave to us her laws, a worthy heritage; but she was barbaric to the end, and gained a civilisation

only as she robbed of art, literature, and religion the
nobler principalities which she conquered.

It is in our own day, however, that we find the supreme example of the antagonism of militarism and
civilisation in the case of Germany.   For centuries, the
German people were peaceful traders, hard-working
peasants, and raptured dreamers.   Political power was
unknown to them, and military greatness undesired.
And these were the days, be it noted, when her life was
purest, and her spirit at its zenith of achievement.   It
was feeble and divided Germany which gave us the long
line of noble mystics from Tauler and Meister Eck-
hart to Herder and Schleiermacher — Martin Luther
and the Reformation — the literature of Lessing, Schil-
ler, Goethe and Heine — the music of Bach, Beethoven,
Haydn, Mozart, and Schubert — the philosophy of
Leibnitz, Kant, Fichte, and Schelling — the scholarship
of Wolf, Strauss, Baur, Niebuhr, and Ranke.   Then,
in the eighteenth century, came the Great Elector and
Frederick, and the beginnings of Prussian militarism.
Then came the Napoleonic Wars, with their poisonous
progeny in the persons of Stein, Scharnhorst, and
Gneisenau.   The days of '48 were a brief awakening
from the creeping hypnotism of the times.   But Bismarck and Moltke, the veritable incarnation of blood
and iron, soon came upon the scene, and Germany was
lost.   From that day to this Germany has been obsessed
with the ideal of force, greediness, power; and from that
day to this, her true life has atrophied and slowly died.
If 1870 marks the beginning of German imperialism, it

marks as well the close of German culture. And if the
political and military doom now impending upon the
Empire can bring any compensation for its attendant
miseries and horrors, it is that the German spirit,
" sleeping, but not dead," may rise and lead the world
again to paths of light.

Force, therefore, has no connection with abundant
life, save as it chokes its springs, diverts its flow, and
poisons its purity. If civilisation flourishes in days
of military splendour, as in Athens after the Persian
Wars, in Venice in the triumphant days of the great
Doges, or in England in the reign of the Good Queen
Bess, it is for reasons extraneous to feats of arms. It
is in spite of war, and never because of war, that the
spirit of man attains. In the case of the antedeluvian
animals, as we have seen, the armaments which they carried were so heavy that their energies were available
for no other and higher purpose than that of physical
maintenance. The battles of these creatures were so
fierce and constant that every nobler instinct of co-
operation, friendliness and compassion was atrophied
from disuse. The same thing is true in the case of
man. It was when brain development began to take the
place of body development, says Alfred Russel Wal-
lace, that the advance of man to the higher reaches of
intellect and spirit had its beginning. Both forms of
development could not go on together. The flesh must
yield place to the spirit, if the spirit was to expand.
And not otherwise is it with nations. Herbert Spencer
traced the true analogy in his *Principles of Sociology,*

in his elaborate account of the passing of militarism
and the rise of industrialism. If the soul is to live, it
must be freed; and the fetters which bind it, and have
always bound it, are those forged by the hand of force.

VI

The failure of force, as a working principle, must
by now be manifest. It is demonstrated by the biological history of the race; it is demonstrated by the
individual and social relationships of men; it is demonstrated by the rise and fall of states. Force and love
— the power that separates and destroys, and the power
that unites and cherishes — here are the two contending giants of the cosmos. They have wrestled long,
and are still wrestling. But little by little, as age
passes into age and æon into æon, force is seen to be
growing weaker and love stronger. "God's in his
heaven," after all! Force is failing, because it is alien
to God. Love is rising, because it is of the very essence
and potency of the Divine. Isaiah had clear vision
when he looked into the future and saw the coming of
the day when force should be wholly overcome, and love,
with its sweet ministers of peace, security and happiness, everywhere supreme. How wonderful, and how
true as well, the picture which he painted. "The wolf,"
he said, "shall dwell with the lamb, and the leopard
shall lie down with the kid; and the calf and the young
lion and the fatling together."! And as the crowning
touch of all, the great prophet proclaimed, that "a little
child," at once the weakest and the loveliest thing of
earth, "shall lead them."

CHAPTER IV

THE MEANING OF NON-RESISTANCE

" I believe in the spirit of peace and in sole and absolute reliance on truth. . . . I do not believe that the weapons of liberty ever have been, or ever can be, the weapons of despotism. I know that those of despotism are the sword, the revolver, the cannon, the bombshell; and therefore the weapons to which tyrants cling and upon which they depend are not the weapons for me as a friend of liberty. . . . Much as I detest the oppression exercised by the Southern slave-holder, he is a man, sacred before me. He is a man, not to be harmed by my hand nor with my consent. . . . He is a sinner before God — a great sinner; yet, while I will not cease reprobating his injustice, I will let him see that, in my heart there is no desire to do him harm . . . and that I have no other weapon to wield against him but the simple truth of God, which is the great instrument for the overthrow of all iniquity and the salvation of the world."— *William Lloyd Garrison.*

CHAPTER IV

THE MEANING OF NON-RESISTANCE

It must be tolerably evident, at this point of our discussion, that the champion of the gospel of force has fallen very far short of discharging the burden of proof which we saw some time ago was laid upon him by the nature of the question. Force, we discovered, was like fire, dynamite, or poison in that it was too dangerous to be used excepting under the most rigid conditions and for the most necessary purposes. Anybody who desires to employ it must prove, beyond peradventure of a doubt, that nothing else will do the work which must be done, and that force itself will do this work successfully.

The attempt to give this proof, however, has failed most lamentably, as we have just been seeing. View it from any angle, subject it to any test, try it under any conditions, and always and everywhere force shows itself to be a failure. It simply will not work — or, if it works at all, accompanies its action with such fearful consequences of ill that the end is lost almost before it is won. Every argument ever offered on behalf of force has sooner or later turned out to be at the worst a calamity and at the best a sadly mixed good. The whole progress of life, at every stage of its existence and in every form of its development, has been de-

113

pendent upon the restriction of force within ever narrower and narrower bounds and the expansion of love
to ever wider and wider areas.   Force, as Jesus clearly
stated, is the wide gate and broad way " that leadeth
to destruction."   To bar this gate and way, and open
wide the strait gate and narrow way " that leadeth unto
life," was the endeavour of the Nazarene, and still remains to-day the unfulfilled endeavour of mankind.

I

This brings us immediately to the discussion of non-
resistance, as the extreme form of pacifism, and the
logical antithesis therefore of force.   And first of all,
to the very particular discussion of the meaning of the
term!   For most people, as I discover from experience, have not the slightest idea of what non-resistance really implies as a philosophy of conduct.   And
this very largely for the reason, as I take it, that the
word which is used to denote this philosophy, is an absolute misnomer!   It is not too much to say that non-
resistance as a word implies just the opposite of what
non-resistance as a programme of life really means.
Therefore do I propose, in the first place, to define non-
resistance from an abstract point of view, with a considerable degree of elaboration.   Then I shall proceed
to illuminate this definition by considering at some
length the teachings and careers of the more conspicuous exemplars of non-resistance in ancient and modern
times.   This somewhat prolonged discussion will give
us, I trust, an accurate conception of what this doc-

trine really involves as a rule of life; and prepare us to
consider the more immediately vital question as to what
we may be able to do with non-resistance.

II

The phrase, non-resistance, has its origin in the
famous passage in the Sermon on the Mount, wherein
Jesus declares his opposition to the Mosaic law of retaliation. "Ye have heard that it hath been said," the
statement runs, "an eye for an eye, and a tooth for a
tooth. But I say unto you, Resist not evil." It must
not be presumed from this fact that there were no non-
resistants in the world before the advent of the Nazarene. On the contrary, as we shall see in the next chapter, there were non-resistants before Jesus, just as there
were kings before Agamemnon. But Jesus gave so
clear a formulation of this doctrine in his teachings,
and exemplified the doctrine with so matchless a degree of heroism in his life, that it is eminently fitting that
it should have become uniquely associated with his name
and have found immortal expression in his words.

An examination of the phrase, to which I have referred, shows that it involves two definite propositions.
On the one hand, there is the statement of fact, " evil ";
and on the other hand, there is the ethical command,
" resist not." There is first the recognition of evil in
the world; and secondly the recommendation as to the
attitude which we are to assume toward this evil. Any
proper understanding of the doctrine involved, therefore, demands an explanation of what Jesus meant by

evil, and what he had in mind when he bade his disciples not to resist this evil.

Many persons have assumed that the word " evil," as used in this connection, refers to everything which may be regarded as in any way obstructive or hostile to the physical and moral integrity of the human race. Thus they have included in the category of evil, such natural phenomena as fires, tempests, floods, and volcanic eruptions — such specimens of organic nature as serpents, wild beasts, and poisonous insects — such unnecessary and baleful horrors of human life itself as famine, pestilence, poverty, and war. These persons have interpreted the word " evil," in other words, in the most literal, which means the most inclusive, sense possible, and, interpreting the command, " resist not," with similar literalness, have come to the obviously ridiculous conclusion that the gospel of non-resistance means flatly that we should offer no resistance to any form of evil.

It should be hardly necessary to point out, in the light of this *reductio ad absurdum*, that a very definite limitation must be placed on this word " evil." Nor will it be in any way difficult to prove that Jesus had this limitation very clearly in mind when he formulated his commandment. Thus, as we read the complete passage, as it appears in the *Gospel of Matthew*, it is evident that the Nazarene was talking not about floods, or snakes, or pestilences, but about human beings and what human beings, in their selfishness and greed, are liable to do to one another. " Whosoever shall smite thee upon the right cheek," is his statement, " turn to him the other also. And if a man sue thee at the law, and take away thy coat, let him have thy cloak also. And whosoever shall compel thee to go a mile, go with him twain." It is perfectly clear, from the context of the passage, in other words, that Jesus was here using the word " evil " not in its universal application to all unfavourable phenomena of the world, but in its narrower application to the sins and aberrations of human conduct. He was speaking not of evil in general, but very particularly of the evil that may be wrought by one man upon another. This means that the doctrine of non-resistance is to be interpreted very strictly as a doctrine of human relationships. The question which it raises is not the question as to what we shall do when we find ourselves set upon by storms or wild beasts or wretched poverty, but what we shall do when confronted with the malicious and violent actions of our fellow-beings.

It is obvious that the non-resistant, in all the great areas of experience outside the comparatively narrow bounds of the human-circle, is privileged to live exactly like other people. He may wear clothes to protect himself against the cold, and raise a roof over his head to shelter him from the elements. He may shoot the lion and the bear, and bruise without compunction the serpent's head. If he plunges into some dangerous wilderness, as Theodore Roosevelt plunged into the forests of Brazil, he may freely follow Mr. Roosevelt's militant example of carrying along a medicine chest to resist the ravages of jungle-fever, and may arm himself with a

rifle to protect himself against the attacks of wild
beasts.   It is not even obligatory upon the consistent
non-resistant to have his door unlocked and his house
unguarded by day and night.   The good Monseigneur
Bienvenu, in Victor Hugo's *Les Miserables,* to be sure,
always left his door open, so that any chance passer-by
might freely cross his threshold.   But it is to be noted
that, while this practice may have been a result of the
saintly Bishop's non-resistance principles, it was defended by him as a practice enjoined upon him by the
ideals of the priesthood.   Just as the door of the phy-
sician's house, he said, should never be closed, so the
door of the priest's house should always be open.   The
matter of placing bolts on our doors has nothing to do
with non-resistance as such.   This principle here comes
into play, not when we bar our homes against unwel-
come or inconvenient intrusion, but when we find ourselves standing face to face with *a man* who has shattered our bolts, and are forced to take some kind of
personal action toward this human invader.

That we are taking no undue liberties with our text,
in thus interpreting the word " evil " to mean in this
connection nothing more than the evil which may be
done by men, is shown most impressively by the fact
that, when the King James Version of the Bible was
revised in the last quarter of the nineteenth century,
this very passage which we are discussing was one of
those which was made to undergo a radical change in
phraseology.   In the Revised Version, we no longer
read, " Resist not evil."   These words have disap-

peared, and in their place appears the much more explicit statement, " Resist not him that is evil." When Jesus laid down this law of non-resistance, in other words, he used not a generic noun, but a personal pronoun and a modifying clause. Which shows us, if anything can show, that Jesus was talking not about evil things but about evil men!

Much more important than the question as to what Jesus meant by the word " evil," is the question as to what he meant by the command, " resist not." It is interesting to learn that when Jesus spoke of " evil," he was really speaking of " him that is evil." But how does this help us any with the problem of non-resistance, for surely " the evil that men do " is even more destructive and terrible than the evil wrought by the blind fury of nature. It is encouraging to know that we may shoot a lion or smite a rattle-snake, but how does this help those of us who have to face not lions or rattle-snakes, but pickpockets, burglars and gunmen?

The very statement of this inquiry reveals the fact that the term, " resist not," is commonly understood in as erroneous a fashion as the term, " evil," which we have just been considering. Most people, undoubtedly, take this phrase to mean exactly what it says — that we shall *not resist* in any way any of the assaults on property and life which evil men may direct against us. The consistent non-resistant must under all circumstances remain inactive, passive, acquiescent. He must accept any injury that may be brought upon him

by a human hand — surrender to any brute that may
attack him. He must be willing to see his home bur-
glarised, himself assaulted, his wife violated, his little
child beaten to death, and yet do nothing in opposition. He must be content to see his country invaded,
ravaged, conquered, laid under tribute by a foreign
foe, and yet lift no sword or rifle in its defence. He
must, in a word, let evil have its own way in the world
of men, and lift not so much as a little finger against it.
The " sea of troubles " may threaten to engulf the
world, but he must on no account " take up arms "
and by " opposing end them " !

Now such a literal interpretation of the words, " resist not," as the above, must be described as just as un-
tenable, and therefore as ridiculous, as the similar interpretation of the word, " evil." It is here that we
are made to see, with perfect clearness, what an absolute misnomer the phrase " non-resistance " is, after
all, and how necessary it is to define and illustrate it
at great length. If passivity, acquiescence, cowardice
of this kind is what non-resistance involves, it is useless to expect that any man worthy of the name will
adopt it as a rule of life ; and it may well be wondered
how in the past it has won the allegiance of so many
pure and knightly souls.

It is evident that there is something wrong somewhere. Let us turn back to our context once again,
and see if we can find out what it is.

In the passage which we are considering, it is no-
ticeable that Jesus introduces his commandment of non-

resistance with the statement, " Ye have heard that it
hath been said, An eye for an eye, and a tooth for a
tooth." Now in this reference to the previous custom
of Israel, as in all the similar references in the Sermon
on the Mount, the Nazarene very obviously had in mind
certain laws in the old Mosaic code. He was thinking
of such a passage as this from *Exodus* —" If any mis-
chief follow, then thou shalt give life for life, eye for
eye, tooth for tooth, hand for hand, foot for foot,
burning for burning, wound for wound, stripe for
stripe "; or this from *Leviticus*, " If a man cause a
blemish in his neighbour, as he hath done, so shall it be
done to him: breach for breach, eye for eye, tooth for
tooth "; or this from *Deuteronomy*, " Life shall go for
life, eye for eye, tooth for tooth, foot for foot." For
centuries the Jewish people had been conducting their
affairs upon this basis of out-and-out retaliation.
They were acting on the principle that injury must be
met with injury, violence with violence, evil with the
same kind of evil. And it was nothing more, and also
nothing less, than this specific principle of action that
Jesus was combating when, after quoting the Mosaic
code, he declared, with unexampled audacity, " But I
say unto you, Resist not evil." Resist not evil with
evil — do not attempt to meet violence with violence, or
force with force. It is necessary, of course, that evil
should be resisted and, if possible, overcome. The
world could not endure for an hour if evil men were allowed to go on unresisted. But do not resist evil with
its own weapons. Do not be guilty of the folly and

iniquity of taking an eye for an eye, a tooth for a tooth, or a life for a life. If this is the only way that you know of resisting evil of this kind, then do not resist at all. For it is better that one eye, one tooth, one life should be taken, unavenged, than that two eyes, two teeth, two lives should be taken for any reason!

That this interpretation may not be thought to be, in any sense of the word, a dodging of the issue or a juggling of terms, let me cite the testimony on this point of Count Leo Tolstoi, who was a literalist in his interpretation of the words of Scripture, if there ever was one. Those who condemn his teachings most severely base their indictment almost entirely upon the liberalism of his exegesis. His critics will in all probability never cease dwelling upon the paradox that the author of the thrillingly imaginative *War and Peace, Anna Karenina,* and *Resurrection,* is also the author of the dry-as-dust treatises on *My Religion* and *The Gospel in Brief.* And yet it is this extreme literalist who, when he comes to consider the phrase, " Resist not evil," tells us, " Christ showed me that the fourth temptation destructive of my welfare is the resort to violence for the resistance of evil. . . . I cannot yield to the first impulse to resort to violence; I am obliged to renounce it, and to abstain from it altogether." And if we want further confirmation of this same fact, we have only to turn from the words of Tolstoi to the life of Tolstoi, which was one long battle against the political, social, and religious evils of Russia, and indeed of all western

civilisation.   He met force — but not with force; he
resisted evil — but not with evil!

Here, now, are the two distinctions or qualifications
which must be kept constantly in mind if we are to
understand aright the doctrine of non-resistance.
" Evil " means " him that is evil "; " resist not " means
resist not with evil; the entire command, " resist not
evil," means resist not the evil of him that is evil with
evil of your own.   St. Paul, in writing to the Romans
in interpretation of this very passage which we are
considering, summed up the whole matter with marvellous precision, when he said, " *Recompense to no man
evil for evil* "!

III

Not yet, however, have we explained all that is involved in the non-resistant principle.   Thus far we
have spoken only of the negative side of the question —
what we cannot do; beyond this lies the positive side of
the question — what we can do — which is so infinitely
more important.   For nothing is more dangerous, and
at the same time more common, than the idea that the
removal of the possibility of resisting evil with evil is
equivalent to the removal of the possibility of resisting
evil altogether.   Let it be set down in this place once
for all, that the evil in the world not only can be resisted, but must be resisted.   It is the first duty, the
whole duty, of man, to hate iniquity and love righteousness — to abhor that which is evil and cleave to that

which is good. There can be no question as to our permanent obligation to make this world the best possible of all worlds by wiping out its evil and fostering its good. The only question involved is as to the methods to be followed, the weapons to be used, in our fulfilment of our duty, and the non-resistant doctrine is an answer to this question. Not ends at all, but means, are what we are concerned with in our discussion of non-resistance. Violent means, as we have seen, are altogether excluded. Now comes the query as to what means can be adopted in place of violence to attain our end. And to this query I venture to submit three suggestions. Paradoxical as it may seem, there are three methods of resisting evil which are not in any sense inconsistent with non-resistance. The most thorough-going non-resistant may — nay, must — resist and overcome him that is evil by one or all of the three ways here laid down.

First of all, as the least effective and least advisable of the three non-resistant methods of resistance, must be named what is commonly known as " passive resistance." The passive resistant may be briefly and accurately described as the complete non-conformist. He is the man who finds himself confronted by some law or condition or circumstance which he regards as evil, and who, refusing from motives of conscience or perhaps only of prudence, to meet this evil with forcible resistance, refuses also to conform or submit to it in any way. Ignoring the bad law or vile condition or evil circumstance as though it did not exist at all, this

man goes on his appointed way with unswerving fidelity,
and suffers without complaint or resistance any consequences, however terrible, which his conduct may bring
upon him.   He resists not actively but passively — not
violently but meekly.   Two or three illustrations, more
or less familiar, will show what passive resistance means.

There has come down to us, from the very early days
of Rome, a stirring legend of the capture and sack of
the city by a horde of Gallic barbarians, under their
chieftain, Brennus.   The Roman army had been defeated on the banks of a river some miles distant, and
the city thus exposed to the invader.   As the Gauls
neared the gates, the inhabitants fled in terror and dismay — all save certain aged men, members of the Senate, who resolved, for the honour of Rome, to face
their conquerors.   They had no intention of fighting,
for, with the dispersion of the army, fighting had become useless.   But they also had no intention of fleeing, and thus abandoning the city without resistance
to the enemy.   Therefore, with fine wisdom and superb
courage, they resorted to the policy of passive resistance.   Donning their robes of office and taking in their
hands their senatorial sceptres, these old and feeble men
sat themselves down in their thrones upon the Capitoline
and, like so many marble statues, awaited the onslaught
of the foe.   Not a finger did they move — not a word
did they speak — and at the same time they offered no
obeisance or surrender.   They simply waited, in calm
repose, for whatever doom the savage Brennus might
pronounce against them.

A more striking illustration, because drawn from the circumstances and conditions of our time, is that of the Passive Resistant movement in England some years ago against the Tory Education Bill. The details of this event are intricate and need not be set down in this place. Sufficient is it to say that, in the ministry of Mr. Balfour, Parliament enacted certain legislation in regard to the public school system of the Kingdom which imposed taxes on Non-Conformists for the support of Anglican instruction. There was a great outcry in protest against this high-handed piece of injustice, and in some cases violent rebellion, as in the case of Ulster and the Home Rule Bill, was insistently urged. Wiser counsels, fortunately, prevailed, and under the lead of the eminent Baptist clergyman, Dr. John Clifford, a Passive Resistant movement of the most formidable description was organised. Offering no forcible resistance whatsoever to the Crown or to the officers of the Crown, Non-Conformists by the thousands, true to their historic appellation, flatly refused to conform. They refused to send their children to the schools — and when punished for this offence, took their punishment without a whimper. They refused to pay the rates — and allowed their houses and goods to be sold for non-payment of taxes without raising a hand in opposition. In more than one instance, they were arrested and imprisoned, but in all instances endured to the bitter end. Nothing could shake their conviction that the Education Bill was a crime; nothing could persuade them to resort to violence against its enforcement by the au-

thorities; but at the same time nothing could swerve
them from their determination to resist that enforcement at any cost.

Another illustration of passive resistance is found in
the life of Jesus of Nazareth.   After his arrest in the
Garden of Gethsemane, Jesus was taken before the Sanhedrin, and later, we are told, before Pontius Pilate, the
Roman Procurator.   There he was asked to plead his
cause, and, according to one version of the record at
least, he refused to speak a word.   He had shown at
the time of his seizure that he would not strike his as-
sailants, or fight against them; and now he showed that
he would not accuse them or even answer their charges.
But at the same time he would not surrender to them.
On the contrary, he would resist them, passively, to the
very end!

Such is the meaning of passive resistance.   It is the
opposite of violence — but at the same time it is the
opposite of mere passivity or acquiescence.   The word
to underscore in the phrase is not " passive " but " resistance."   Passive resistance means most emphatically
resistance to evil — and a most effective kind of resistance as well!   Take the old legend of the Roman
Senators.   When the Gauls climbed the hill and looked
upon the aged men in their curile chairs, the story runs
that they were so surprised and over-awed by the noble
spectacle that they dropped their spears and shields,
and one after another approached, like worshippers to
a shrine, and stroked the snowy beards of the Senators
with reverence.   Had it not been that one of these men,

less self-controlled than the rest, raised his sceptre and smote one of the Gauls for his audacity in touching him, their lives, and the city itself, would have been spared. The Passive Resistant movement in England made the enforcement of the Education Bill impossible, and was one of the decisive influences in the downfall of the Balfour Cabinet. And as regards Jesus, it may be said that it was his attitude more than anything else which made Pilate marvel and moved him to declare that he could find no evil in him.

Passive resistance effective? Think of what would have happened in Europe in the summer of 1914 if the Christians and socialists, who were pledged against international war, had steadfastly refused to take up arms! There are reports that some socialists in Germany and Austria were shot to death because they would not answer the mobilisation orders. A well-authenticated story has come to England from Hungary of certain members of the ancient sect of Nazarenes — non-resistants like the primitive Christians — who were butchered because they would not enter the army. Such isolated protests, however sublime, were of course ineffective. But suppose all had been faithful. Thousands would undoubtedly have perished — but the war would have been made impossible. Not violence, but passive resistance, is the potent weapon. Not to strike, but to endure, is again and again the way to victory.

But passive resistance is not the only, nor yet the most effective, mode of legitimate resistance to evil. Sometimes, for reasons that must be obvious, it is the only way; and sometimes also it is the most effective. But usually there is open to us that more active and aggressive way, exemplified by all great prophets and teachers, of resisting evil by a method dictated by the fact that the evil with which we are concerned is the evil which may be visited by one man upon another. In wrestling with storm or flood, we are dealing with physical phenomena, and have no help but in the wise utilisation of physical energy. In battling against wild animals, or even lunatics, we are engaged with creatures moved by physical instincts, and subject therefore to no discipline save that of physical force. With man, however, this is never the case. By the very nature of his being, man is endowed with reason, and open therefore to the appeal of thought. By the very necessities of his bodily mechanism, he is controlled by motives, and therefore amenable to intelligent suggestion. A man, just because he is a man, lives and moves and has his being on the plane of the mind and not of the body, of the spirit and not of the flesh — and therefore can be approached and swayed and mastered upon this plane more wisely, and assuredly more worthily, than upon the lower animal plane. A myriad examples attest the power of education, persistently applied, over all the evil that can be wrought by the devices of man's heart.

Take such an episode of history, for example, as that of the exposure and defeat of the fell conspiracy of Catiline against Rome by the intelligence and eloquence of Cicero. The great orator, as we know, was no non-resistant, and certainly no genuine idealist. He would have felt no reluctance about appealing to arms against his fellow-Senator, had he believed that such an appeal were wise. And had he made the appeal, all the forces of the Republic would have been placed at his entire disposal for the defeat and capture of the arch-traitor. But all of these customary weapons of defence Cicero cast resolutely aside. Knowing full well the scope of his mental resources and especially the magic of his tongue, he assailed Catiline and his followers not with a legion but with an oration. Four times he rose in his place in the Senate Chamber and indicted Catiline to his face. Four times he recited the case against him — four times he challenged him for very shame to seek acquittal or to withdraw from the high office which he disgraced. Four times he called upon his fellow-citizens to hear and note the truth. With the result that Catiline was hounded from the Senate, driven from the city, and banished at last in exile from his country. Without so much as the drawing of a sword or the lifting of a spear, solely by the power of clear thought and valiant speech, the most dangerous conspiracy in Roman history was frustrated and its leaders exposed and scattered.

Another and still more impressive illustration of the power of reason is that of the Revolution in France in 1789. It is common to think of this stupendous event as a hideous and yet triumphant exemplification of the virtue of force as applied to certain political and social Gordian knots. We recall the Bastile, the field of

Mars, the feast of pikes, the guillotine of Danton, the
sword of Napoleon — and straightway declare that this
great day of deliverance was a thing of blood and iron.
As a matter of fact, however, nothing could be farther
from the truth.   Before the sword was the pen.   Before Parisian mobs and Napoleonic guards, were books,
pamphlets, and encyclopedias.   Before Robespierre,
Danton, Marat, Pichegru, were Rousseau, Diderot, Hol-
bach, D'Alembert, Voltaire, and all the rest of that
great cluster of thinkers whose rise, like that of flaming stars, proclaimed the dawning of the new day of
freedom.   Take Voltaire alone!   In his biographical
study of this colossal genius, John Morley declares that
Voltaire's life was so potent an influence in the overthrow of the vast structure of superstition, tyranny
and misery which was Bourbon France, that his career
must be told not in terms of biography but of history.
He is fairly to be described, says Morley, not as a man
but as an epoch.   A little, shrivelled dwarf, feeble all
the time, sick most of the time — hiding away in dark
corners and out-of-the-way places from the wrath of
kings and cardinals — journeying madly across frontiers and seas in flight from prison, torture and execution — this mighty man for a period of full seventy
years wielded such a pen as has never been wielded before or since by mortal man.   Letters, pamphlets,
plays, poems, novels, histories, poured by the thousands
from his asylums — all of them arrows dipped in wrath,
feathered by scorn, and aimed straight as a shaft of
light at the entrenched abominations of the times.   The

world is old, but it has never seen another such fighter against evil as this dauntless Frenchman, who could not lift a sword, trembled at bloodshed, and hated war as he hated hell. Single-handed, with a pen dipped in ink as his only weapon, Voltaire offered resistance to the worst abominations of the worst country in the worst century of modern times — and more than any other man or force, delivered the country, and through it all of Europe, from its woe. Pikes and swords, mobs and armies — these, after all, were but accidents, frothy spume upon the great currents of the mighty deep which Voltaire and his associates had stirred.

And so we might go through all the history of ancient and modern times, and find the same thing everywhere to be true. The man whose life marks the turning point of history, was an artisan who talked to people like himself, and died like a sheep going to the slaughter. The men who conquered Rome and laid the foundations of modern times were Christians, sworn to non-resistance and practising the same. The men who scattered the darkness of the Middle Ages and wrought the wonders of the Renaissance were quiet scholars in cells of monasteries and halls of learning, like Erasmus and Thomas More. The man who overthrew Catholicism in half the Christian world and precipitated the resulting storm of the Reformation, was a priest who was sworn by his oath of office not to use the sword of violence. The man who delivered England in the long fight against the Cavaliers was quite as much Milton, with the pen that wrote the *Areopagitica,* as Crom-

well, with the sword that won Naseby and Marston
Moor. The speeches of Patrick Henry and Samuel
Adams, the pamphlets of Thomas Paine, and the Declaration of Thomas Jefferson, were the determining
forces of the American Revolution. The great battle
for emancipation in this country was won not by men
who fought on any field of battle but by a single non-
resistant who owned a printing press and published a
newspaper called *The Liberator*.[1] And the most potent
movement of our time, socialism, is a movement which
has definitely banished the advocates of violence from
its ranks, and sought its ends by education, organisation and the ballot.[2]

The whole history of humanity, from the standpoint
of progress, is the history of the pen and not the sword,
of the spoken word and not the iron deed, of the
thinker and not the soldier. Say all that can be said
about weapons of violence, and you can only declare
that they end in the worst way what thought has begun
in the best way. " The only things that get done in
this world are done by words," says the Captain in
Charles Rann Kennedy's *The Terrible Meek*, in explanation of the necessity of putting Jesus to death for
" sayin' a few words." Why, even in this day of universal violence, the supremacy of thought is still manifest. Here is Belgium, for example, devastated, pil-

<hr/>

[1] Lowell wrote with perfect truth of William Lloyd Garrison —
" In a small chamber, friendless and unseen,
    Toiled o'er his types one poor, unlearned, young man,
    The place was dark, unfurnitured, and mean,
    Yet there the freedom of a race began."
[2] See Robert Hunter's *Violence and the Labor Movement.*

laged, swept from end to end. Liège, Dinant, Namur,
are hopeless ruins; Antwerp, the mightiest fortress in
Europe, is in the hands of the enemy; her army of
thousands of men is broken and shattered. Everything, upon which was placed reliance in the days of
her pride and strength, is gone. Nothing is left —
save only those things which no might of arms can ever
destroy and which are destined to save her as a people.
First among the things of Belgium " that cannot be
shaken " is a certain treaty written in the year 1839.
Torn into shreds as a mere " scrap of paper " by Von
Bethmann-Hollweg, it is for that very reason a sacred
thing which will eventually do more for Belgium's
security than all her armies and all her forts. A second
thing that belongs to Belgium to-day, more precious
by far than the sword of Albert, is Maeterlinck's written protest against her violation. What the soldiers
of the king could not do, the words of the poet have
already done. And still another thing that stands like
a bulwark in Belgium's defence — a bulwark which shall
stand when not a stone is left upon another in any of
her fortresses or cities — is the pastoral letters of Cardinal Mercier. Here are instruments not only of
preservation but of restoration, which put to scorn
" the armies of the aliens."

Talk about swords, guns, forts, dreadnaughts, sub-
marines, Zeppelins! Nothing is so potent as thought.
A word is irresistible. An idea is omnipotent.
Well has Bulwer-Lytton affirmed that " the pen is
mightier than the sword." Conquerors rise and fall

like the empires which they build —" the captains and
the kings depart" like the vanished pomp of Nineveh
and Tyre. But the prophet lives and conquers, long
after his body has been broken, burned, dismembered.
In spite of its apparent "foolishness," preaching
stands; all the might of a hundred kings and a thousand marching armies shall not prevail against it.
Swinburne sums it all up in one stanza of flaming
verse —

> "And shall ye rule, O kings, O strong men? Nay!
> Waste all ye will and gather all ye may,
> Yet one thing is there that ye shall not stay,—
> Even Thought, that fire nor iron can affright."

Not yet, however, have we reached the end. One
thing more there is that the non-resistant can do in
legitimate resistance against evil — and this the wisest,
noblest and most effective thing of all. He can have
resort, or make appeal, to love, as indicated by Jesus
himself in his immortal proclamation, "Love your enemies, bless them that curse you, do good to them that
hate you, and pray for them that despitefully use you
and persecute you."

The evil which we are discussing, as we have seen
again and again, is the evil involved in human relationships. The whole problem before us, in other words, is
that of "evil communications" between one person and
another. The very fact, however, that two persons, by
the mere doing of this kind of evil, are brought in touch
with one another, opens at once the way of love. If
one person hates, the other can love; if one person

seeks to injure, the other can seek to benefit; if one attempts to destroy, the other can attempt to save. A lie can always be met by a truth, a curse with a blessing, an evil with a good. Love has its opportunity in any relation between persons, whether that relation be joined by force of evil or force of good. And if it acts, it " never faileth "! Thus it is that the non-resistant, in the highest and best sense of the word, is not the man who endures passively, nor yet fights rationally, but the man who loves profoundly. The non-resistant disarms his enemies by serving them, conquers them by loving them, overcomes their evil by his good. The non-resistant is pre-eminently the lover and servant of his kind — and to this extent and for this reason the one personage who is supremely useful. " They are lovers and benefactors," says Emerson, in his *Lecture on War*, " men of love, honour, and truth — men whose influence is felt to the end of the earth — men whose look and voice carry the sentence of honour and goodwill — and all forces yield to their energy and persuasion."

The best example which I know of this highest form of positive non-resistance is given to us by Victor Hugo, in his *Les Miserables*, in the person of the good Bishop Myriel, a man who was not a genius but simply loved, who did not seek to get gold out of the earth but pity out of the hearts of men, who sought to do good to all in return for whatever either of good or evil was done to him. The supreme test of his soul came, of course, on the night when the convict, Jean Valjean, given food

and shelter in the Bishop's home, fled with the basket
of silver and was arrested by the gendarme.   Anger at
the betrayal of his kindness, the thought of punishment for crime, the consideration for social welfare —
all these may very well have been present in his mind;
but all were forced to yield to pity for frailty, or love
even for the most ungrateful of " brethren."   Refusing
to recognise the theft, he takes his two silver candle-
sticks from the shelf and gives them to the frightened
convict, and bids him go and " sin no more! "

Here, in such an act as this, do we have the non-
resistant spirit at its best.   And here also, by the same
token as we shall see, do we have the non-resistant spirit
at its highest point of efficiency.   To forgive, to serve,
to love supremely — to meet injury with service and
evil with good — this is at once to conquer every difficulty, stay every peril, and win mankind.   See Jesus
hanging on the cross, praying for the forgiveness of
those who knew not what they were doing in slaying
him — and instantly converting the soul of the Roman
centurion who had crucified him!   See Stephen, yield-
ing to those who stone him, praying to God to " lay
not this sin to the charge " of those who smote him —
and at once winning the allegiance of " the young man,
Saul," who held the garments of his executioners!   See
Garrison led through the streets of Boston with a halter
about his neck, unresisting, unreviling — and claiming
on the spot the life-long devotion to his cause of Wen-
dell Phillips!   As surely as violence makes enemies, so
surely does love make friends.   Why, love can do any-

thing. Love is the greatest thing in the world. It cuts
through steel more quickly than any acid; it conquers
flesh more surely than any sword. The only reason
why we do not know its potency, and believe in it, and
use it, is that we have never dared to try it. We lack
the supreme courage of faith. But some there are who
have tried it — and never vainly. These are they to
whom St. John refers in his first epistle, when he speaks
of those who " have overcome the world." And it is
with sure vision that he goes on to explain their triumph by the assertion that " these are of God."   " For
love is of God," he says, " and every one that loveth is
born of God and knoweth God . . . There is no fear
in love, for perfect love casteth out fear. God is love;
and he that dwelleth in love, dwelleth in God and God
in him."

IV

Such is the meaning of non-resistance! On the negative side it is the refusal to resist " the evil that men
do " with other evil. It is the firm denial of either the
efficacy or the right of resorting to force for the purpose of overcoming force. It is, in fewest possible
words, the abandonment once for all of physical force
as a method of destroying evil and establishing good.

Contrary to almost universal opinion, however, this
great refusal does not in any sense of the word imply
a weak and cowardly acquiescence in evil and indifference to good. Paradoxical as it may sound, and contrary to all apparent implications of the word, non-

resistance must be understood as involving resistance
to falsehood, dishonour, greed, lust, violence, hate, of
the most persistent and heroic type.   The non-resistant, if he be a true non-resistant, fights as bravely as
anybody for God's kingdom.   But just because he is
fighting for God's kingdom he believes that he must
fight, not as the devil fights, but as God fights.   He
thinks it vain to defeat the devil outwardly by surrendering to him inwardly.   He believes it futile to uproot
Prussian militarism from the soil of Germany by planting it deep in the soil of France and England.   He is
certain that God is served by his own spirit — and, unless all revelation is false, this spirit is the spirit of
love.   From this viewpoint, non-resistance means one
thing, which can be expressed very simply — *the lifting
of resistance to evil from the physical to the moral
plane!*

Let it be repeated, therefore, definitely and finally,
that non-resistance is no counsel of cowardice, and the
non-resistant no minion of fear.   Non-resistance is
moral militancy, spiritual chivalry, the knighthood of
the Kingdom.   St. Paul, a true non-resistant, described
true non-resistance in the great passage in his letter
to the Ephesians where he exhorted his followers to
" put on the whole armour of God, that (they might)
be able to stand against the wiles of the devil."   Pic-
turing the terrible evils, which must be fought and destroyed —" principalities, powers, the rulers of the
darkness of the world, spiritual wickedness in high
places "— he proclaims, " Wherefore take unto you the

whole armour of God. . . . having your loins girt about with truth, and having on the breastplate of righteousness: and your feet shod with the preparation of the gospel of peace; above all, taking the shield of faith; . . . and take the helmet of salvation, and the sword of the Spirit, which is the word of God." Having thus armed themselves, he promises his disciples that, " strong in the Lord and in the power of his might," they shall " be able to withstand in the evil day," and " quench all the fiery darts of the wicked."

CHAPTER V

EXEMPLARS OF NON-RESISTANCE (Ancient)

"With mercy and forbearance shalt thou disarm every foe. For want of fuel the fire expires: mercy and forbearance bring violence to naught."—*Buddha.*

CHAPTER V

THERE can be no better way of illuminating the interpretation of non-resistance submitted in the last chapter than that of turning to the vast treasuries of biography and discussing what certain men have actually said and done in regard to this rule of life. By this method of procedure, furthermore, we shall not only get a clearer definition of our doctrine, but we shall also find ourselves strengthened in our faith by the knowledge that some of the noblest figures in the history of humanity have been teachers and exemplars of the non-resistant principle. For the purpose, therefore, in the first place, of emphasising what we have said about the positive, aggressive and militant character of non-resistance, and, in the second place, of showing that, in our advocacy of this gospel, we are by no means alone, but on the contrary in the goodly company of some of the greatest heroes of ancient and modern times, we shall proceed to call the roll of some of the more conspicuous exemplars of our cause. It is obvious that our list must fall very far short of being complete; but it will at least be long enough, we trust, to achieve the ends we have in view.

I

First of all, among the non-resistants of the ancient world, must be cited the shadowy and yet strangely impressive figure of Lao-tse, a teacher of religion in China before Confucius. This man, it may be safely affirmed, is the only real prophet of the spirit that the Chinese people have ever produced, for his more famous and influential rival, as a matter of fact, was not a seer at all, but only a shrewd expounder of a not very exalted type of expediential ethics. Taoism, the religious system of Lao-tse, is the only native religion, in the strict sense of the word, which China has ever known.

That Lao-tse was a consummate genius is evident from the profound impression which he made upon his contemporaries and transmitted to posterity. Of the details of his life and teachings, however, we know practically nothing. In both of these respects, this Chinese sage reminds us irresistibly of Heracleitus, the famous philosopher of early Greece, whose outlines are hidden in the impenetrable mists of remote antiquity. He was born, in all probability, somewhere about the year 604 B.C. His father, strangely enough, seems to have been an officer in the king's army. We know that during the greater part of his career he was a librarian, or keeper of the royal archives, in the court of the sovereign of Chow. Beyond these very rudimentary facts or surmises, we are sure of nothing.

One story, illuminating in its way, comes down to us, of a meeting between Lao-tse, when he was an old man, and Confucius, who was at the time apparently a young man. According to the record, Confucius undertook a long and painful journey for the express purpose of meeting and conversing with the venerated teacher, Lao-tse. Returning to his disciples after the visitation, Confucius described his amazement at what he had seen and heard in the following terms: " I know," he said, " how birds can fly, how fishes can swim, and how beasts can run. The runner, however, may be snared, the swimmer may be hooked, and the flyer may be shot. But there is a dragon — I cannot tell how he mounts on the wind through the clouds, and rises to heaven. To-day I have seen Lao-tse, and I can only compare him to the dragon."

This story is almost certainly apocryphal — a mere legend of unhistoric days. But it shows, with perfect accuracy, how the spiritual message of Lao-tse must have impressed a teacher like Confucius, who was ignorant of all the deeper mysteries of the spirit, and whose gospel never rose above the shallow levels of a kind of dry, uninspired, more or less platitudinous philosophy of common-sense practicality. It was quite impossible that these two alien souls should have any understanding of one another. To Confucius, the great Lao-tse, with his lofty vision of the universal and eternal, must indeed have appeared like the dragon who mounted by unknown paths to heaven and could not be snared by the devices of men.

Turning from the life of Lao-tse to his teachings, we find at once the certain fact that here was a noble and consistent exemplar of non-resistance. So fragmentary are the sayings which are left to us, that it is almost impossible to ascertain from just what point of view he came to the acceptance and inculcation of this idealistic doctrine. What seem to have been the workings of his mind can best be suggested, perhaps, by a reference to a familiar piece of English literature, which seems to reflect in our modern language, in the strangest way in the world, the hidden thought of this ancient seer. I refer to Matthew Arnold's poem, entitled *Self-Dependence*, wherein he pictures himself as standing at the prow of a great ship, which is sailing across the vast reaches of the sea.

> "Weary of myself, and sick of asking
> What I am or what I ought to be,"

he ponders upon the restlessness of human action, and the strange unsatisfied yearnings of human thought. And as he tries to still the perturbations of his own spirit, he becomes impressed with the great repose of the surrounding universe. He listens to the steady washing of the waves against the vessel — he looks upon the quiet shining of the stars in heaven — he feels the soft blowing of the gale against his cheek. And out of the great spaces of the night there comes to his troubled spirit the suggestion as to how the heart of man can find content and peace. Speaking of the things of nature, the poet says:

> "Unaffrighted by the silence round them,
> Undistracted by the sights they see,
> These demand not that the things without them
> Yield them love, amusement, sympathy.

> "And with joy the stars perform their shining,
> And the sea its long moon-silvered roll,
> For self-poised they live, nor pine with noting
> All the fever of some differing soul.

"Bounded by themselves and unregardful
In what state God's other works may be,
In their own tasks all their powers outpouring,
These attain the mighty life you see."

Strangely enough, it is this high thought of the English apostle of culture of the last century, which seems best to interpret the philosophy of the Chinese seer who lived some six hundred years before the birth of Jesus. Lao-tse, so far as we can judge from the few sayings which have been preserved to us from his writings, seems always to have been primarily impressed by the unvarying processes of the natural world — the forces of nature and the laws which controlled these forces. Every day he watched the sun rise in the morning and go to its setting in the evening without haste or confusion. Every night he beheld the stars march reposefully across the heavens, and look down, as if in pity, upon the fevered ways of men. He saw great rivers coursing to the sea, and the sea itself rising and falling in rhythmic beat upon the shore. Nowhere was there fret or fury, confusion or waste or chance. Nature apparently did all that she wanted to do, and received all that she wanted to receive, without clamour, excitement, violence, or death. And contemplating these phenomena as the English poet contemplated them, Lao-tse spoke to men, as the English poet spoke in his verses, urging upon their attention and imitation the example of the natural world. From some such experience and reflection, we may be reasonably sure, the great sage came to his message of gentleness and repose, which stands out in our late day as the one unmistakable feature of his gospel. He exhorted men to be quiet, kindly, sympathetic; he instructed them not to fret or struggle, not to " strive nor cry "; he warned them against endeavours to outmatch their neighbours in strength or cunning, or to rival others in powers or possessions. And then he went on to emphasise the majesty of repose, the valour of gentleness, and the unconquerable power of humility. " Of all the weak things in the world," he said, " nothing exceeds water; and yet of those which attack hard and strong things, I know not what is superior to it." And the same fact, he went on, is true of men. " The weak," was his declaration, " can conquer the strong, and the tender the hard. Therefore the superior man, conscious of being strong, is content to be weak."

Here, in this exposition of the power of the gentle life, is the unmistakable note of non-resistance. But Lao-tse did not stay his flight at this point; he rose at once, like Confucius's dragon, " on the winds " of faith " through the clouds " of doubt, to the " heaven " of perfect vision. Impressive is it to note, six centuries before the advent of Jesus, the appearance of a teacher who imparted to his disciples exactly those principles of moral recompense which glorify the gospel of the Nazarene. " To those who are good," he said, " I am good; and to those who are not good, I am also good — and thus all get to be good. To those who are sincere I am sincere; and to those who are not sincere, I am also sincere — and thus all get to be sincere. To recompense injury with kindness, this is the law of life." Confucius, it will be re-

membered, never accepted this principle.   On the contrary, he laughed it to scorn.   Thus when one of his
disciples pointed out to him that Lao-tse had taught the
doctrine of returning good for evil, Confucius replied,
undoubtedly with that tone of positive assurance that
always characterises the practical man — Not at all;
you should not recompense injury with kindness, for if
you do that, what are you going to give the kind man?
" Give to the kind man kindness, but to the unkind man,
give nothing more than justice."

Preaching thus the thorough-going gospel of goodwill, it is not surprising to learn that Lao-tse translated
his theories into definite social policies which were unique
in his day and still remain unfulfilled in ours.   Thus
this forerunner of spiritual idealism denounced the
practice of capital punishment, on the ground that it
was a violation of the law of love.   More remarkable
still, he inveighed against the barbarous punishments
for crime which, then as now, were ruthlessly ad-
ministered in Chinese prisons.   Most remarkable of all,
in an age of almost universal ignorance and barbarism,
he declared against war.   I cannot find that he ever
laid down any absolute dictum against war.   But he denounced it freely as the consummation of all evil, asserted that it should never be practised except under the
most extreme circumstances, and said that " he is the
wise king who keeps his people in the paths of peace, and
he an unwise and foolish king who leads them into the
paths of strife."

Here, certainly, is a non-resistant!   Whether there

is any connection between the teachings of this prophet and the traditional practices of the Chinese people it is difficult to say. The books of Confucius have had an immensely wider and deeper influence than those of Lao-tse; and the modern religion of Taoism has little of the gospel of its reputed founder left in it. But certainly it does not seem altogether rash to venture the supposition that the pacific temper of Chinese life is to some degree a result of Lao-tse's philosophy, or at least that both have their origin in some more ancient influence not yet disclosed to human knowledge.

II

The second exemplar of non-resistance is Buddha, the founder of the greatest and most beneficent of the world's religions, with the single exception of Christianity. There is no need in this place to tell at any length the familiar story of the life of this great teacher. His birth in the palace of his father, the prince and soldier — the careful shelter of his early years from all knowledge of pain and misery — his marriage to the beautiful princess, Yasodhara — the birth of his only child, a son — his discovery first of pain, then of disease, and last of death — his determination, under the impact of this revelation, to devote himself to the alleviation of human ill, and his consequent abandonment of his family, home and political responsibilities — his years of wandering, as a poor mendicant, in search of the way of salvation — the moment of supreme revelation beneath the Bodhi tree — the preaching of the sermon at Benares, which corresponds in the history of Buddhism to Jesus's Sermon on the Mount — the gathering of his disciples and organisation of his sacred order — the long years of his teaching, the wide spread of his influence, his old age, his death — these facts are familiar as constituting one of the most romantic stories in history. Sufficient is it for our purposes to point out that throughout all the period of his long life, from the time he left his father's court to the time he expired in the arms of his disciples, he exemplified with unvarying uniformity the precepts of non-resistance.

More important for us than the story of his career, is the question as to the line of thought which led this great prophet to the acceptance and practice of the non-resistant principle. And fortunately, in this case, as not in the case of Lao-tse, we are left in no manner of doubt as to the answer to this inquiry. The record of Buddha's thought is full and clear.

At the bottom, of course, of all his teaching, is the recognition of the fact of suffering. Buddha saw suffering everywhere. " Birth," he said, " is suffering, age is suffering, illness is suffering, death is suffering, contact with what we dislike is suffering, separation from what we like is suffering, failure to attain what we crave is suffering . . . in brief, all that makes bodily existence is suffering." Buddhism, after all, has its origin in what must be described, with however much reluctance, the blackest kind of pessimism to the very end.

Now as it was this recognition of suffering which

awakened Buddha to his sense of a mission to mankind, so it was an endeavour to discover the cause of suffering and the cure of suffering which engaged all his thought as a religious teacher. And very early in his search for the way of salvation, he came face to face with the great fact of violence. A large part of the suffering in the world was undoubtedly the direct result of the violent practices visited by men upon their fellows. Greed, selfishness, fear, lust, hate, all these were constantly finding expression in action based upon physical force. Nay, more than this, virtuous motives were dictating the use of force quite as frequently as evil passions, with the same results of pain and woe. If suffering ever is to be conquered, violence, for whatever purpose used, must be abolished. Therefore, with almost unexampled thoroughness, did Buddha denounce the use of force, and seek to eliminate it from human life. Violence, he declared, can accomplish nothing but suffering. It can only pile up evil upon the earth continually. The man who resorts to its use, for however worthy an end, is only defeating his end and at the same time adding to the accumulated miseries of the race.

But Buddha did not stop with the proclamation of this negative gospel. On the contrary, he advanced at once the positive message of gentleness, kindness, and compassion. These are the things, he said, that bring balm to the wounds of men, and surcease therefore to their suffering. These are the things which, while they add nothing to the evil of the world, add immeasurably to its good. And then, moving straight along the pathway trod by Lao-tse and later followed by Jesus, he came to the great goal of forgiving love. Startling is it to find these three great teachers, separated from one another by thousands of miles of space and hundreds of years of time, rising to the same great heights of vision and formulating the same great law of life. " Recompense injury with kindness," said Lao-tse; " love your enemies," said Jesus; and now comes Buddha with the words, " The man who foolishly does me wrong, I will return to him the protection of my ungrudging love; the more evil comes from him, the more good shall go from me. . . . Let a man overcome anger by love, let a man overcome evil by good,[1] let him overcome the greedy by liberality and the liar by truth."

As we study the religion of Buddha, it is interesting to note, that, unlike the religion of Lao-tse, it has no social applications whatsoever. Throughout his life, Buddha was a teacher of the individual, and the way of salvation which he laid down was a way for the individual. Therefore do we look in vain among his sayings for any application of his gospel to poverty, war, the treatment of prisoners, etc. One statement only, apart from his general formulations of the laws of gentleness and sympathy, can here be quoted — and this not so

---

[1] " Overcome evil with good "— St. Paul, in *Romans* 12. See Edwin Arnold's rewriting of this saying in his *Light of Asia* —
" Also I think that good must come of good
And ill of evil — surely unto all —
In every place and time — seeing sweet fruit
Groweth from wholesome roots, and bitter things
From poison-stocks; yea, seeing too, how spite
Breeds hate, and kindness friends, and patience peace."

much because it has any reference to our present discussion as because of its amazing anticipation of a point which we amplified at considerable length in our chapter on " The Fallacies of Force."

It will be remembered that in our consideration of Bernhardi's reliance upon biological phenomena for the substantiation of his doctrine of force, we showed that the combative monsters, who fought and tore one another in the primeval " ooze and slime," were the very animals which had disappeared in the course of ages of evolution, and that the weak, gentle, gregarious creatures were the ones which had withstood the crucial test of survival.   Now here in the case of Buddha, who lived some two thousand five hundred years before Charles Darwin and the modern school of evolutionists, do we find the following saying —" Three cubs the lioness brings forth, four the tigress, but one the cow, yet many are the meek cattle, few the beasts of prey.   The fierce and grasping soon decay; the universe preserves to the peaceful the heritage of the earth." [1]   It seems almost incredible that Buddha could have observed and formulated this biological law; and yet this statement is as well-accredited as any which is reputed to have come from his lips.   Here, six hundred years before Christ, is the summing up of the whole gospel of evolution in its bearing upon the principle of non-resistance.   Buddha, like Lao-tse before him and Jesus after him, saw clearly that it is the weak who conquer the strong in the long

[1] " Blessed are the meek for they shall inherit the earth "— Jesus, in *Matthew* 5.

run, and that as a consequence the way of love is the
way of life. Verily, verily, General Bernhardi and his
school are farther behind the times than we had supposed!

III

The third exemplar of non-resistance, whom I shall
name, brings us to the familiar ground of Jewish history
and the familiar record of the *Old Testament.* I refer
to Isaiah, commonly regarded as the greatest in the long
line of the prophets of ancient Israel.

In order to understand the teachings of this man, it is
necessary to remember that, unlike Lao-tse and Buddha,
and unlike also most of his predecessors and successors
in the prophetic line, Isaiah was not primarily a religious teacher at all, but a politician or rather statesman. He was not a cloistered student, not a wandering mendicant, not a priest, not even a man of the people, but all his life an aristocrat, a courtier, a friend of
kings and a counsellor in the ministries of state. It is
for this reason that his recorded writings have so exclusively to do, not with the ethical problems of individual life, but with the political problems of Israel,
and the vast issues of international relationships. And
it is for this reason also that his attitude as a non-resistant has a greater interest for us than that of Lao-tse
or Buddha, or perhaps even of Jesus. For there are
many of us who are pretty much convinced of the inef-
ficacy of force and the efficacy of goodwill in the quiet
and sheltered ways of individual existence, but are ex-

ceedingly dubious about these principles when they
come to be extended to the larger, more intricate and
therefore more perilous problems of the nation and of
society at large. In Isaiah we have a supremely able,
courageous and spiritually-minded man who made just
this doubtful extension of the non-resistant gospel to
the affairs of state — and therefore an immensely significant example of the meaning and practicability of
our doctrine.

There were two episodes in the long career of Isaiah
as a statesman and prophet which put his non-resistant
principles to the test. They may be cited as all-sufficient illustrations of his thought and conduct.

The first episode occurred in the year 734 B.C. It
was in anticipation of that invasion from the east which
resulted only a few years later in the fall of Samaria
and the conquest of the Northern Kingdom, that Pekah,
the king of Israel, and Rezin, the king of Syria, undertook to persuade Ahaz, king of Judah, to join with them
in a coalition against the Assyrians, believing that the
time had at last come when together they could overthrow the Chaldean hosts and thus protect their lands
from destruction. Now the motive behind this pro-
posal seemed worthy, and its occasion propitious; therefore was Ahaz tempted to clasp hands with his royal
contemporaries and join in their hostile enterprise.
When he looked far to the east, however, and saw in all
its splendour and might, the stupendous military power
of Assyria, he became frightened and hesitant. Thus
did he blow now hot, now cold, eager to smite his enemy,

longing for the booty of a successful war; but, a coward
at heart, never quite daring to take the final step. At
last, after long waiting, Pekah and Rezin, both of them
men of some boldness, grew angry as well as impatient,
and decided to force Ahaz to join them. Therefore did
they turn their armies south into Judah instead of east
into Assyria, and marched upon Jerusalem.

Terror-stricken at this sudden and unexpected turn
of affairs, the wretched Ahaz was about to appeal to
Assyria, of all countries, for help, when, at the supreme
crisis in the nation's affairs, Isaiah came upon the scene.
His advice was at once comforting and terrifying. You
are perfectly right, he said, to hesitate about joining
in any desperate coalition against Assyria. The three
nations, Israel, Judah, and Syria, can never hope to secure any permanent advantage over this mighty power
to the East; an attack can only lead to utter destruction in the end. But you are all wrong in seeking now
to form an alliance with Assyria, in order to ward off
the invasion of Pekah and Rezin. Assyria may promise
protection, but she will not give it; and any alliance of
any kind means the ultimate merging of your kingdom
into the Assyrian empire. The thing for you to do, he
continued — and here is the greatness of his message!
— is to stand aloof from all alliances and coalitions,
and steadfastly refuse to make war. Even now, when
your foes are advancing against you, it is the part of
wisdom for you to sheath your sword and place your
confidence in Jehovah. God is our God, who will safeguard his people who put their trust in him!

It is needless to say that a coward like Ahaz had no confidence in such desperate counsel as this. Surely hope is far gone when one has no other reliance but God! Therefore did the king cast his fate into the hands of Assyria — and the inevitable straightway came to pass. Marching west with his swarming legions Tiglath-Pileser, the Assyrian despot, overthrew the armies of Syria and Israel, captured the capital cities, Damascus and Samaria, ravaged the prostrate countries from end to end, and carried the population off into captivity. Then, distrusting Ahaz and contemptuous of his friendship, he invaded the land of his ally exactly as he had invaded the lands of his enemies, and was only turned aside by a surrender on the part of Ahaz which was equal in humiliation if not in terror to that of Pekah and Rezin. Only when the temple of Jehovah had been stripped of its gold and silver, the daughters of Ahaz passed over to the pleasures of the great king, and hundreds of captives of high degree committed to his hands as hostages, did Tiglath-Pileser consent to spare Judah and return to his own dominions. The kingdom was saved, but at what a loss of wealth, happiness, and honour!

Anticipating exactly such an outcome as this, Isaiah, upon hearing of Ahaz's alliance with Assyria, had erected in one of the public squares of Jerusalem, a great sign bearing the inscription, " Swift spoil, speedy prey." The prophecy was clear — that he who lifted the sword would always become the " swift spoil " and " speedy prey " either of his enemy or of his friend.

And the prophecy was fulfilled. Ahaz escaped Pekah
and Rezin, only to fall into the clutches of Tiglath!

The second episode, to which I have referred, took
place twelve years later, in the year 722 B. C. Sargon,
the successor of Tiglath-Pileser on the throne of Assyria, had been assassinated, and the great soldier, Sennacherib, had taken his place. Revolution broke out in
the West immediately on the death of Sargon, and
among those who took advantage of this opportunity
for independence was Hezekiah, the king of Israel.
Sennacherib's first move was to put down the rebellion
in his own kingdom. This done, he marched straight
to the West and invaded Egypt, with the Pharaoh of
which Hezekiah had joined alliance. The land of the
pyramids was soon conquered, and then came the turn
of Israel. Advancing rapidly eastward, the great king
ravaged and burned and slaughtered on every side, and
at last, breathing frightful vengeance, marshalled his
host about the walls of Jerusalem and besieged the city.
It was at this moment, when the most formidable of
armies, under one of the greatest of soldiers, was as-
saulting the citadel, that Isaiah came to Hezekiah and
spoke that message which stands, and must stand forever, I believe, as one of the most remarkable utterances
of all time. " Woe," he said, " to the rebellious children that go down into Egypt for help, and trust in
chariots because they are many, and in horsemen because they are strong; but unto the Holy One of Israel
they look not, neither seek the Lord! . . . Now the
Egyptians are men, and not God, and their horses are

flesh, and not spirit; wherefore both he that helpeth shall stumble, and he that is helped shall fall. . . . As birds flying, so will the Lord of Hosts defend Jerusalem; defending also he will deliver it, and passing over he will preserve it. Turn ye unto him, from whom the children of Israel have deeply revolted."

Then followed one of the most extraordinary accidents of history. Isaiah had told the king that, if he defended the city, it would be destroyed; but that if he trusted to God alone, it would be saved. The idea seemed preposterous; but Hezekiah, in the desperateness of the situation, knew nothing else to do but look to the Lord. And lo, in a single night, the vast army which was besetting Jerusalem on every side, suddenly broke camp, returned to the east, and never again invaded Israel. What took place, no historian is able definitely to say. Some surmise that a revolt had taken place in Assyria — others, that news of an invasion from some unexpected source was received — still others, that pestilence had broken out in the camp and was decimating the troops. The last is probably the most likely supposition. But whatever the cause, the fact still remains that the siege was lifted and the city saved. And from that day forward, it may be added, Isaiah was a man of unquestioned authority in the political affairs of the kingdom.

Here, now, in these two striking episodes, do we have impressive evidence of the thoroughness and courage of Isaiah's policy of non-resistance. To many historians, the prophet's attitude on both of these occasions has

seemed to be the very acme of unreason and immorality.
Some have even gone so far as to suggest in Isaiah's
case, as later in Jeremiah's, the charge of treason.
Thus Ernest Renan, discussing these events in his *History of the People of Israel,* asked if " one does not seem
to be reading the words of a rabid socialist of our own
day, declaiming against the army, making mock of patriotism, and predicting with a kind of savage joy future disaster? " From the standpoint of the traditional and still universally accepted ideas of statecraft
and patriotism, Renan is undoubtedly correct in this indictment; and those who read the words of Isaiah as inspired utterances and clamour for armies and navies,
foreign coalitions, and wars on every provocation, may
well take note of his fearless criticism. But some of
us may be pardoned, perhaps, if we believe that Isaiah,
whether justified by events or not, was right in his
counsel of perfection, and seek for some statesman-
prophet of our own time to " profit by his example."
Isaiah, in a position of great responsibility, anticipated
Jesus in asserting that " they that take the sword
shall perish with the sword," and is still unmatched by
any public leader in his trust in God and the things
of righteousness.

IV

Our last example of non-resistance in the ancient
world must be Jesus of Nazareth. At first sight it
might seem as though we needed to spend very little time
in explaining the attitude of the Carpenter upon this

question, for the evidence is familiar and would seem to be unimpeachable. We shall deceive ourselves, however, if we lightly assume that the founder of Christianity is everywhere accepted as a non-resistant, and that we can use the authority of his name without substantiating our interpretation of his gospel. Nothing has been more marked, for example, since the outbreak of the Great War in Europe, than the endeavour of those who believe in war, or at least in this particular war, to prove that Jesus was not a non-resistant, and that the Christians of Germany, England, and France were under no spiritual obligation, therefore, to refrain from taking up arms against their enemies. Strange as it may seem to those of us who have always accepted the Christian tradition in this regard without hesitation, there are those who are ready to argue that our conclusions are wrong, and, like the devil in the old saying, quote scripture to suit their purpose. Which means that we must assume nothing upon this question, but, if we can, prove everything!

It would be a long and undoubtedly tedious task to search the Scriptures for evidence upon the question of Jesus's attitude toward the use of force in human affairs. Therefore is it fortunate that no such exhaustive survey of our problem is required. For all the arguments ever offered in contradiction of the assumption that Jesus was a non-resistant are based upon one or all of four very brief passages in the Synoptic Gospels. If we can dispose of these, the whole case in opposition falls to pieces, and our original conception stands unimpaired.

First among these four passages which seem to invalidate the non-resistant interpretation of Jesus's life and teachings, is the familiar statement in the thirteenth chapter of *Mark*, " When ye shall hear of wars and rumours of wars, be not troubled, for such things must needs come to pass." Here, it is argued, is Jesus foretelling the wars that are vexing the earth even in our day, and laying down in so many words the principle of their necessity. How can it be contended that Jesus is a non-resistant when he distinctly says that the very things, against which the non-resistant stands fronted in deadly opposition, " must needs come to pass "?

The absurdity of this argument is so apparent that it is hardly necessary, I take it, for one to waste time and strength in answering it. Surely there is some difference, is there not, between saying that it is inevitable that certain things shall transpire in the future, and saying that it is right and proper that such things should transpire? I pick up a letter written by Count Tolstoi to the London *Times* some years before his death, in which he states that, under the conditions then prevailing in Europe, it is certain that sooner or later the continent will be engulfed in a universal cataclysm of arms. Ergo, I must infer that the rumour that the great Russian was a non-resistant can be no longer credited! I read Romain Rolland's vast novel, *Jean Christophe*, and find in the last volume a

startling forecast of the outbreak of the present War of
the Nations. Ergo, I must presume that M. Rolland
welcomes the conflict and approves of all that Germany
and Austria did to precipitate it! I turn the pages of
H. G. Wells's *Social Forces in England and America,*
and, coming to his essay on *The Possible Collapse of
Civilisation,* find him anticipating the horror which the
armaments of modern nations have brought upon the
world. Ergo, I must take it for granted that Wells
does not hate war, does not believe in disarmament, but
on the contrary is to be counted among the Treitschkes
and Bernhardis, the Crambs and Robertses, of modern
times! Is not the folly of such a mode of argument
too patent to need serious refutation? When Jesus declared that " wars and rumours of wars . . . must needs
come," he simply showed that he understood the stupidity of human reason, the blindness of human greed,
the immorality of national statecraft. He simply
prophesied that, so long as the temper of the heart and
the conditions of society remained as they were, there
could be no " peace on earth, goodwill toward men."
He said what would be — not what ought to be! And
coupled this with a grand assurance of faith, that " such
things " need not trouble us, since the time must come
when " such things " shall not be!

Another passage which is always cited in this connection is the famous text from the tenth chapter of
Matthew, " Think not that I am come to send peace on
the earth; I came not to send peace, but a sword."
Here is a statement which seems to be conclusive, and

therefore incontestable. Jesus declares categorically that his mission is not one of peace at all, but one of war. He comes to earth not to unite men, but to send a sword among them. It is evident that he not only believes that " wars and rumours of wars " shall " come to pass " of their own accord, but that he proposes to make some of those " wars and rumours of wars " himself.

Such a literal interpretation of this martial text seems to be inevitable — at least until we read on in this same chapter a little farther. " I came not to send peace, but a sword," are his words. But immediately thereafter, in the same passage, he goes on to say, " I am come to set a man at variance against his father, and the daughter against her mother, and the daughter-in-law against her mother-in-law." These sentences obviously belong together — they are part of the same thought, or sequence in the same discourse. And are we to infer therefrom that Jesus came into the world for the single, distinct purpose of breaking up families and severing households — that his appointed mission was to turn fathers against their sons, and daughters against their mothers, and daughters-in-law against their mothers-in-law?

The mere suggestion takes us at once to the *reductio ad absurdum* which is involved in any attempt to interpret literally, " I came not to send peace, but a sword." What Jesus was emphasising here, in his vivid oriental fashion, was the radical and therefore divisive character of the gospel which he had come to preach.

His message of pure idealism went to the roots of things. It separated instantly the sheep from the goats — the worshippers of Mammon from the worshippers of God. Right in his own household, he had seen it divide himself from his mother and his brethren. And what had taken place in his home, he felt certain was bound to take place in many others. The preaching of the Kingdom would sever fathers from sons, and mothers from daughters. Such divisions were not to be welcomed, much less plotted and planned, but were to be accepted when they came. They were simply the altogether regrettable and yet inevitable results of the proclamation of a new truth, a new commandment, a new age! Let no man seek for compromises — or, having put his hand to the plough, look back — or, having enlisted, seek to return and bury his dead. "He that loveth father or mother more than me is not worthy of me; and he that loveth son or daughter more than me is not worthy of me. And he that taketh not his cross, and followeth after me, is not worthy of me." Thus spoke the Master his awful challenge of allegiance — and thus he lifted the sword that cleaved those who heard from those who would not hear!

More serious than either of these two passages which we have cited, is the third, which appears in the story of the Last Supper as told by St. Luke. Jesus and his disciples were conversing together after the evening meal, and he was telling them something of the perils which lay before them. "And he said unto them, When I sent you without purse, and scrip, and shoes, lacked ye anything? and they said, Nothing. Then he said unto them, But now, he that hath a purse, let him take it, and likewise his scrip; and he that hath no sword, let him sell his garment, and buy one." And when he had said this, we are told, that they said, "Lord, behold, here are two swords." And he said unto them, " It is enough."

This passage has always proved troublesome, not only to non-resistants, but to all students of the gospels, who have without exception found it difficult to reconcile with the actions of Jesus on other and similar occasions. Apart from all questions of his non-resistant attitude, this speech of his simply does not seem to fit in, somehow or other, with the rest of his career. Therefore do we find various attempts to explain it or even argue it away. What these are, we need not here enumerate. Renan, who declares flatly in his *Vie de Jesu*, that Jesus was momentarily overcome by fear, and Nathaniel Schmidt, who surmises in his *Prophet of Nazareth* that the incident in all probability never took place as here recorded, are perhaps typical. What is important for us to observe is, that all higher critics of the gospel narrative agree that here is something that does not fit in with the rest of the picture, something that needs special study and consideration, something that must be explained; and that they all straightway proceed to find some explanation which is different from that which the passage seems to imply upon its face! What we have here, to my mind, is simply a bold endeavour on the part of Jesus, through the figure of the sword which he had used so many times before, to impress upon his over-sanguine and therefore heedless disciples the seriousness of the situation which was before them, and thus to prepare them for disaster. The whole atmosphere of the Last Supper was that of farewell. Every word of the Master was that of forecast of arrest, punishment, death. The spilt wine, the broken bread, the promised betrayal, the judgment of Peter — all pointed straight to Gethsemane, the Sanhedrin, and Calvary. The situation has changed, was the message of the hour — our enemies are upon us. There was a time when we could go " without purse, and scrip, and shoes," but not now! If therefore there be any one among you who cares particularly about saving his own skin, he cannot do a better thing than sell his cloak and buy a sword, for this is a time for swords! The incomparable irony was at work here, as on so many other occasions in the Master's speech. And as usual it was totally misunderstood. He may have had in mind many things, when he thus instructed his followers. But that he actually bade them to buy swords and defend themselves against arrest, is too preposterous for discussion. It is put absolutely out of court by the great event which transpired only a few moments later in the Garden, when Peter drew a sword against the servant of the High Priest. " Put up thy sword again into its place," said Jesus, " for all they that take the sword shall perish with the sword."

But one passage more remains to be considered, and this the most serious of all. I refer, of course, to the

cleansing of the Temple. That this event took place
as recorded is unquestionable. That it constitutes an
act of open violence is similarly unquestionable. Any
such explanation as that piously offered by Adin Ballou
in his *Christian Non-Resistance,* that Jesus may have
driven the money-changers from the court-yard, but
there is no evidence that he struck any one of them, is
of course the most flagrant kind of hair-splitting.
What we have here is a well-authenticated violation of
the principle of non-resistance — and why not accept
it as such? The episode is chiefly remarkable in the
life of the Nazarene, not for anything which it teaches
in itself, but for its inconsistency with the rest of his
career. Never at any other time, so far as we know,
did he precipitate riot or himself assault his enemies.
But this time he did — this time he failed to live up to
the inordinately exacting demands of his own gospel of
brotherhood. Nor is the circumstance at all difficult
to understand! Jesus came to Jerusalem tired, worn,
hunted. He knew that he walked straight into the arms
of his enemies, and undoubtedly therefore straight to
his own death. Weary, desperate, confused, he came to
the Temple to pray — and here, right before the altars
of his God, were the money-changers — here in the
sacred places, the type and symbol of that com-
mercialised religion which he most abhorred and which
he knew was certain in the end to destroy him. What
wonder that a mighty flood of anger surged up in his
soul, and for the moment overwhelmed him. What
wonder that he seized the rushes from the floor, and

swept the place clean of its profaners. It was mag-
nificent, we grant you, but it was not war, in Jesus's
sense of that word. This was a moment of defeat, and
not of victory!

Such are the passages upon which those, who deny
that Jesus was a non-resistant, found their case.
Whether we have explained these passages satisfactorily
or not, is after all not a matter of great importance.
For even though every one of the four were to be interpreted as our militant friends would have us believe,
and even though the four were to be multiplied to fourteen or forty, we should still be obliged to hold to the
non-resistant character of Jesus's life and teaching.
Whatever our interpretations of separate speeches and
episodes, three general facts in regard to the work of
the Nazarene stand unimpeachable.

In the first place, whatever may be said about separate incidents, the whole spirit of Jesus's life, as reflected in the four gospels, and in every apocryphal
and patristic memory of him that has been preserved to
us, is that of a man who believed profoundly in the
gospel of love; whatever may be said about isolated
passages, the whole burden of Jesus's teaching is that
of the gospel of forgiving injuries, doing kindness, and
fostering goodwill. The Nazarene had his inconsistent
moments, like the rest of us. There is nothing easier
than to go through the gospels and point out the contradictions in the record. But whatever his occasional
lapses from his own august ideals, his power, his desire,
his spirit, are plain beyond possibility of confusion.

He condemned and eschewed violence. He deprecated and avoided the use of force. At his best moments he sought to " turn the other cheek," to love his enemies, to do no evil for any cause. Not by one or two, or even four, exceptions, which can by hook or crook be found in one of the most stressful careers in history, must the man be judged, but by the whole rule of his life. The workmanship may here and there be defective, but the design is plain.

Secondly, at the supreme crisis of his life, when he was put to the ultimate test of his convictions, Jesus made perfectly plain the import of his doctrine. When he was set upon in the Garden of Gethsemane, three things were at stake: First of all, his own life. Secondly, so far as he could foresee at the moment, the lives of his well-beloved disciples who had left all and followed at his bidding. Thirdly, again so far as he could foresee, the whole destiny of the reform movement which, at some cost, he had initiated and carried forward in Israel. Now, had Jesus's own life alone been placed in jeopardy by the action of Caiaphas, he might well have disdained to resort to arms. This, certainly, is understandable. But what shall we say when we see him refusing to use the sword offered him by Peter, to defend his disciples and perpetuate his work? If ever there is excuse or reason for the use of force, it is in defence of the persons of those we love, or of the cause of truth which we espouse. Here, if anywhere, it is agreed, are sanctions of violence. And yet Jesus steadfastly refused to avail himself of them.

Any one who can look upon Gethsemane, the Sanhedrin, the house of Pilate, and Calvary, and deny that Jesus was a non-resistant, seems beyond the reach of reason.

Lastly, as we shall see at length in the next chapter and need therefore only mention in this place, it is to be noted that the men who knew Jesus, and the men who knew the men who knew Jesus, were so convinced that he was a non-resistant that, even in the face of the cruelest martyrdom the world has known, not one of them lifted the sword in self-defence. They preferred to die rather than to take up arms, and many there were who walked the path of death in obedience to their faith.

These three facts cannot be denied. Any teachings that seem to contradict, and any conduct that seems to fall short of, the perfect idealism embodied in these facts, must be counted as of small significance. If Jesus was not a non-resistant, then there are no non-resistants. We are talking about creatures as grossly fabled as the roc or unicorn.

v

Here, now, are the four supreme exemplars of non-resistance who come to us from ancient times. In the early days of the Great War, it was the fashion to speculate as to what might have happened in Europe if the socialists had but stood fast by their pacifist principles. Is it not worth speculating at any time, in much the same way, as to what might have happened in the world at large long since, if the professed disciples of these four great religious prophets had from the beginning been faithful to their gospel?   The total population of the world in 1910 was estimated in round numbers to be 1,652,945,000.   Of these, 483,000,000 were Buddhists and Taoists, 610,000,000 Christians, 11,-000,000 Jews — a total of 1,104,000,000.   Is it too much to assert, in the light of these figures, that, if these millions were " faithful to the heavenly vision " seen and revealed by their prophets, wars would cease forthwith and peace at last be established among mankind?

CHAPTER VI

EXEMPLARS OF NON-RESISTANCE
(Modern)

"Peace is of all things the best and happiest. War on the contrary is the blackest villainy of which human nature is capable. . . .

"The object of war is to do all possible injury to the enemy. But can we hurt essentially without hurting at the same time and by the same means ourselves? . . . What is there not to be feared in it and from it? . . . Great are the evils which must be submitted to, in order to accomplish an end itself a greater evil than all that have preceded it. Indeed, if we were to calculate the matter fairly and form a just computation . . . no men of sound mind or honest heart would ever rush headlong into the dangers and difficulties (of violence) when they may enjoy the blessings of peace with little trouble"—Erasmus, in *The Plea of Reason, Religion and Humanity Against War.*

CHAPTER VI

THE earliest exemplars of non-resistance in the modern world were the early Christians, not a few of whom like Stephen, died for the sake of the cause which they had espoused without offering resistance to their enemies. Pre-eminent among these primitive witnesses, for the vividness of his words as well as the heroism of his deeds, was Paul, the apostle to the Gentiles.

I

Paul first makes his appearance in history as the " young man " who guarded the " clothes " of the executioners of Stephen and " consented " unto the killing of this first of all the martyrs. Later on he is described as one of the most active and ruthless of the persecutors of the little bands of Christians which were scattered throughout Palestine. Terrible is the passage in *Acts*, which speaks of him as " breathing out threatenings and slaughter against the disciples of the Lord," and going " unto the high priest " for " letters to the synagogues " that he might be duly commissioned to " bring bound unto Jerusalem " any that he " found of this way, whether they were men or women." At this time, as later, intense in his convictions and thoroughgoing in his actions, Paul found

177

it entirely consistent with his Pharisaic Judaism
to wield the fire and sword of persecution. The tradition of Judas Maccabeus had long since overshadowed
that of the great Isaiah! But the very moment that he
became converted to Christianity, he swung far over to
the other extreme, and in accordance with what he regarded as the teaching and example of Jesus, became as
ardent a non-resistant as he had formerly been a champion of force. Through all his long service as a
missionary to the Gentile world, " in labours abundant,
in stripes above measure, in prisons more frequent, in
deaths oft . . . thrice beaten with rods, once stoned,
. . . in journeyings often, in perils of robbers, in perils
by the heathen, in perils in the city, in perils in the
wilderness, in perils among false brethren, . . . in
weariness and painfulness, in watchings, hunger, thirst,
fastings, cold and nakedness," he never swerved from
his obedient practice of that love which he described as
" the fulfilling of the law." No man ever preserved
greater fidelity to the ideal of the non-resistant life
under more trying circumstances than Paul. And no
man, be it said at the same time, ever gave more valiant
service against what he regarded as falsehood and evil.

Nor did his service end with his deeds. More valuable in certain ways than anything that he did, were
the deathless words which he wrote in interpretation of
the Christian gospel. All through his epistles there
sounds the constant appeal to his followers to " live at
peace with all men," and again and again he describes
with unequalled clearness and power the meaning of

peace.   Nowhere in all literature — not even in the
gospels themselves — is there a more precise and beautiful elucidation of the non-resistant doctrine than that
found in the twelfth chapter of *Romans*.   More satisfactory than the famous " resist not evil " passage, of
which it is frankly a re-statement, are the sublime words,
" Bless them which persecute you; bless, and curse
not. . . . Recompense to no man evil for evil. . . .
Avenge not yourselves, but rather give place unto
wrath; for it is written, Vengeance is mine, I will repay,
saith the Lord.   Therefore if thine enemy hunger, feed
him; if he thirst, give him drink: for in so doing, thou
shalt heap coals of fire upon his head.   Be not overcome of evil, but overcome evil with good."

II

Cruel as were the trials of the early followers of
Jesus, however, the non-resistant aspect of Christian
life only came into real prominence with the extension
of the movement to the great centres of the Roman
world, and its consequent appearance as an important
element in the life of the Empire.   Then came the clash
with the public authorities, as a result of the refusal
of the Roman citizens converted to the new religion to
serve in the army.   There was more than one reason, of
course, why the early Christians declined to enter the
ranks of the legions.   First of all, they could not con-
scientiously take the oath of obedience to the Emperor
which was required of every legionary.   In the second
place, they were unwilling to place upon the Emperor's

shrine the offerings exacted of every soldier and thus worship the ruler as a divine or semi-divine being. Furthermore, they were well aware, if they enlisted, that they were liable to be summoned at any time, in obedience to the whim of the Emperor or even of a provincial officer, to arrest their fellow-Christians, torture them and put them to death. More important than any such reasons as these, however, is the simple fact that conversion to Christianity, in this age of the world's history, involved conversion to the ideal of non-resistance. No man, so it was believed in this benighted era, could be a soldier of the Empire and at the same time a follower of the Nazarene. To draw the sword, even in the public service of the country, was a flagrant violation of Jesus's law of life. Therefore did they refuse; and many were those who walked the bloody path of martyrdom as the price of this refusal.

The writings which have come to us in abundance from the church fathers of the first three centuries after Christ, give ample evidence of the depth and thoroughness of the early Christian attitude upon this issue. The idea of non-resistance in its most extreme form is written all over the pages of this patristic literature. In one of the most famous of the letters of the great teacher, Justin Martyr (*circa* 150 A. D.), we find a citation of the passage from Isaiah prophesying the day when " nation shall not lift up sword against nation, neither shall they learn war any more," followed immediately by the impressive declaration of Justin, that " this prophecy is already being fulfilled, since we who formerly used to murder one another, not only now refrain from making war upon our enemies, but also, that we may not lie nor deceive our enemies, willingly die confessing Christ."

Another striking testimony comes to us from the great Tertullian (*circa* 200 A. D.), the ablest and most zealous of the Christian leaders of his day. Retorting upon some of his pagan critics, who had accused the Christians of all sorts of crime, especially the crime of non-resistance, Tertullian says, " Shall (the Christian) apply the chain and prison, torture and death, who is not even the avenger of his own wrongs? Shall it be held lawful to make an occupation of the sword, when the Lord proclaims that he who takes the sword shall perish by the sword? " And then repudiating the charge of cowardice brought against his brethren, because they refused to enlist in the legions, he continues, " For what wars should we not be fit, we who so willingly yield ourselves to the sword, if in our religion it were not counted better to be slain than to slay? "

Especially impressive is the testimony of Lactantius (*circa* 260–325 A. D.), not only because of the uncompromising character of his words, but also because of the comparatively late period of his career. Already by the end of the third century, the early passion for non-resistance, as for various other Christian ideals, was beginning to cool, but Lactantius spoke forth as boldly as any of those who had preceded him in the earlier and less corrupt periods of Christian life. " When God forbids us to kill," he says in *The Divine*

Institutes, "he not only prohibits us from open violence, which is not even allowed by the public laws, but he warns us against the commission of those things, which are esteemed lawful among men. Thus it can never be lawful for a righteous man to go to war, since his warfare is in righteousness itself; nor to accuse any one of a capital charge, since it makes no difference whether you put a man to death by word or by sword, since it is the act of putting to death which is prohibited. Therefore, with regard to this precept of God, there can be no exception at all . . . it is always unlawful to put a man to death."

So do the evidences of Christianity multiply. Adin Ballou, in his *Christian Non-Resistance*, has gathered together a series of some of the more striking and pithy sayings of the early writers upon this point. "One says, 'It is not lawful for a Christian to bear arms.' Another, 'Because I am a Christian, I have abandoned my profession as a soldier.' A third, 'I am a Christian, and therefore I cannot fight.' A fourth, 'I cannot fight, if I die; I am not a soldier of this world, but a soldier of God.'" It is evident that, in these primitive days at least, there was no compromise upon the question whatsoever. More than one, as for example a certain Maximilian, died rather than take up arms and fight against the invaders of the Empire. Even though the nation was destroyed by barbarians, they still believed that they must not kill.

Of course the charge was frequently brought against these early Christians, as it is against pacifists to-day, that if their conduct became a rule of universal conduct, it would mean the end of civilisation.   Thus Celsus, the opponent of Justin, wrote in one of his controversial epistles —" You will not bear arms in the service of the Empire when your services are needed; and if all people should act upon this principle, the Empire would be over-run by barbarians."   To which statement it was unfalteringly replied that this matter was in the hands not of men but of God!   If God desired the barbarians to over-run the Empire, then this was a part of " the divine plan " [1] and must be endured. Even though this part of the divine plan could not be understood, that other part of the divine plan, the law of love, was perfectly plain to every conscience.   Therefore must this law be heeded, though the end of the world come.   " Fiat justitia, ruat coelum! "   " Even though St. Peter himself should descend out of heaven, and should come to us with the declaration that we must take up arms for the sake of saving Rome from the barbarians," said one of the Fathers, " I would not believe it; for the words of Jesus are more sure than even such a miracle as this."

III

By the time that the third century A. D. was well under way, it was evident that the original zeal of Christian discipleship was beginning to wane, and its primitive characteristics to adapt themselves more and more

---

[1] How much a part of "the divine plan," or a necessary stage in the evolution of civilisation, this barbarian invasion was, not even these early Christians could have imagined!

closely to the worldly environment of the Empire. By the time that Constantine was converted and Christianity made the official religion of his dominions, the process of spiritual disintegration was far advanced, and only needed this crisis of success to become complete. It is common to speak of this year, 312, as the date which marks the conquest of the Roman Empire by the Christian church; but much more accurate would it be, to my mind, to describe it as the date which marks the conquest of the church by the Empire. For at this fateful moment, the religion of Jesus disappeared, like a hidden river, not to emerge again for more than a thousand years. Like every hidden river, the lost stream of spiritual life made green the fields beneath which it found its way, and nourished many a fair growth of blossom and fruit. But it was seldom seen of men, and was almost as much lost as though it had never been.

From this date on, the history of Christianity is the history not of a redemptive religion, but of a corrupt ecclesiastical state and a repressive theological system. Not Jesus, but Augustine and Thomasius, Gregory and Innocent, are the dominating figures. The world, and not the church, has won!

Now one of the most surprising results of this conquest of Christianity by the Empire, is the practical annihilation of the doctrine of non-resistance, which had played so conspicuous and heroic a part in the early history of the church. Even before the con-

version of Constantine, Christians here and there had
begun to give way, especially on the vital issue of joining the army; but from the time that the Emperor was
numbered among the followers of the humble Nazarene
and proclaimed the cross as the symbol of victory on
the field of battle, the cause was for the time being almost entirely lost.   The army now became the weapon
of the church; and service in the army, therefore, a test
of discipleship.   Here and there, to be sure, would
rise up a stalwart apostle, who, like another Lactantius, would remind the world of the recorded teachings of the Master.   But these were " voices crying in
the wilderness," and they soon subsided.   The great
officers and teachers of the church were now not only
very complaisant on this matter of militarism, but were
themselves soldiers.   Bishops wore armour and rode
into battle side by side with " men of iron."   Legions
were recruited to conquer foreign lands in the name of
Christ.   Bloody conquerors, like Charlemagne in Sax-
ony, were blessed for their feats of arms, which brought
unnumbered thousands of helpless captives to the
waters of baptism.   And at last, as a fitting climax,
came the Crusades, with all Christendom transformed
into an armed camp for the slaughter of the Paynim
and the recovery of the Holy Sepulchre.   Never was
so rapid and complete a revolution!   In five centuries
the religion of the cross had become the religion of the
sword.   And so triumphantly has the sword prevailed
down to our own day, that it is possible for a conserva-

tive historian, like John Morley, soberly to affirm, that "more blood has been shed for this cause (Christianity) than for any other cause whatsoever!" [1]

It would be wrong, however, to imply that the non-resistant idea wholly disappeared from the hearts of men, even in the black midnight of the Middle Ages. The hidden river of pure Christianity was not always a hidden river. Here and there it came rippling to the surface, as living water, and revealed thereby the presence of the stream. All through the Mediæval period, in other words, there appeared little groups of men and women who held to the old ideas and clung to the old practices of the primitive church. These sects, as they were called, were far removed from the main thoroughfares of Christian life. They were unfailingly condemned as heretical, and frequently persecuted with the most terrible severity. Altogether outside the pale of official Christianity, they played little part in the history of the church and exerted little tangible influence upon the world's development. But they at least remained "faithful to the heavenly vision"— kept burning bright and clear a light in dark places — and preserved to a more sympathetic era the type of early Christian life and thought. It is impressive to note some of the characteristics of these heretical bodies, all of which, it is needless to point out, were consistently non-resistant. [2]

In the first place, their membership was invariably drawn from the ranks of the common people — in most

[1] See his *Voltaire,* Chapter I.
[2] See "Voices in the Wilderness" in *Christ and War.*

cases the poverty-stricken populace of the country-sides. Rare indeed was it to find any person of education, wealth or social respectability associated with these sects. Peasants, artisans, travelling journeymen, strolling players, seers and saints of doubtful lineage, these were the kind of men and women who comprised these strange groups of spiritual outlaws — men and women, it should be noted, who were much nearer the type of those who heard gladly the preaching of the Nazarene than the ecclesiastical princes who monopolised his name.

In the second place, these heretical sects were at one in their predominant interest not in the sacraments of worship or the articles of theological instruction, but in the things of the spirit. Christianity was to them not an institution to be supported, nor a creed to be learned, nor a ritual to be performed, but first and foremost, a way of life. They were concerned not with the definitions of the Godhead, but with the commandments of God. They were interested not in the nature of Christ, but in the nature of the Christ-life. What to do, whom to serve, how to live — these, and not intricate theories of transubstantiation or supererogation, were the problems of religion. And to the settlement of these problems, in the light of the Master's teachings, they devoted the glad service of their days.

Lastly, it is to be noted, that these obscure and heretical sects were all of them composed of men and women who were ceaseless readers of the Bible, and more or less literal interpreters of the scriptural text.

The Roman church knew perfectly well what it was doing when it declared that the uninstructed reading of the Bible was dangerous business, and forthwith took the sacred book from the hands and eyes of its communicants. It was obvious, even to a Mediæval bishop, that there was a serious discrepancy between ecclesiastical Christianity and the religion of Jesus, and that it was important that this discrepancy should not be made apparent by indiscriminate reading of the Bible. It is no accident that such reading was as uniformly characteristic of these Mediæval sects as it was of the primitive churches of the second century.

It will be instructive, as well as inspiring, to name some of these sects and consider for a moment some of the ideals which they tried to serve in these dark and terrible years of Christian history.

Here, for example, are the Cathari, who first appeared in Bulgaria in the ninth century. By the eleventh century, they had spread abroad through the neighbouring countries, and had attracted so much unfavourable attention, that they were honoured with persecution. The word Cathari, significantly enough, means "the pure men." In some places they were called the Slavoni, because of their origin among the Slav population of southeastern Europe. Still more frequently they were styled the "Weavers," for the obvious reason that most of them were weavers, or artisans who supported themselves by some kind of hand labour. These Cathari were primitive Christians in the literal sense of the word; and of course were non-resistants of the uncompromising type. Therefore is it a matter of record that when the persecutors of Rome fell upon them with fire and sword and rack — pillaged their homes, tortured their old and young, and slaughtered men, women and children, all alike without compunction — they raised not a hand in opposition. Without any attempt at self-defence, they died for the faith that was within them.

An equally noble, and much more famous sect, is that of the Waldenses, which appeared in the twelfth century. The Waldensian movement, as it is called, goes back to Peter Waldo, a rich merchant of the city of Lyons. In 1170, he heard for the first time the story of the rich young man who was told by Jesus to sell all his goods and give them to the poor. Good Waldo acted at once upon this commandment of the Master, and, like St. Francis after him, went forth to preach the gospel of goodwill. From the very beginning, non-resistance was an important part of his message. And it is somewhat noteworthy that he based his teaching in this regard, not merely upon the words of Jesus, but also upon those of Moses. The non-resistant principles of the Nazarene, he said, were only a logical extension of the Mosaic law, " Thou shalt not kill." For two centuries, the followers of Waldo were faithful to his teachings in this as in all other regards. Hunted from one end of Europe to the other, tortured, slain, mutilated, they refused to take up the sword. The

Waldensian persecution constitutes one of the noblest as well as one of the blackest pages of religious history.

A still more remarkable group of non-resistants in the Middle Ages is that of the followers of John Wycliffe in England. An eloquent preacher, profound scholar, ardent reformer, a man of nervous energy and kindling magnetism, the translator of the first English Bible and the founder of the epoch-making school of Lollards, the great Wycliffe is the noblest ornament of English history down to his own day, with the single exception of King Alfred, and unquestionably the brightest light that glowed in the darkness of the Middle Ages. His life, like that of Voltaire, was in many ways an epoch in the progress of the race.

A non-resistant always, there were few things against which Wycliffe inveighed more persistently than the practice of the priests of the church in taking their places in the line of battle. " Men say," is his word on this issue, " that Christ bade his disciples sell their coats, and buy them swords. But Christ taught not his apostles to fight with the sword of iron, but with the sword of God's word, which standeth in meekness of heart and in the prudence of man's tongue." Long after John Wycliffe himself had passed away, and his followers were being harried in the land, these Lollards, as they were dubbed, remained steadfast in their allegiance to the non-resistant idea and commended it in their preaching as one of the cardinal principles of Christian faith. " Men of war are not allowed by the

gospel, for the gospel knoweth peace and not war,"
was the unvarying language of their speech.

But the influence of Wycliffe was by no means limited to England and his persecuted Lollards. Far
abroad, to the distant borders of Bohemia, was it carried by journeying artisans and students. Here in
this alien soil were the seeds of his word planted; and
here did they later spring up into the rich harvest of
the Moravians, who constitute one of the most beautiful of all the heretical orders of the Middle Ages.
Faithful in all things, they were especially faithful to
the doctrine of non-resistance. Says one of the historians of the Moravian church —" No weapon did they
use except the pen. They never retaliated, never re-
belled, never took up arms in their own defence, never
even appealed to the arm of justice. When smitten
on the one cheek, they turned the other also." And
this is true not merely of yesterday, be it recorded, but
of to-day as well. For the Moravian church, in spite
of long persecution, still flourishes in Bohemia, and
only a few years ago despatched a large delegation to
the great International Congress of Religious Liberals
in Berlin.

Not so much an heretical sect outside the church as
a great movement of reform within the church, and
yet to be classified, from our point of view at least,
among the movements which we are here describing, is
that of the Franciscans. By general consent is the
story of the good St. Francis counted as the most beautiful in the records of Mediævalism. Born in wealth

and reared in luxury, this man lived a life, through all
his early years, of idleness and dissipation. He played
day and night with the sportive youths of his " set ";
marched light-heartedly to battle when his native city
was at war, and fought valiantly be it said; travelled
on pleasure bent wherever fancy might lead him.   Then
came   the   sudden   emotional   upheaval — strangely
enough when he was fighting in battle; the long struggle
for inward peace, and at last the surrender to the in-
sistent call of his soul.   Stripping himself literally
naked, he forsook family, friends, everything that he
had known, and gave himself unreservedly to the service
of the poor, the diseased and the fallen.   Then came
the gathering of his disciples, the building of his monasteries, and at last the great Order, the history of
which marks one of the noblest pages in all the long
story of Christianity.

The work of St. Francis, in its essential character,
was pre-eminently emotional; but behind it was at
least one consistent idea, namely, that of reproducing,
in one of the most corrupt ages of European history,
the exact pattern of the life of Jesus.   Francis set
himself deliberately to the task of living as he believed
that Jesus lived, and he educated all his personal followers in the same habit of life.   It is not surprising,
therefore, to learn that, in his personal experience at
least, he was a scrupulous non-resistant.   Very touching, as an illustration of his practice, is the story of
the robbers who broke into the monastery one night.
A monk, who was a doorkeeper or watchman, set upon

the intruders and succeeded in driving them away.
Awakened by the disturbance, St. Francis heard the
excited tale of the sentinel and, greatly displeased at
his violence, despatched him down the road as fast as
his legs could carry him to overtake the robbers and
bring them back. This the monk somehow or other
succeeded in doing; whereupon St. Francis received the
robbers in his private room, spread the board with food
and drink for their refreshment, and in general so overwhelmed them with kindness that they fell on their
knees in repentance and begged to be received into the
fellowship of his Order.

That this story is historically true, may well be regarded as doubtful; but that it is spiritually true is
beyond question. This is the kind of thing which St.
Francis was always doing, and the kind of thing which
he was always commending to his disciples. These
followers, it will be remembered, he divided into three
groups. Only one of these did he bind to the literal
performances of the life of Jesus, mindful in his unfailing charity that " the flesh is weak." But to this he
granted no qualifications, and therefore among other
things, pledged them to non-resistance. This very
flower of the Franciscan Order was forbidden to use
force for any purpose or under any conditions. Going
through the world unarmed, they were to practise
peace, and manifest to all mankind the omnipotence of
love.

IV

Mention of the Moravians and Franciscans brings us at once to the period of the Reformation, which involves one of the most remarkable phenomena in the history of non-resistance. In the beginning, nearly all the great leaders of the Protestant revolt were out-and-out non-resistants. The explanation of this fact is undoubtedly to be found in the further fact that the whole reforming movement of this age had its origin in a rediscovery of the Bible. For generations the scriptures had been safely hidden from the laity, and used by the clergy only under the most severe restrictions. Now, under the impulse of the quickening spirit of the Renaissance, came a new interest in the sacred literatures of Judaism and Christianity; and, with the reading of the text which this prompted, a new understanding of the past and especially of the teachings of the Nazarene. In the case of the reformers, as inevitably in the case of the various heretical sects which we have named, this meant a revival of primitive Christianity, and of non-resistance as a vital part of primitive Christianity. In its incipiency, Protestantism was as truly a non-resistant movement as Waldensianism or Lollardry. Martin Luther, for example, in the early years of his revolt against Rome, was an advocate of the pacifist principle. For this reason in particular, was he violently assailed by Sir Thomas More, who, in spite of his *Utopia*, was in many things an eminently practical man. Luther valiantly held his ground, however, and, at the crowning moment of his life, in his sublime defiance of Charles V at the Diet of Worms, gave to the world one of the bravest examples of non-resistant action since the crucifixion at Golgotha. Later on, however, when Luther entered upon his long career of compromise, he found it convenient to rid himself of some of his ideals, and non-resistance was one of the first to go.   Henceforth he was glad to have the Protestant princes serve him and his cause at any cost of suffering and bloodshed. And when the wretched peasants, stirred by his own preachings of liberty, sought release from the intolerable burdens of their lot, he not only urged the nobles to defend themselves against attack, but actually incited them to harry and slaughter without mercy until the uprising was suppressed. The most regrettable episode in the history of Protestantism, in many ways, is Martin Luther's conduct in relation to this Peasants' Revolt.

John Calvin also was a non-resistant in his early years. Thus in one of his writings we find the statement, " Trust in the power of man is to be unconditionally renounced; if there is need, God will work a miracle to save his church." When, however, Calvin undertook the administration of the city of Geneva and found himself confronted by French Catholics to the west, German Catholics to the north, Swiss Catholics to the east and Italian Catholics to the south, to say nothing of varieties of hostile Protestants inside and outside of his seat, he found it convenient to change his tactics. From this time on, he never scrupled to use force, not only for defence, but for the active furtherance of his plans of government and social control; until at last, like Luther, he touched the lowest depths of infamy in his burning of Michael Servetus. No better illustration of what I have called " the logic of force," can anywhere be found, than in the case of these two great leaders of Protestantism, who, abandoning their non-resistant ideals for expediential motives, were led, the one into the cruelties of the Peasants' War and the other into the calculated horror of Servetus's murder.

One man, conspicuous in this epoch, stood firm. On his dying day, as in his early youth, the great scholar and teacher, Erasmus, was a relentless hater of war and an ardent lover of peace. Untiringly by voice and pen, did he condemn appeal to the sword; and in his multitudinous writings he has left to us some of the strongest arguments and noblest appeals upon this theme in the literature of his or any other age. His *Plea of Reason, Religion and Humanity Against War*, with its eloquent portrayal of the horrors of war and the beauties of peace, its relentless exposure of the perils and fallacies of force, and above all its telling analysis of the teachings of Jesus and the apostles, remains to this day the classic utterance of modern times upon the peace question. Only the half-heartedness of our modern peace-advocates, their fear of a thoroughgoing statement of their own gospel, has left this matchless treatise unknown to the people of our time.

v

Aside from Erasmus, the Protestant movement has on the whole little to offer us on the question of non-resistance, until we come to the seventeenth century and the advent of the Quakers. Then do we receive an illustration of our theme which constitutes, as it must ever constitute, I believe, the most persuasive of all arguments in support of the non-resistant philosophy of life.

It is important to note that the Quaker movement had its beginning at a time when England was being rent and torn with war to a degree unknown since the bloody days of Lancaster and York. It was when Charles and Cromwell, in other words, were locked in deadly combat, and all men were summoned to join the ranks either of Cavaliers or Roundheads, that George Fox and his despised Quakers proclaimed their gospel of peace and resolutely refused to take up arms. This was most decidedly no academic or theoretical crusade. It was an announcement and trial of the non-resistant principle at a time which was least propitious and consequently most dangerous. When the supreme test of his ideals came, George Fox was in prison under the guard of the soldiers of Cromwell. Knowing of his great influence over his followers and desirous therefore of securing his allegiance, the Puritan officers offered to set him free and give him a high position in the army of the Commonwealth, if he would publicly renounce his non-resistant folly, take up arms, and bid his disciples to do the same. The temptation was a bitter one. Fox was weak and sick; his prison was as dark and filthy as all the prisons of that cruel day; chains were on his hands and feet; and so long as he was thus confined, his voice was stilled. Never for a moment, however, did he falter; on the contrary, he hurled the challenge of the officers straight in their teeth and revealed to them the cause of all the woes that contending warriors were then visiting upon England. "I told them," he records in his *Journal*, "I knew from whence all wars arose, even from lust, according to James's doctrine; and that I lived in the virtue of that life and power that took away the occasion of all wars . . . I told them I was come into the covenant of peace, which was before wars and strifes were."

What was done by Fox on this occasion, was done with equal valour on later occasions of greater or less agony, by his gentle followers without number. The consistent bravery and almost miraculous success of the Quakers in living out their doctrine, under the most trying conditions, stands as the most convincing demonstration available of the entire practicability of non-resistance, as we shall point out at length in the succeeding chapter. In this place, we would speak of the Friends only as exemplars of the gospel, and exemplars of altogether extraordinary courage and pertinacity.

Take, for example, the notable case of Richard Sellar, a fisherman of the city of Scarborough, England. In 1665, this man was impressed on an English man-o'-

war, in the good old-fashioned method of recruiting in
vogue in those days.   When he was seized by the sailors
he refused to go on board; and his captors were obliged
to tie him up in a bag and throw him on to the ship
with a derrick.   Once aboard, he refused to obey
orders to work the cannon, load the guns, handle the
ammunition, and the rest.   Whereupon he was thrown
on deck, heavily ironed; and kicked about like a foot-
ball by the angry sailors.   Why the man was not
kicked to death, remains to this day a mystery.   Still
obdurate, in spite of the frightful mauling to which he
was subjected, he was at last taken before the captain
of the ship, and put on trial for his life.   Condemned
of course on his own confession, he was sentenced to
suffer the hideous penalty of being put into a large
cask, through the sides of which huge iron nails had
been driven in a hundred places, and rolled about the
deck until he was dead.   Without a word of complaint,
Sellar made ready for the frightful ordeal and calmly
awaited the appearance of the cask.   By this time,
however, the inconceivable patience and goodwill of
the Quaker fisherman had made its impression not only
upon the officers, but even upon the hardened sailors.
Somehow or other, contrary to all expectations, they
did not relish the idea of carrying out the sentence of
the court, and put the matter off from day to day.
Then suddenly a ship of the enemy was encountered,
and in the battle which ensued, Sellar made himself so
useful and showed himself so brave in caring for the
wounded under fire, that after the fight was over, the

captain took him to the nearest port, and, releasing him, gave him service-papers which protected him permanently from impressment.

Here is only one of the Quakers of the seventeenth and eighteenth centuries, who at greatest hazard of comfort and safety, triumphantly vindicated the efficacy of the doctrine which they had espoused. The instance is typical, not exceptional. Nor do we have to return to these distant days for illustrations from Quaker history. Our own Civil War furnishes examples of striking impressiveness. Thus when the Southern States found themselves hard pressed for soldiers in the closing days of the Rebellion, they began to seize Quakers, who up to this time had been excused from service, and order them to the front. In every case, the Confederate authorities were met with a point-blank refusal to take up arms, and in every case resolved to push the matter to the limit. Hundreds of Quakers were tried for treason before drum-head court-martials, and nearly all of them were convicted and condemned to be shot. In many cases, they were actually seized, blindfolded, and stood up against a wall before a firing-squad. But not a single recalcitrant, so far as I have been able to ascertain, was put to death. Execution was psychologically impossible in the face of such patient and unprotesting courage. Here again, as always with the Quakers, we have example not only of the sublimity but also of the practicability of non-resistance. [1]

[1]For above, see Wilson's *Christ and War.*

VI

Mention of the Civil War brings us to the consideration of that remarkable group of non-resistants who appeared in New England in the first half of the nineteenth century.   The years from 1810 to 1850, as we know, were years which witnessed a marvellous intellectual and spiritual awakening throughout the northern states.   The Transcendental movement, the anti-slavery movement, the women's rights movement, the Unitarian movement in theology, the socialist or communist movement which culminated in the Brook Farm and Hopedale experiments, the founding of the Concord School of Philosophy, the rise of the poetic group in Cambridge and Boston, the organisation of the Radical Club, the educational reforms of Horace Mann, the social service activities of Joseph Tuckerman, Dorothea Dix and Dr. Howe — all these were so many different phases of the most potent revival of the spirit that this country has ever seen.   And one among all the others was the movement of non-resistance!

Conspicuous among the teachers and exemplars of this ideal in the early days was Ralph Waldo Emerson, who, in his *Lecture on War,* first delivered in 1833, set forth the clearest and most exalted exposition of the doctrine to be found in American literature.   His *Journals,* so recently published in ten elaborate volumes, throw interesting side-lights upon his thought on this subject in the earlier days of its development. Under date of October 3, 1831, for example, he writes,

" I wish the Christian principle, the ultra principle of
non-resistance and returning good for evil, might once
be tried fairly." And again, under date of October
27, 1839, he says, " But to return to the principle of
non-resistance — I believe that that principle should
be trusted."

The mighty change in Emerson's thought and feeling, which was wrought by the shocking events in the
last half of the fifties and the climactic events of the
Civil War, did not leave his non-resistant convictions
unshaken. On the contrary, under the stress and
strain of this stupendous upheaval in American life,
they tottered and tumbled to the ground. Thus, for
example, we read that in 1857, in the days of the Kan-
sas-Nebraska struggle, John Brown came to Concord
and delivered a lecture, which Emerson heard. A note
on this lecture in his *Journals,* reads as follows —
" One of his good points was, the folly of the peace
party in Kansas, who believed that their strength lay
in the greatness of their wrongs, and so discounte-
nanced resistance." When, a few months later, John
Brown and his gallant band went down to Harper's
Ferry and by the capture of the United States Arsenal, declared open war against the Southern slave-
power, we find Emerson giving a lecture in Boston and
referring to Brown, then confined in the Virginia prison
awaiting trial, as " that new saint, than whom none
purer or more brave was ever led by love of men into
conflict and death,— the new saint awaiting his martyrdom, and who, if he shall suffer, will make the gal-

lows glorious like the cross." Later on came the outbreak of the war. In the early part of 1861, according to the biography by Mr. Cabot, Emerson visited
the Charlestown Navy Yard and, looking about at the
cannon and shells, exclaimed to a friend, " Ah, sometimes gunpowder smells good."

It is obvious from these facts that it is unfair to
cite Emerson as a champion of non-resistance. He re-
pudiated his faith completely and finally under the
impact of the closing years of the struggle against
slavery. Nevertheless, if the Concord philosopher
cannot be called non-resistant, his earlier writings can!
His *Lecture on War* is the classic American utterance
on this theme.

But if Emerson finally severed his connection with
the non-resistant movement of the forties and fifties,
others remained faithful to the cherished ideal, even
through all the dreadful years of this saddest epoch
in American history. Towering head and shoulders
above the rest of these stalwarts is of course William
Lloyd Garrison, who fought through the anti-slavery
struggle from beginning to end, a leader of the leaders
in that great battle of the giants, and kept his non-
resistant principles inviolate to the close. Never, even
in the days when feelings ran highest and crises were
most acute, did he yield for a moment to the easy
temptations of violence. When the fugitive slave
riots burst upon Boston, for example, he steadfastly
counselled against forcible resistance to the government officers. Even in the days of the rendition of

Anthony Burns, when mobs were racing through the streets and raging about the court-house and prison, when Parker and Phillips and Higginson were moving heaven and earth to secure the prisoner's release, Garrison, as his biographers point out, stuck to his printing office and calmly set his type. The publication of *The Liberator* on time was more important, to his mind, than the liberation of any escaped slave! And when John Brown made his attack on Harper's Ferry, we find Garrison writing, " Judging John Brown by the code of Bunker Hill, we think he is as deserving of eulogy as any who ever wielded sword or battle-axe in the cause of liberty. But we do not or cannot approve any indulgence of the war-spirit. John Brown has perhaps a right to a place by the side of Moses, Joshua, Gideon, and David, but he is not on the same plane with Jesus, Paul, Peter, and John."

Side by side with Garrison, must be named John Greenleaf Whittier. Serving as the poet of the movement of which Garrison was the prophet and organiser, Whittier, like Garrison, refused to use any weapons but the reasoning mind and the impassioned heart. His comment on the John Brown exploit, in a letter to his non-resistant friend, Lydia Maria Child, under date of October 21, 1859, tells the whole story of his attitude. Referring to the " brave but sadly misguided Captain Brown," he continues, " We feel deeply (who does not?) for the noble-hearted, self-sacrificing old man. But as friends of peace, as well as believers in the Sermon on the Mount, we dare not lend any coun-

tenance to such attempts as that at Harper's Ferry.
. . . God is now putting our non-resistant principles
to the test. I hope we shall not give the lie to our
professions. I quite agree with thee that we must
judge of Brown by *his* standards; but at the same time
we must be true to our settled convictions, and to the
duty we owe to humanity."

VII

Along with the Quakers and the Transcendentalists
as non-resistants must be named the socialists. That
these international labourites are non-resistants has
never been asserted, so far as I know; and it may seem
strange to make this assertion at just this time when
the socialists of Europe are eagerly supporting the
Great War. But that the socialists, when they are
faithful, are pacifists in the true sense of the word,
non-resistants in the sense of the word here employed
in our discussion, is to my mind beyond question. For
fifty years they have steadfastly resisted every effort
to introduce violence as a weapon in their arsenal of
revolt. Bakounin and his terrorists were driven from
the International at what threatened to be the cost of
the life of the movement. Sorel and his syndicalists
have fought a gallant but losing fight for recognition.
Haywood and his I. W. W. have been forced to conduct
their propaganda in America altogether outside of the
socialist ranks. Again and again, as the ruthless
power of capitalism, in defiance of every statute of law
and every precept of morality, has abused and tor-

tured them, have the socialists been tempted to take
up the sword in self-defence.   But with a wisdom which
might well be the model of priests of the church and
ministers of the state, they have refrained.   Great is
this example!   In spite of the War of the Nations,
which swept socialists away only as it swept away Jews,
Christians, and professional pacifists, these socialists
must be described as the supreme exemplars in our
time of the sublimity and efficacy alike of the non-resistant ideal.

VIII

It remains for us to name but one other modern exemplar of non-resistance — and this the colossal moral
giant, Leo Tolstoi.   To do justice to this mighty man
in this place is quite impossible, nor is it necessary, for
the story of his life and the record of his teachings
have already found their way into the treasure-houses
of the race.   Already before his body has crumbled to
dust, the great Russian has become enrolled among the
immortals.   Suffice it to point out that Tolstoi, like
St. Francis, came to the discovery of his convictions
after years of dissipation and of valiant service in
bloody wars.   *Sebastopol* and *War and Peace* stand as
permanent witnesses of what Count Tolstoi knew of war
and warriors.   Then came his spiritual awakening, described in his *Confessions* — his discovery of primitive
Christianity and the religion of Jesus, narrated at
great length in his *My Religion* and *The Gospel in Brief,*
and finally those heroic days of abnegation and

steadfast witness against wrong, which lifted him in moral stature far above his contemporaries in every land until, for a period of a generation, " he bestrode the world like a Colossus." Living in the most barbaric land of Christendom, Tolstoi was the most consistent Christian of modern times. As a non-resistant, he can be compared to nobody who has lived and taught since the earliest days of primitive Christianity. He converted few to his viewpoint; and in the light of present events, it may well seem as though he lived in vain. But his memory, like a great sun shining upon wintry snows, abides, and will some day turn the world to fragrance and to beauty.

IX

Here are the more conspicuous non-resistants of modern times. They are not many. But the important fact to note is, that never at any time since Jesus perished upon Calvary, have these champions of goodwill failed to appear and " bear witness to the truth." The teachings of the Master have been lost, forgotten, perverted, flouted; superstition and barbarism have overwhelmed the earth like the Darkness of which Lord Byron sang the dreadful song; wars have devastated the earth a thousand times, and rumours of wars forever beset with terror the hearts of men. But still has the torch been passed from hand to hand of the faithful, and shone like a beacon in the night.

And significant is it to observe that, in this age of ours, the darkest that the world has known since that which looked upon the decline and fall of the Roman Empire, the non-resistant principle is undergoing such a renaissance as it has not seen since the advent of the Quakers, two centuries and a half ago. The light of the spirit cannot be quenched! The voice of truth cannot be silenced! God reigns, and Christ still walks the earth!

> "O pure Reformers! not in vain
> Your trust in human kind;
> The good which bloodshed could not gain,
> Your peaceful zeal shall find.

> "The truths ye urge are borne abroad,
> By every wind and tide;
> The voice of nature and of God
> Speaks out upon your side.

> "The weapons which your hands have found
> Are those which Heaven hath wrought,
> Light, Truth, and Love; your battle-ground
> The free, broad fields of Thought.

> "Oh, may no selfish purpose break
> The beauty of your plan,
> No lie from throne or altar shake
> Your steady faith in Man!" [1]

[1] John Greenleaf Whittier.

CHAPTER VII

THE PRACTICABILITY OF NON-RESISTANCE

" ' Resist not evil' means never resist, never oppose violence; or, in other words, never do anything contrary to the law of love. . . . Christ said this in words so clear and simple that it would be impossible to express the idea more clearly. . . . Nowhere did he say that obedience would be difficult; on the contrary, he said, ' My yoke is easy and my burden is light '. . . . How was it, then, that believing or trying to believe that he who said this was God, I still maintained that it is beyond my power to obey? . . . As I reviewed my past history, I perceived that I had drunk in this idea (of impracticability) with my mother's milk, . . . and all my after life had only confirmed me in this strange error. . . . From infancy to manhood, I learned to venerate what was in direct contradiction to Christ's law. . . . The whole organisation of my life agreed in calling Christ's teaching impracticable and visionary, and by words and deeds taught what was opposed to it. Thus my error rose. . . . But now I understand. . . . This commandment is like a key which opens everything, but only when it is thrust into the lock."— Leo Tolstoi, in *My Religion.*

CHAPTER VII

It may be taken for granted, at this point in our argument, that we have some understanding of the meaning of non-resistance, in its positive as well as negative aspects, and some knowledge as to how it has been interpreted and practised by great souls of ancient and modern times. The very elaboration of our study of these phases of the subject, however, has perhaps only aggravated our desire to get at close grips with the question as to whether or not non-resistance is practicable. Just here, after all, in this matter of workableness, is the crux of our whole problem. Everybody is ready to admit the beauty of the conception of non-resistance as a conception; but is anybody prepared to justify it as a practical way of life? The " tabernacle " of theory is superb; but is there any way of bringing this " tabernacle " down out of heaven and placing it on earthly foundations? We call it a way of life, but is it anything more, in the last analysis, than a way of death? Is not the consistent non-resistant a suicide?

I

It is obvious that the discussion of this question cannot longer be avoided. But it must also be admitted, as we have before suggested,[1] that such discussion can only be entered into with reluctance. For is there not something essentially unworthy, indeed almost degrading, in complicating the discussion of a great conception of the spirit with inquiry as to its efficacy in the outer world of practical affairs? It would seem as though it were the business of those who profess themselves to be spiritual beings, especially of those who claim allegiance to such out-and-out idealists as Isaiah or Jesus, to consider primarily not what is practicable but what is right, and having found the right, to serve it with all their "mind and heart and soul and strength," whether it be practicable or not. It would seem as though it were the unescapable duty of those who worship God and pray to God for the coming of his Kingdom, to try to learn the will of God and then to try to do this will whether it be easy or be hard. To consider results, to ponder expediences, is very like surrendering the unique privilege of the soul to live in a higher realm than that of earth. Whether true or not, it has the appearance at least of reversing the charge of Jesus that we "fear not them which kill the body . . . but rather him which is able to destroy both soul and body," by making the preservation of the body and not the salvation of the soul our chief concern.

Leo Tolstoi, it has always seemed to me, spoke the perfect word upon this subject in the immortal letter addressed to the people of the Czar on the occasion of

[1] See above, Chapter I, pages 33–36.

the Russio-Japanese War, which was published in the
London *Times* under the title of *Bethink Yourselves*.
Appealing for non-resistance at the moment when the
enemies of the Empire were thundering at the portals
of Manchuria, Tolstoi takes up the familiar charge
that his doctrine is impracticable — that, if the people
of Russia were to respond to his summons to lay down
arms, the country would straightway be over-run by
the Japanese and in due course added to the Mikado's
dominions.   " To this question," answers Tolstoi, with
the unshakable conviction of the true prophet of righteousness, " there can be no other answer than this —
that whatever be the circumstances, I cannot act otherwise than as God demands of me.   What will happen
immediately or soon from my ceasing to do that which
is contrary to the will of God, I do not and cannot
know — but I believe that, from the fulfilment of the
will of God, there can follow nothing but that which is
good for me and for all men."   Then, mounting to a
still higher plane, he continues, " The religious man is
guided in his activity not by the presumed consequences
of his action, but by the consciousness of the destina-
tion of his life. . . . For him there is no question as
to whether many or few men act as he does, or of what
may happen if he does that which he should do.   He
knows that besides life and death nothing can happen,
and that life and death are in the hands of God whom
he obeys."   Therefore " the religious man acts thus
and not otherwise, not because he desires to act thus,
nor because it is advantageous to himself or to other

men, but because, believing that his life is in the hands
of God, he cannot act otherwise."

Here, as applied to the particular question of war
and peace, is the rule of life as laid down and practised by every true prophet of the soul who has ever
lived. Here is the faith of Buddha as he left his
father's court and entered the paths of beggary, of
Isaiah as he fronted the cowardice of Ahaz and Hezekiah, of Jesus as he "set his face steadfastly toward
Jerusalem," of Justin Martyr as he answered Celsus's
charge of treason, of Savonarola as he indicted Pope
Alexander and Prince Lorenzo, of Luther as he defied
Charles V with the immortal declaration "God help
me — I cannot do other," of every hero who has preferred the approval of his conscience to the applause
of the multitudes, the sanctity of his spirit to the uses
of the world. On the low levels of ignoble strife for
profit, security, success, the air is heavy with the poisonous fogs of expediency. But there are heights to
which have climbed the strong and brave, where ideas
practical and impractical are dispersed like mists before the sun, and we breathe the tonic air of pure
idealism. Or rather, shall we not say that, on these
heights, the mists are absorbed in the sunlight, the
practical merged with the ideal, and the vision of what
we may call the higher expediency thereby disclosed?
Rising to these spiritual summits, in other words, we
get the far view of the horizon instead of the near view
of rocky barriers. We behold the vast reaches of eter-
nity instead of the narrow confines of time. And lo,

there dawns upon our sight the abiding truth that the ideal, after all, is nothing more nor less than that which is practicable in the long run!

For what great truth was ever practicable in the days when it was first discovered and proclaimed? How practicable was the religion of Jesus, when the Nazarene proclaimed it to the world of Caiaphas and Pilate — how practicable even to-day? How practicable was the gospel of democracy when the first man, whoever he was, stood up among the brutish serfs of his day and generation and declared that governments " derive their just powers " not from the will of kings or the whims of aristocracies but " from the consent of the governed "? How practicable was the doctrine of women's rights when first acclaimed by Mary Wollstonecraft in her *Vindication of the Rights of Woman,* or even later in this country by Lucy Stone and Susan B. Anthony? How practicable was the movement for the emancipation of the three million ignorant slaves of the South, when Garrison set up his printing-press in Boston, or even later when Lincoln wrote his immortal proclamation? Every great endeavour of the spirit, just because it is an endeavour of the spirit, is absolutely impracticable at the outset. Indeed, nothing at all is practicable, until it is made so by the will of dauntless men. And those men of the past whom we most truly reverence and deeply love at the present moment are none other than those who, bearing all things, believing all things, hoping all things, enduring all things, working steadfastly in face of opposition, remaining patient under ridicule and denunciation, dying that the cause may live, have made the impracticable to be practicable, and the ideal to be real. " I did not know that it could not be done," said one of these spiritual creators, " so I went ahead and did it."

All of which has its very immediate application to our problem of non-resistance! Some time this gospel, so impracticable at the present time, is going to be made practicable by the will of humankind. Some time it is going to become as much of a social commonplace as political democracy, or Negro freedom. And it is for those of us who are convinced of its validity, to begin right here and now the work of establishing its efficacy as a practical philosophy of life. This work will not be easy and pleasant. We shall be denounced as fools, cowards, and perhaps traitors. Position, influence, reputation may have to be sacrificed without other recompense than that of inward peace. If war swept down upon America as upon Russia in Manchuria, and we remained faithful as did Leo Tolstoi, we might possibly have to suffer loss of freedom, of property, and in the last emergency, of life itself. But this principle is no different from any other, and cannot be established therefore in any other way than by the fearless witness and willing suffering of those who believe. As true for peace as for war, is the immortal *Quatrain* of Emerson —

> " Though love repine and reason chafe,
>   There comes a voice without reply,
> 'Tis man's perdition to be safe,
>   When for the truth he ought to die."

II

But *is* non-resistance impracticable at the present time? So we have admitted, momentarily, for the sake of our argument on behalf of pure idealism; and so unquestionably would the overwhelming majority of men assert at the present time! Already have we summarised the dubious questions which throng upon the mind the instant that the challenge of non-resistance is encountered. But are these questions valid? Is our admission even momentarily sound? Is the majority opinion upon this matter anything more than the evidence of prevailing ignorance and instinctive fear? Is not the practicability of non-resistance already proved, and our case therefore already established?

This is the question now before us. And no sooner do we enter upon its consideration, than we find ourselves treading familiar ground. Already in our study of what we called " the fallacies of force," [1] have we seen how impracticable is the use of force in all human relationships, and how the whole story of the progress of humanity in this regard is the story of the gradual abandonment of force and the search for some wiser and more gentle method of procedure. In the relations of husband and wife, of parent and child, of employer and employé, of warden and convict, of king and subject — in all of these relations, we have found that man has long since become convinced of the futility of force as a law of life, and has been ceaselessly

[1] See Chapter III, pages 82–97.

struggling to discover and to put into practice some higher and safer law.

At the time that we were considering this matter, we were interested in the negative rather than the positive aspects of the question. We were interested primarily in what man was finding to be a failure — namely, force — and not what he was trying to establish as a successful substitute for this failure. Now, however, that we have considered the meaning of non-resistance and observed some of the ancient and modern exemplars of non-resistance, it is all at once become evident that here is the new thing which, little by little, with much hesitation and many fears, the human race is learning to use in place of the old, discredited, fallacious resort to violence. For centuries our various human relationships have been in process of shifting from the basis of force to the basis of non-resistance!

And what do these centuries of trial teach us but the unfailing practicability of the non-resistant principle? Enter any home where the husband holds the wife to himself by the compulsion not of bonds but of love; go into any household where corporal punishment is unknown, discipline precise, and obedience absolute — where the children rush gladly into the father's arms, bring to him their secrets, confess to him their errors, seek his counsel, accept his reproof, and imitate his example; search the industrial field in vain for the chain and the whip of old-time slavery, and observe in their places the free comradeship of common labourers in a common task of co-operative achievement; go to

Oregon, and see unguarded convicts working on the
public highways and in the state forests — or to Colorado, and see Judge Lindsey handling his juvenile de-
linquents without a suggestion of compulsion — or to
Sing Sing, and see a prison run by convicts for the
benefit of convicts instead of by guards for the benefit
of guards; live in the United States, where soldiers are
almost never seen, where a decision of the Supreme
Court, however unpopular, is enforced by popular consent and not by official compulsion, where the government, without arms, enjoys a security which is the
despair of Czars and Sultans; — and here, in all these
cases, do you find demonstrations of the perfect practicability of non-resistance.   In all of these relationships
of life — domestic, industrial, political, social — non-
resistance is being tried to some extent or other.   And
just to the extent that the trial is complete, in courage
and good faith, it tends to work; and just to the extent that the trial falls short of completeness, from
fear or scepticism, it tends to fail.   Non-resistance —
in other words, moral compulsion or moral suasion —
is itself the only force that is practicable.   Love is
stronger than any chain that has ever been forged by
the hand of man.   Righteousness, honour, goodwill,
are bulwarks mightier than any fortresses that have
ever been builded of rock or steel.   The Psalmist is
right —" God is our refuge and strength "; when we
put our trust in him we need not fear, for he " shall
not be moved, though the earth be removed and though
the mountains be carried into the midst of the sea."

III

All this is evident. Denial of the successful substitution of love for force in various fields of human relationships is no longer possible at this late day. And yet, this demonstration does not satisfactorily answer our inquiry, as to the practicability of non-resistance. For this question, in the last analysis, after all, concerns itself not so much with the slow substitution of love for force, as with the immediate abandonment of force altogether; and an abandonment not merely in the even flow of every-day affairs, but in the violent upheavals of the great crises of life and death. When we are dubious about the feasibility of non-resistance, we have in mind not the children in the home or the labourers in the factory or even the convicts in the prison, but those ultimate questions of the security of property and life which constitute the final test of any theory of individual conduct and social order. Is it possible to walk the crowded ways of life, go to all kinds of hidden places, associate with all sorts and conditions of men, and never lift up the hand of violence or resort to the protection of the officers of the law? What are you going to do if an enemy insults you or libels your reputation? How are you going to protect your home from burglary and your property from theft? What is your method of procedure if a highwayman holds you up on a dark street, or a ruffian assaults your wife, or a brute undertakes to beat to death a little child? Or what would you recommend

in such a recrudescence of barbarism as is now afflict-
ing more than half the world? Would non-resistance
avail anything in Serbia, Bulgaria, or Poland — or
indeed anywhere in Europe under such conditions as
are now prevailing? Let us talk of specific things —
grapple with particular situations! Let us get away
from the consideration of abstract ideals on the one
hand, and vague surveys of the course of human progress on the other! Let us face this question of practicability in its naked reality! What are you going to
do when you face the loaded pistol of a murderer, or
witness the rape of your wife, or see your native soil
invaded by the armed hosts of a revengeful and savage
foe? " That," as Hamlet says, " is the question."

At first sight, I must admit, I am tempted to be impatient at this attempt to shift our basis of discussion
from the broad grounds of social law to the very narrow ground of individual accident. I am reminded of
the shrewd reference of Ralph Waldo Emerson, in his
discussion of non-resistance, to extravagant dilemmas
of this kind, which he compares to " those problems in
arithmetic which in long winter evenings the rustics
try the hardness of their heads in ciphering out." It
seems ridiculous to the last degree that the acceptance
of a great ideal of human conduct should be made thus
conditional upon the solution of moral riddles. And
yet, after all, such riddles as these cannot, in fairness,
be evaded. For if the gospel of non-resistance cannot
prove itself to be practicable in just such contingencies
as these which have been enumerated, then it can avail

us very little. A boat must float not only in still
waters but in stormy seas. An automobile must move
ahead not only on smooth roads but up steep hills and
through deep mires. An aeroplane, if it ever is to be
generally serviceable, must fly not only in quiet breezes
but in sudden gales. And so with non-resistance. It
must work when it is most necessary that it should
work. It is when life and death are in the balance that
it must not fail. Hence the cogency to our argument
of just such riddles as these which have been proposed,
and the fairness of the insistence that they be answered.

IV

One thing still remains, however, to be pointed out,
before we proceed to the direct consideration of our
problem. I refer to the fact that, in order to establish
what we are calling the practicability of non-resistance, it is by no means obligatory upon us to prove
that this principle will infallibly work in each and
every relation of life — that it will never fail under
any circumstances. What we are trying to do here,
after all, is not to establish an invariable law of action,
but to offer a reasonably efficacious substitute for the
more or less futile method of force. And in order to
do this, the most that we have to do, from the standpoint of strict logic at least, is to demonstrate that
one is likely to win out more frequently and more effectively by appeal to non-resistance than by resort
to force. For how often does force insure to us secur-

ity under such conditions as are laid down in the riddles
outlined just above?   How likely am I to get the better of the highwayman, who suddenly bars my road
with a levelled revolver, and thus to protect my purse
from capture and my body from injury, by attacking
my assailant with bare hands?   What is the chance of
my being able to protect my wife from rape or a little
child from a beating, if I precipitate a fight with the
consummate brute who can alone undertake the doing
of such hideous offence?   What did it avail Belgium
to marshal her armies and hold her forts against the
irresistible advance of the German legions?   We are
speaking, it is to be remembered, not of honour but of
security — not of what is morally creditable, perhaps,
but of what is practically efficacious.   And from this
standpoint is it not easily apparent that in each and
every case the appeal to force is the direct choice of
injury and destruction?   Physical resistance under
such circumstances, as actually in the case of Belgium,
is suicidal.   Non-resistance cannot be less secure; it
may very easily be more secure.   It would seem, after
all, in this matter of alternatives, that our " yoke "
of preference is " easy " and our " burden " of proof
is " light."

Not so, however, says the champion of force!   Resistance to the highwayman or the invading army may
be desperate, as you say; force may fail far more often
than it succeeds, as you seem to imply.   But it is at
least more practicable, even under such hazardous circumstances, than non-resistance; for in the one case,

you at least do, or attempt to do, something, on behalf of your purse, or your wife, or your child, whereas in the other case, you do not do, or attempt to do, anything at all. You simply hold up your hands, surrender, acquiesce — let the robber take your purse, the ruffian misuse your wife or child, and the invader overrun your country, without so much as raising a finger or firing a shot in opposition. In resorting to force, under however disadvantageous circumstances, you at least have some chance of accomplishing something; but in "non-resisting"—if there be such a word!—you have no chance at all, for you submit at the very start and give a free hand to your assailant to work his will unhindered. Certainly there can be no comparison between the two methods, either as regards honour or feasibility.

So it would seem at first glance! Further consideration of the problem, however, will show that there are at least two serious errors involved in this reply.

In the first place, there is the error of assuming that, because you attempt to do something by resort to force, you are therefore doing something effective on your own behalf. It is true that you are "doing something" when you offer violent resistance to your assailant; but it is also true that you are doing the very thing which he expects you to do and for which therefore he is amply prepared. In other words, you are doing what, in all reasonable probability, will injure your assailant least and yourself most. You are doing the one thing which is bound to fail, and leaving undone

many things which may possibly succeed. You are
certainly no match for your assailant in physical
strength, but you are very likely much more than his
match in wits, in patience, in self-control, in goodwill.
Why do the insane thing of meeting him on his own
ground — of accepting his choice of weapons? Why
not dictate your own terms of battle, and thus have
some chance of accomplishing your end?

But in non-resistance, you say, you do nothing at
all? Surely physical resistance, however hazardous,
is better than servile surrender?

Here is the second error in this reply. For surely
it must have become apparent long before this, if our
argument has not been all in vain, that non-resistance
means anything but inaction, abject surrender to evil.
Non-resistance is a positive and not a negative thing
— it is attack not submission, but attack on the high
ground of the spirit and not on the low ground of the
flesh. "No man," says Emerson, with his customary
acuteness of thought, "ever embraces the cause of
peace for the sole end and satisfaction of being plun-
dered and slain. A man does not come the length of the
spirit of martyrdom without some active purpose, some
equal motive, some flaming love." And one such purpose at least of non-resistance is that of which we have
just now been speaking — the shifting of the ground
of battle from the plane where the defendant is at a
hopeless disadvantage to the plane where he has at least
an equal, and in all probability has an infinitely superior, chance of winning out. The non-resistant, in

other words, quite apart from his deep-rooted conviction that love is the highest duty of his life, has a
clear idea that, if he resorts to violence in his dealings
with those to whom violence is as the very breath of
their nostrils, he is bound to be overcome, but that if he
resorts to a duel of wits or a competition of goodwill,
he is pretty certain to emerge triumphant. He does
not surrender or run away. He will die rather than
see his wife and children abused without his interference
— die rather than see his native land invaded and laid
waste. But he will fight the good fight in his own element. He will choose the weapons. And the weapon
in this case, as in every case, will be love. And who
that knows the power of love can doubt its efficacy, even
in the most dreadful emergencies of life? Think of
what Paul has to say of love! "Love suffereth long
and is kind; love envieth not; love vaunteth not itself, is
not puffed up, is not easily provoked, thinketh no evil;
rejoiceth not in iniquity, but rejoiceth in the truth;
beareth all things, believeth all things, hopeth all
things, endureth all things." Do you wonder that,
when the Apostle has listed this catalogue of virtues,
he ends up with the triumphant declaration, "love never
faileth"? Of course it "never faileth." Love softens
all enmity, disarms every foe. It is at once the sword
that conquers and the armour that wards. The
fallacies of force are apparent; but not less apparent
are the virtues of love.

V

Our faith in the practicability of non-resistance, however, is still an assertion, and not yet a demonstration. Two things must now be said in confirmation of this faith.

First of all, it is almost uniformly true that such violent experiences as are pointed out in the test-questions submitted above, very seldom fall to the lot of the man who is a lover of his kind and therefore a " peace-maker." " Such cases," says Emerson, in his *Lecture on War*, " seldom or never occur to the just and good man." The true non-resistant, as a general rule, does not get into trouble, for the reason that he does not make trouble, seek trouble, or expect trouble. He leaves all such experiences as these to the advocate of force, who, because he lives in the realm of violence, regards violence as the invariable condition of existence.

A good example of this truism came to me some months ago in the person of a gentleman who had heard me discussing certain aspects of the non-resistant question in the pulpit. He informed me that he had lived most of his life in Mexico, and was to return within a fortnight to that turbulent and war-stricken country. Would I advise him, now, to go back to his old haunts unarmed? Did I believe that the non-resistant doctrine would work for an instant under such conditions as prevailed in nearly every part of the Republic? He himself, he said, had little use for any such preposterous ideas. His equipment had never included less than seven revolvers or rifles, and he was quite ready to testify that, on many occasions the presence, and on more than one occasion the prompt use, of these weapons, had alone secured him from attack and possible death. He then went on to tell me about the Mexican people — their dirt, their cruelty, their treachery, their incapacity. Scorn curled his lips; hatred darkened his brow; " dagos," " greasers," " niggers," were the contemptuous epithets that tripped from his tongue. It was obvious enough that this man had nothing but bitterness in his heart for these sorely beset people of the southern Republic — and that, with such a temper behind his actions, nothing but trouble could dog his footsteps. If he did not find trouble in his dealings with the Mexicans, he would certainly make plenty of it in short order. So I advised that, in his case, not seven guns, but " seventy times seven," were an advisable equipment — and I ventured to express my doubt if even the " seventy times seven " could save him in the end.

Then I thought of the men — one at least of my own acquaintance — who had roamed Mexico for years unarmed, loving these intensely lovable people and serving them whenever opportunity offered, and never at any time meeting trouble or suffering injury. I thought of Livingstone threading the jungle pathways of central Africa, surrounded on every hand by the savagest people on the surface of the globe, and everywhere finding his goodwill matched by the goodwill of his dusky friends. I thought of General Scott of the

United States army, just at that moment doing, alone and unarmed, what regiments of soldiers had failed to do — subdue the revolting Indians of Utah by the sheer power of understanding and affection.

Do we encounter no peace or security in the world? Do we see no gentleness and goodwill in the hearts of men? Is not the trouble with ourselves? " Thou find'st it not? " says James Russell Lowell —

> " I pray thee look again,
> Look inward thro' the depths of thine own soul.
> How is it with thee? Art thou sound and whole?
> Doth narrow search show thee no earthly stain?
> Be noble! And the nobleness that lies
> In other men, sleeping but never dead,
> Will rise in majesty to meet thine own:
> Then wilt thou see it gleam in many eyes,
> Then will pure light around thy path be shed."

It is useless to deny, however, that even the noblest lover of his kind may now and then encounter accident. The non-resistant's house can boast no certain immunity from burglary, his wife may fall victim to assault, his land may be precipitated into war by the mad folly of militarists and thus exposed to hostile invasion. What, under such unusual circumstances, is he to do?

The answer is easy — he is to appeal with calm poise and sure reliance to the spiritual weapons of reason and goodwill. And abundant are the illustrations, to be drawn from history and personal experience, to prove that such appeal is not in vain.

First of all, take such a comparatively trivial mat-

ter as a personal affront or insult! Adin Ballou, in
his *Christian Non-Resistance,* tells a story of two
students in a certain college years ago, who had long
been friends, and who one day fell into a misunderstanding. One of the two young men, a Southerner of un-
governable temper, proceeded to berate his comrade,
and finally demanded satisfaction on the field of honour.
The other young man refused to be in any way disturbed, ignored the challenge to a duel, and persisted
in the declaration that he was not conscious of having
done any harm, but that if his friend would point out
his offence he would be glad to make amends. The answer was only a new torrent of abuse and insult.
Whereupon the second man replied that he had always
been the friend of his college-mate, always would continue in that friendship, and expressed the hope that
the old relations would soon be resumed. The effect
of this conduct was of course inevitable. It takes two
to make a quarrel! Before the interview was over, the
Southern lad was overtaken with shame, came to himself, and grasped the hand of his forgiving friend in a
new and stronger bond of affection.

Such an experience can be duplicated in nearly every
life. In my own case, I have frequently taken advantage of the insulting letters which occasionally come to
the desk of every clergyman, to try experiments along
this line. Thus when a particularly objectionable
epistle has reached me from somebody in my own city,
I put on hat and coat, go straight to the home or business office of my correspondent, send in my card and

ask to be received. Nothing can be more amusing to
the deliberate plotter of such a wicked scheme than the
confusion, embarrassment, and chagrin of my host when
I enter his presence, show him his letter, express regret
that I have been so misunderstood, and offer to make
explanations, or, if I have unwittingly done him injury,
give reparation. Experiments of this kind have taught
me that Paul was far more cruel than kind when he
recommended pouring " coals of fire " upon a victim's
head! In every case, however, where I have acted upon
this policy, I have put my assailant immediately on
the defensive, received from him sooner or later profuse
apologies, and ended once for all the possibility of further insulting letters from that particular source.
Verily, verily, a " soft answer turneth away wrath ! "

But what about the protection of property? What
are we going to do when we are halted by a highwayman, or our homes are entered by burglars, or our es-
tates ravaged by the depredations of the heedless or
hostile public? Here again the answer is the same, and
the evidence not lacking!

Thus there is the story of Dr. Ramsay, a Methodist
non-resistant clergyman of England. " He was dependent for his living upon the quarterly collection
made by his people, which was barely sufficient . . . to
support his family. On the night that one of these col-
lections was taken up, he was obliged to preach six miles
distant from his home, and the night was too stormy to
allow his return. During the night, two robbers broke
into his house, called up Mrs. Ramsay and her sister,

and demanded to know where the money was. Mrs. Ramsay, in her night-dress, lit the candle, and leading the way to the bureau that contained the precious deposit, procured the key, opened the drawer, and pointing out the money as it lay in a handkerchief, said, ' This is all we have to live on.   It is the Lord's money. Yet, if you will take it, there it is.'   With this remark she left them, and returned to bed.   The next morning, the money to a penny was found undisturbed."

A story of the same kind has come within my own experience.   It concerns two women who lived alone in a house in a great city.   The one was an invalid, dangerously afflicted with some kind of nervous disorder; the other was a nurse.   On a certain night, the house was entered by burglars.   The nurse, awakened by the disturbance, had but a single thought — that of saving her patient from what might be the fatal shock of fear or excitement.   Hastily donning a robe, she immediately went down-stairs, all oblivious of peril, entered the dining-room where the burglars were packing the silver, and with perfect calmness informed the astonished invaders of the presence of the invalid and asked them to leave at once with as little noise as possible. Whatever they desired to take with them, she added, they were welcome to.   Immediately, in answer to this friendly appeal, with every indication of solicitude and genuine embarrassment, the burglars gathered up their tools and hastened away, without so much as purloining a single spoon.

More important, however, than the fact that prop-

erty can be protected by methods such as these is the
further fact that property can be rendered to all intents and purposes immune from attack by a frank extension of these methods.   Two examples will illustrate
what I mean.

On January 26, 1915, I received a letter from a
lawyer of New York City, which read as follows:

" My purpose in writing you is to inform you of a
fact in real life, within my knowledge, which seems to
me stronger than the fiction of Bishop Myriel's confidence in his fellowmen as evidenced by his omitting
locks and bars from his house.   A leading San Francisco man, now dead, for many years owned a beautiful
country estate situated about an hour's ride by boat
and rail from his place of business.   It consisted of
many acres a considerable distance from any other
habitation on a well-travelled highway leading to Mt.
Tamalpais.   He maintained there a residence for his
own use, and several cottages for the use of his guests.
And there was not a lock or bolt on a single door in any
of them — nothing but a common latch.   Shortly before his death I visited this place as his guest, and saw
in these houses vast quantities of the most expensive
household furnishings, linens and silverware, sculpture,
bronzes, china, and paintings.   He was a collector of
works of art, and kept perhaps $100,000 worth of per-
sonal property in these houses.   For weeks at a time
he left the entire property absolutely alone, without
even a caretaker, except for the occasional visit of a
servant from his city home.   At the time of my visit

he told me that he had never lost the slightest article and that no one had even attempted to enter the premises with wrongful purpose. He told me that if it were not to protect his property from the weather he would have no doors at all. He said men could always be trusted more safely than they could be feared, and he lived up to his ideals. There are many people in San Francisco who can verify the above. His widow lives there, and I will be glad to give you her name and address if you wish to confirm this."

I immediately replied to this letter, asking for permission to use the remarkable information therein conveyed. This was granted in a letter from my correspondent, under date of January 27. Later on, I received a third letter, dated February 19, as follows:

" Referring to my letters to you under date of January 25 and 27, I beg to state that, desiring to refresh my recollection of the matter, I wrote Mrs. ———,[1] the widow, enclosing the correspondence with you. I to-day have a reply in which she confirms my statement, except that she thinks that my estimate of the total valuation of the personal property may be a little higher than it was at any one time, though it was very large and may have been as much. She gives me the additional information, which may be of use to you, that later on, due to the urgency of herself and other members of her family, Mr. ——— was induced to put locks and bolts on some of the doors, and to keep some

[1] The name is on my files, but is here withheld for obvious reasons.

one at the place all the time; and that afterwards they were troubled by thieves and vandals."

The second illustration is gathered from my own experience. Some months ago I was the guest of a distinguished business man in a city of the Middle West. My host was the owner of a beautiful estate, situated just on the outskirts of the city, and comprising many acres of woods, pastures and gardens. In the early days of his possession of this land, the gentleman to whom I refer had taken care to protect his property with fences, gates, armed watchmen, etc.; but during this period invasions and depredations were constant. After a while, in disgust perhaps at his ill-success, he decided to change his policy. Guards were discharged, gates unlocked, fences removed, and announcement made to the citizens of the community that the property was open freely to the public on condition that certain reasonable wishes and regulations, which were duly posted, were complied with. Since that time, the land has been used by thousands of people — and to-day it is to all intents and purposes a public park! — but no damage has been done and no property lost.

While riding through this estate one day, we stopped at a greenhouse, located on the edge of a large stretch of cultivated ground, right beside a public highway. As we entered to examine the vegetables and flowers, I noticed that the door was unlocked, no watchman or even gardener in sight, and that in addition there were wash-rooms for men and women on either side of the entrance passage-way. I at once inquired if the greenhouse was regularly left wide open and unguarded in this way, and was informed that this was the case. Experience had shown that this was the only way to protect the place from attack. Every effort was made to attract visitors and make them welcome — with the result that not a blossom was ever plucked or a tool disturbed. In other words, this man had perfect confidence in the goodwill of his fellow-citizens — and this confidence had not yet been abused!

Such illustrations as these go far toward proving the perfect security of property when handled on the nonresistant principle. It only remains now to consider the question of our persons. Is the doctrine of nonresistance equally practicable when applied to crises affecting the security of life? What about assaults, hold-ups, riots — all conditions of social unrest and disturbance? Will reason and love work here, or shall we be wise and prepare ourselves for the occasional resort to force?

That force is never necessary, even under the most trying circumstances, is shown conclusively by the conduct of Jesus on the one occasion in his career when he was placed in the position of defending another from violent death. This was a position of peculiar difficulty. On the one side was a wretched woman, who had been " taken in adultery," and who, by the accepted law and custom of the age, was doomed to death by stoning. On the other side, was not one man or a group of men, but a mob raging against the guilty woman and waiting only the word of the leaders to destroy her. What did

Jesus do under these terrifying conditions? Did he
threaten the crowd with punishment? Did he throw
himself between the crowd and its crouching victim in
an attitude of menace or defiance? Did he strike madly
right and left, in the vain hope of putting the mob
to flight, in the sublime determination to die himself
rather than to stand by and see the woman die? He
might have done any one of these things, not without
credit to himself. But if so, we may be sure that his
efforts would have been futile. He would have but
stirred the throng to wilder fury and doomed the woman
to a more fearful death! Instead of resorting to violence of any kind, however, he simply spoke some words,
and then, turning away, began to write upon the sand.
Could anything have been more utterly ridiculous!
And yet, we are told that when Jesus finished his writing and looked about him, the mob was dispersed and
the woman saved!

It is difficult to find another incident to match this,
for the same reason that it is difficult to find another
personality to match the Nazarene. Other episodes,
only less striking, however, are not uncommon. The
famous story of Archbishop Sharpe, a distinguished
churchman of England, comes immediately to mind.
According to the account of the essayist, Jonathan Dy-
mond, " Archbishop Sharpe was assaulted by a footpad
on the highway, who presented a pistol and demanded
money. The Archbishop spoke to the robber in the
language of a fellow-man and of a Christian. The man
was really in distress, and the prelate gave him such

money as he had, and promised that, if he would call
at the palace, he would make up the amount to fifty
pounds. This was the sum of which the robber had
said he was in the utmost need. The man called and
received the money. About a year and a half afterwards, this man came again to the palace, and brought
back the same sum. He said that his circumstances
had become improved and that, through the astonishing
goodness of the Archbishop, he had become the most
penitent, the most grateful, and happiest of his species."

Similar stories of this same kind, as of Robert Bar-
clay and Leonard Fell, the English Quakers, of John
Pomphret, the English Methodist, of Rowland Hill, the
well-known London preacher, could be multiplied almost
indefinitely. No man who has had faith and courage
enough to put the non-resistant principle to the test
even under the most trying conditions, but has his tale
of triumph to narrate. All these personal anecdotes
I put one side, however, to come the more speedily to
the experience of the Quakers, as a group, which constitutes not only a demonstration of the practicability of
non-resistance, but, entirely apart from this particular
subject here under discussion, one of the most glorious
episodes of history.

VI

The story of the Quakers is everywhere the same.
The chapter which has special interest for us, however,
is that pertaining to the coming of the Quakers to North
America in the seventeenth century, and more particu-

larly their settlement in the colony of Pennsylvania, under the leadership of William Penn. All the world has of course heard the thrilling story — how Penn and his Quaker followers landed on the banks of the Schuylkill River unarmed, met with the savage and suspicious redskins under the famous oak tree, and gave to them the hand of friendship. " The Great God," said Penn in his address to the Indians, " hath written his law in our hearts by which we are taught and commanded to love and help and do good to one another. It is not our custom to use hostile weapons against our fellow-creatures, for which reason we come unarmed. Our object is not to do injury but to do good. We are now met on the broad pathway of good faith and goodwill, so that no advantage is to be taken on either side, but all is to be openness, brotherhood, and love, while all are to be treated as of the same flesh and blood."

If the experience of the other colonies of the Atlantic seaboard was any criterion, Penn and his followers, by this crazy action, were only preparing themselves for inevitable destruction. Any wise militarist of Massachusetts, Connecticut, Maryland, or Virginia could have told him of the treacherous character of the North American Indians, their bloodthirstiness, their unexpected raids with tomahawk and torch — and the absolute necessity therefore of being armed to the teeth in preparation for, and security against, attack. But the Quakers did not know, or, if they did know, they did not believe ; and thus they came to this wilderness without so much as a sword or a rifle, and settled down to es-

tablish a "city of brotherly love." And lo, they succeeded! While other settlements, well armed and
watchful, were every now and then being attacked and
burned, and their inhabitants slaughtered or carried off
into hideous captivity, the little Pennsylvania colony
enjoyed uninterrupted prosperity and happiness. The
Quakers had no forts, no soldiers, not even any arms.
They lived in the midst of a savage people who knew
that they were defenceless against attack. And yet, in
spite of this fact — or, shall we say, because of it! —
they knew no war "for more than seventy years."
"Whatever the quarrels of the Pennsylvania Indians
were with others," says one of the Quaker historians,
"they uniformly respected and held, as it were sacred,
the territories of William Penn. . . . The Pennsylvania
colony never lost a man, woman, or child by them, which
neither the colony of Maryland nor that of Virginia
could say, no more than the great colony of New England." "The flowers of prosperity," says Charles
Sumner in his *True Grandeur of Nations*, "smiled in the
footprints of William Penn. His people were unmolested and happy, while other colonies, acting upon
the policy of the world, building forts and showing
themselves in arms, were harassed by perpetual alarms,
and pursued by the sharp arrows of Indian warfare."

And what ended the happy reign of peace? Why
did not the immunity of the Quaker colony from Indian
warfare continue, not seventy years merely, but indefinitely? The answer is significant! By reason of the
very security which its non-resistant policy had

achieved, Pennsylvania began to attract settlers from other colonies. In course of time these non-Quaker settlers came to outnumber the Quakers, and, like all practical persons, learning nothing from experience, insisted upon erecting forts upon the frontier, and organising and drilling a militia force. In other words, Quaker principles were abandoned by those who could not and would not see the connection between these principles and the uninterrupted peace which had long blessed the Pennsylvania colony. Security was no longer sought in " brotherly love," but in the sword. With the result, that security was lost forever. From the very moment that the Quakers were outvoted in the Pennsylvania legislature, and their non-resistant policy thus overthrown, peace with the surrounding Indian tribes came to an end, and war therefore a matter of frequent and disastrous occurrence.

All sorts of attempts have been made by American historians to " explain away " this impressive demonstration of the practicability of non-resistance, by asserting that there were certain unique conditions in Pennsylvania which did not pertain in the other English colonies. Thus some historians argued that the Susquehanna Indians, with whom Penn had his dealings, were a particularly amiable and unwarlike tribe of savages. Other historians, not having heard that these members of the bloodthirsty Six Nations were themselves Quakers, or not believing it, argue on the other hand, that the Susquehannas had just gone through a long and cruel war, and were too exhausted to enter

upon hostilities with the colonists.   All such special explanations as these, however, fail to account for the further fact that the Quakers who chanced to live in other
settlements, such as those in New England or Virginia,
which were constantly harried by Indian warfare, enjoyed exactly the same immunity from injury as that
enjoyed by the Pennsylvanians.   The other settlers in
other places lived in armed houses, carried weapons
wherever they went, and in case of attack from the
forests fled at once to the block-houses prepared for
these occasions.   The Quakers, however, true to their
principles, lived in houses which were undefended, never
carried arms of any kind, and, when the Indians came
sweeping down upon the villages, went undisturbed about
their daily tasks as though nothing unusual were hap-
pening.   And what was their fate?   Were they the
first to be butchered in cold blood?   On the contrary,
they were the only members of these communities who
were left unharmed.   In all the Indian fighting of these
early colonial days, only three Quakers, so far as we
know, were slain.   And these were Quakers, who, under
stress of great alarm, were persuaded to arm themselves
against attack!   Two were men who were accustomed
to go to their labour unarmed; " but a spirit of distrust
taking place in their minds, they took weapons of war
to defend themselves, and the Indians, who had seen
them several times without them and let them alone . . .
now seeing them with guns, and supposing that they
were designed to kill the Indians, therefore shot them
dead."   The other was a woman; who, on the occasion

of a raid, had remained in her habitation, not deigning to go to the block-house for protection.   Later, becoming frightened, she fled with her children, and on the way was killed.

The surest test to which the peace principles of the Quakers were ever subjected, however, was that which came in Ireland, on the occasion of the memorable Rebellion in 1798.   Two years before this outbreak occurred, the Quakers, anticipating serious trouble, met together in their meeting-houses and publicly destroyed their firearms which they were in the custom of using for game.   This they did, so one of the statements ran, " to prevent (arms) being made use of to the destruction of our fellow-creatures and more fully and clearly to support our peaceable and Christian testimony in these perilous times."   In other words, they did just the opposite of what the Belgians did last year.   Instead of arming themselves against those who they feared were getting ready to attack them, they went out of their way to proclaim their defenselessness.   Feeling sure that war was coming, they prepared not for war, but for peace.   And what was the result?   For two years, from 1798 to 1800, the Rebellion raged.   Thousands of men were killed, hundreds of women outraged, fields were ravaged and towns destroyed.   Victory alternated from side to side, and by both sides were the Quakers " despised and rejected."   The Protestants viewed them with scorn because they would not fight for the Protestant cause or even pay military taxes; the Catholic insurgents hated them because they would

neither profess the true faith nor help them fight for
Irish freedom. Threats and insults were heaped upon
them by both parties. More than once they were
brought face to face with death. But, steadfast in
their faith and practice, they everywhere escaped. In
course of time their homes became known as sure havens
of safety, and were sought out by fleeing women and
wounded men. At last, their unfailing deeds of kindness to both Protestants and Catholics had their inevitable effect, so that toward the close of the Rebellion,
whichever party would enter a village after a victorious
fight, the cry would go up, " Spare the Quakers — they
do good to all, and harm to none!" It is worthy of
memory that, in all these dreadful months of ravage and
slaughter, only one Quaker is known to have been killed.
This was a young man who, being afraid to trust peace
principles, put on a uniform and went to the garrison
for protection. This man was later captured by the
enemy, and he was killed. " His dress and arms spoke
the language of hostility," says the historian, " and
therefore invited it."

VII

The Quakers, however, are not the only organised
group of modern times, whose experience gives us
demonstration of the practicability of the non-resistant
principle. More remarkable, in certain ways, is the
story of the famous sect of the Bahaists.

If there are any conditions amid which the practice of
non-resistance would seem to be as impossible as it

would be ignoble, these conditions are certainly to be found in the Empire of Turkey. The horror of the Armenian persecutions, through many generations past, is a case in point. Here have inoffensive and unoffending Christians been set upon by the bloodthirsty emissaries of the Sultan and his ministers, and visited with such indignities, sufferings, agonies as few other peoples, in all the long history of human misery, have ever been called upon to endure. Villages levelled to the ground — country-sides put to the sword — populations driven like sheep into wilderness and desert, there to perish of thirst, hunger, exposure and exhaustion — men by the hundreds shut up in churches and burned alive — women by the thousands ravished, mutilated or spared only for captivity in harems — children abandoned, murdered, torn limb from limb, tossed in idle sport from spear to spear — what words are adequate to describe the enormity of these crimes! And who can dare to argue, in the face of such crimes, that non-resistance is a practicable law of life? Would it have availed these wretched Armenians anything to have offered no resistance to their Turkish murderers? Would they have won any security or saved any lives by submitting tamely to the hand of the oppressor? And even if prudence might have dictated such a course of action, would it not have been the height of cowardice to have acquiesced? Was it not the duty of every man to resist to the death the violators of his home, and of every woman to fight to the last in defence of her own honour and the safety of her children? Is it not sufficient, in a word, to encounter one experience of this kind to see to what a *reductio ad absurdum* we are speedily brought by any thorough-going discussion of this question?

In answer to these inquiries just two things are to be said. First of all, it must be noted that the appeal to force has in this case accomplished nothing in the way of guaranteeing to the Armenians immunity from attack, or protecting them from unmentionable horrors when attacked. Neither the arms of the Armenians themselves, nor the enormous armaments of the Christian nations of Europe and America to which appeal for aid has repeatedly been made, have restrained the blood-stained hand of the Turkish oppressor. Indeed, it may fairly be asked if the tradition of Christian militancy as made known to the Mohammedan through many centuries gone by, and the call of the Armenians to an armed Christendom for protection and redress, have not served to aggravate, if not actually create, the situation? In any case, Armenian massacres have been for years a constantly recurring event in Turkish history; and the outbreak of the Great War was the signal for worse atrocities than have ever been known before. The appeal to force is a failure!

But would non-resistance have been a success? To this we answer, Yes — and for the simple reason that, under exactly similar circumstances, it *has* succeeded! For the Armenians are not the only religionists in the Mohammedan world who have been ruthlessly perse-

cuted.   Side by side with them, through many years,
suffered and died the followers of the Bab.   Shot to
death himself in a public square in Tabriz in July, 1850,
this noble prophet of the soul left behind him many disciples who devoted themselves, like the early apostles of
Christ, to the preaching of his gospel to a hostile world.
Very speedily the Mohammedan authorities became
alarmed, especially after an unsuccessful attack upon
the life of the Persian Shah by a crazed Babi, and persecution of the most terrible character was set on foot.
In the frenzied massacres which followed, thirty thousand men, women and children were cut down in cold
blood.   Outrages of every description were practised,
cruelties of the last degree of refinement perpetrated,
upon defenseless and terrified populations.   The leaders
were seized, some of them killed and others imprisoned.
Baha o'llah, the successor of the Bab, was stripped of
his property, imprisoned in a noisome dungeon, and at
last banished from the kingdom.   In Turkey, where he
took refuge, he was in 1868 doomed to the prison of
Akka in Palestine, where he remained till his death.
And here also, for a period of forty years, languished
his disciple and later successor, Abdul Baha.

Thus far the story of the Bahaists is that of the
Armenians.   But now appears the difference.   Instead
of meeting violence with violence, or appealing from the
sword of Mohammed to the sword of Christ, the followers of the Bab, like the early Christians in Rome,
dedicated themselves resolutely to the ideal of non-re-

sistance. Not a sword was drawn or a staff lifted in defence of their homes and persons against the assaults of their enemies. Protests were uttered, prayers offered, appeals to pity spoken — but no resort was had to violence of any kind. With the result that slaughter very soon ceased, persecutions ended, prison doors opened; and Bahaism is now taught and practised by millions of devotees without interference by the authorities! Long before Baha o'llah died, he saw his followers protected from attack by the sheer power of their own endurance, patience and unfailing goodwill. In his old age, he was himself released from prison, so great was the impression made upon his jailers " by the uniform kindness and fairness the Bahaists displayed toward each other and toward their keepers." Abdul Baha, also, after forty years of suffering, has won similar immunity by similar ways of the spirit, and is now permitted a latitude of speech and action within the confines of Islam which would not under any circumstances be granted to a native Christian. Again has love done its perfect work. Again has the spirit triumphed, where the flesh has failed. Well does an historian of this movement declare that " religious faith, in our own times, once more revealed its secret power to triumph over the agony of fire and steel." [1] Nor is any record to be found of denunciation of these martyrs for cowardice or shame in thus enduring and hoping all things!

[1] See Horace Holley's *The Modern Social Religion*, page 160.

VIII

To the Quakers and the Bahaists must now be added the socialists, who are exemplars, from the wider viewpoint at least, of all the best that we mean by non-resistance. The story of the mighty and successful battles which they have waged against the capitalistic despotisms of modern times presents many illustrations of the perfect efficacy of the pacifist method of attack, but none is quite so cunning and inspiring, perhaps, as that of the triumphant twelve-years' fight of the German socialists against Bismarck and the Hohenzollerns.

In October, 1878, as a result be it noted, of a succession of terrorist outrages, there was passed by the German Reichstag, after a battle royal between the Chancellor on the one side and Bebel and Liebknecht on the other, an anti-socialist law which was intended to cut off every legal and peaceable means of advancing the socialist cause. The chief measures of the law [1] prohibited the formation or existence of socialist organisations, so restricted the right of assembly that all socialist meetings, festivals and processions were made impossible, interdicted all socialist publications, both domestic and foreign, confiscated all socialist books and printing presses, and forbade the collection of money on behalf of socialistic activities either by private assessment or public appeal. Persons violating these prohibitions were liable to punishments varying from a fine of 500 marks or three months' imprisonment to expul-

[1] See Robert Hunter's *Violence and the Labor Movement.*

sion from a certain neighbourhood or governmental district. Ample powers for enforcing these prohibitions were lodged in the local and national police.

For the moment it seemed as though the enactment of this law marked the end of German socialism. Societies were instantly dissolved, newspapers and magazines suppressed, printing establishments confiscated, and agitators imprisoned or expelled. " Within a few weeks," says Mr. Hunter, " not a thing seemed left of the great movement of half a million men that had existed a few weeks before." Here, if ever, was a case where violence would seem to have been justifiable. Where or when can be found a state of affairs which more nearly meets the condition of *ultima ratio* laid down by Professor Rauschenbusch? [1] Had arson, assassination, and general murder broken loose throughout the Empire, it would be difficult to condemn the utilisation of such methods of force. Nor were the terrorists of the time slow to see the opportunity and to point its moral. " All measures are legitimate against tyrants," cried Johann Most from the safe refuge of London, and here certainly was tyranny at its very worst.

In spite of the extreme provocation of the situation, however, the German socialists stood steadfast against resort to violence. Instead of fighting, they gave themselves to the development of an underground socialist movement that proved most baffling to the police. In a hundred mysterious ways the propaganda was ceaselessly conducted throughout the Empire. Papers were

[1] See above, Chapter II, page 45.

passed from hand to hand; meetings were held in vacant fields and darkened cellars; funds were raised to support agitators whose dangerous duty it was to keep the fires burning in hidden places.   In spite of all that Bismarck and his minions could do — in spite of martial law, fines, imprisonments, banishments — the agitation went on. Month after month, year after year, reports came to the Chancellor of the continued life of the movement, and, what was more astounding, of its rapid growth. In 1886, infuriated beyond measure by the failure of his programme, Bismarck arrested nine of the socialist deputies in the Reichstag on charges of belonging to a secret and illegal organisation.   All the accused were convicted and sentenced to imprisonment for six or nine months.   But even this did not avail to stop the movement.   Slowly, surely, without the firing of a single gun or the throwing of a single bomb, the work went on from strength to strength.   Whereas the socialist vote in 1878, when the law was enacted, was 450,000, in the election of 1890 it mounted to 1,427,000.   Defeat was apparent; and in spite of all Bismarck's pleas to the contrary, a disgusted Reichstag, in September 30, 1890, repealed the law.

Never was there a greater victory — and never a victory which showed more convincingly the irresistible momentum of moral, as contrasted with physical, power. Had the German socialists, in their hour of despair in 1878, resorted to violence, there can be no question but what they would have been destroyed root and branch. Such resort was indeed the very thing for which Bis-

marck in his secret heart most ardently hoped, for the
game of blood and iron was the one game in which he
knew himself to be supreme.   With aggravating per-
sistency and marvellous patience, the socialists kept to
the non-resistant path, and thus made certain their ultimate victory.   Liebknecht summed up the whole matter
when he said: " He [Bismarck] has had at his entire
disposal for more than a quarter of a century, the
police, the army, the capital, and the power of the State
— in brief, all the means of mechanical force.   We had
only our just right, our firm conviction, our bared
breasts, to oppose him with, and it is we who have conquered!   Our arms were the best.   In the course of
time brute power must yield to moral factors."

IX

The experiences of the Quakers, the Bahaists and the
socialists give us indication of what can be accomplished
along the lines of non-resistance not only by individuals
but by groups of individuals.   They suggest the possibility at least of a practicable extension of the non-resistant principles to the great field of international relationships, and a satisfactory answer therefore to those
basic questions of peace, security and national idealism
which have been raised up all anew, as we have seen,[1] by
the present war.   Fortunately, however, we are not left
any more to speculation in this field than in the other,
Experimentation along these lines by nations has of
course been rare as compared with experimentation by

[1] See Chapter I, pages 10–18.

individuals.   But instances exist, and are convincing!

Take, for example, the problem of international peace.   We have already seen at considerable length the utter failure of the militarist theory of preserving peace by preparing for war.[1]   Always have nations prepared for war, just as the militarists have advised, and always has war, and not peace, been the result.   It is obvious, or at least it should be obvious, that there is no solution of our problem along these lines.   This being the case, it might well be asked if it is not possible that there may be "something" in the pacifist theory of disarmament as a guarantee of peace — especially in view of the fact that one trial has been given to this theory with completely successful results!

Just one hundred years ago, in 1815, England and America agreed to a policy of almost complete disarmament along the four thousand miles of boundary line between the United States and Canada.   One or two ships of ridiculously light tonnage and only a single gun each, were to float upon the Great Lakes, but aside from this the frontier was to be open.   Practically speaking, there was to be absolute disarmament so far as the relations between these two great countries of North America were concerned.   From that day to the present, this condition of affairs, happily achieved by President Monroe and his minister, John Quincy Adams, has continued; and from that day to the present, there has been peace.   The treaty effecting this arrangement, be it noted, was signed very shortly after

[1] See Chapter III, pages 98–102.

the close of the War of 1812, when feeling was bitter between Canada and America. At various times, disputes of great intricacy and full of fighting possibilities have arisen, as witness the " Fifty-four Forty or Fight " crisis of the '40s. But in spite of every difficulty and temptation, peace has held for an entire century. And who that can reason at all along the lines of cause and effect, can deny that the absence of weapons of war is one of the chief reasons, if not actually the sole reason, why war has not come? Extend this policy, now, throughout the world. Let all national frontiers be like that of Canada and the United States rather than like that of Germany and France. Let all statesmen take example of Monroe and Adams rather than of Bismarck. And who can doubt that war would be no more? Peace will come when we really believe in peace enough to walk steadfastly in its ways. So, and not otherwise, can the problem now before us be permanently solved.

The one hundred years of peace between America and Canada might well be taken also to illustrate the one possible solution of our second problem, that of national security. For where is there an American citizen, even on the frontier between these two countries, who feels any sense of insecurity because we have no forts on the northern borders of Maine or Minnesota or Washington, and no dreadnaughts floating upon Lake Erie or Lake Superior? On the contrary, is not every American citizen conscious of a profound sense of security as he looks toward Canada, for the very reason that there is not a gun upon that border which menaces our safety?   Compare the feelings of Americans toward Canada to-day with the feelings of Frenchmen toward Germany, or Germans toward Russia, two years ago — and we begin to realise, perhaps, what is the true relation between armaments and national security.

That there may be no dodging of issues and evading of questions, however, I propose to go to the extreme upon this matter, and cite as an illustration of security won by non-resistance methods, the case of China.   The Celestial Empire is usually taken by the militarists as the supreme example of the failure of non-resistance as a practicable national policy.   But why?   Let the pages of history be turned from the most ancient days unto our own, and where is there a single people which has achieved such security as the Chinese?   Egypt, Chaldea, Persia, Athens, Macedonia, Rome, Spain — all have gone.   Not a nation has endured beyond a certain span of centuries — save only China.   And China has endured, century after century, æon after æon — and here she stands to-day, as firm, as impregnable, as ever.   Invading armies, to be sure, have crossed her borders.   Her sovereigns have been overthrown, and alien dynasties placed within her palaces.   In recent times, ports have been wrested from her control, and concessions of territory exacted, by western peoples. But how nearly have these insignificant details of political experience touched the national life?   How have the people of China as a whole been affected by a change of royal houses or the lifting of a foreign flag above

Hong-Kong or Kiow-Tschau? The impressive fact is
not that occasional attacks have been made upon her
territory, but that no attack has touched the integrity
of her civilisation. Chinese sovereigns have fallen,
Chinese cities have been stolen, but the Chinese people
have endured, like the sands that meet the mounting and
receding seas. They have seen a score of conquerors
come and go, and promise to see another score of our
own and later times similarly disappear — and still
they remain the same! If by security we mean survival
— and what does security mean if not this? — what
people has ever stood the test like these mysterious ori-
entals? All other nations have drawn the sword, and
perished by the sword. This nation has drawn no
sword, or has done so only upon rare occasions under
the disastrous leadership of militaristic dynasties, and
behold, she lives! The inference is indubitable — that,
if security is our problem, here is our answer!

But who would have security at such a price as this?
Who wants to survive, if he must survive as a Chinaman? Is it not better to be a dead lion than a live dog
— to perish grandly like Rome than to exist forever
like China?

This raises at once our third question — that of national idealism. And let it be said at once of the pacifist, that he has no more admiration for Chinese civilisation as such than the militarist! But he quite fails
to understand wherein the peculiar and uninspiring
character of this civilisation has anything essentially
to do with resistance or non-resistance. The Egyp-

tians, in their worship of dead ancestors, their rearing
of temples and tombs, their reverence for tradition,
their expediential philosophy, their stolidity, bear striking resemblance to the Chinese — but the Egyptians
were militarists of the fiercest type.   The Quakers, on
the other hand, in their non-resistant ideas, are of one
mind and heart with the Celestials; but one may look
to the Quakers in vain for any of those religious and
racial characteristics which set the Chinese apart from
other peoples.   The fact of the matter is, there is on
the one hand no essential connection between the character of Chinese civilisation and the non-resistant principle; and on the other hand nothing essentially inconsistent between any other type of civilisation — our nation for example — and the non-resistant principle.
Non-resistance may be practised by any people successfully, just as its opposite, militarism, has been practised by a long succession of peoples unsuccessfully.
What we have in the case of the Chinese is simply the instance of one people, which, by some fortuitous con-
course of circumstances, was induced to follow this particular law of life.   That this one people chanced to
exemplify certain characteristics which do not stir our
admiration, matters nothing either one way or the
other.   The Quakers, equally non-resistant with the
Chinese, exemplify, on the other hand, everything that
is beautiful in the moral and spiritual life; in many
ways they must be regarded as the very flower and
fruitage of our Christian civilisation.   To argue that
the Quakers are thus spiritually supreme because they

are non-resistant would be as inaccurate as to argue
the opposite of the Chinese. In neither case is non-
resistance a vital part of the group-character under
discussion. It is as consistent with the highest as well
as with the lowest type — can be made as much a rule
of life for the best as for the worst civilisation. What
we have here is simply a principle of action which allows
whatever civilisation may adopt it to survive and thus
develop to the uttermost every element that it chances
to contain. If the militarist principle of action be
adopted, development is interfered with, diverted from
its true course, cut off untimely by repressive, cor-
ruptive, and destructive forces of a wholly extraneous
character. Non-resistance furthers survival, and hence
gives a chance for full fruition. The Chinese and the
Quakers, each in their own way, are finished products.
What they are is all they ever can be. Which means
from the standpoint of national idealism, that non-resistance is the " saving element."

X

Such are the evidences of the practicability of non-
resistance. It may be contended, of course, that all
these cases are, after all, exceptions. But to this full
answer has already been given by Charles Sumner in his
oration already referred to more than once. "If it
be urged," he says, "that these instances are exceptional, I reply at once, that it is not so. They are indubitable evidence of the real man, revealing the divinity of humanity, out of which goodness, happiness,

true greatness can alone proceed.   They disclose sus-
ceptibilities confined to no particular race, no special
period of time, no narrow circle of knowledge or refinement, but are present wherever two or more human beings come together, and strong in proportion to their
virtue and intelligence."

The instances here cited, so far from being exceptions, are definite illustrations of the workings of two
absolute spiritual laws.

The first of these laws is this — that like always produces like.   Reason conduces to reason, hate stirs up
hate, love generates love.   " Cast your bread upon the
waters," said Jesus, " and it will come back to you
again."   " As ye sow," said Paul, with the same moral
truth in mind, " so shall ye also reap."   Nothing can be
more certain than that, if you distrust a man, you will
alienate him; if you have trust in a man, you will encourage him to goodwill; if you love a man, he will love
you in return.   This law is all summed up in the writings of one of the more remote groups of early Christians, where appears the remarkable saying, " Love your
enemies, and you will have none."

And the second spiritual law exemplified by this evidence is this — that the spirit is always superior to the
flesh, and the flesh therefore always subordinate to the
spirit.   Wherein is man superior to the brute if not in
the possession of those spiritual qualities which make
him in very truth to be " but a little lower than the
angels "?   Wherein is " the wise man," as Socrates
called him, superior to the ordinary man, if not in in-

telligence, reason, patience, self-control, compassion, love, as contrasted oftentimes with fleetness of foot, strength of muscle, and power of physical endurance? It is spirit that elevates, purifies, and, in the final struggle, conquers. To trust to the spirit, is to trust to nothing less than the immortal soul, the universe, God. Who can stand before such a marshalling of power? Robert Browning sums up all of this great law in his poem *Instans Tyrannus*, where he tells us how the slave conquered his murderous master.

> "Did I say 'without friend'?

says the beaten master, referring to his victim, as he tells the tale of defeat.

> "Say rather, from marge to blue marge
> The whole sky grew his targe
> With the sun's self for visible boss,
> While an arm ran across
> Which the earth heaved beneath like a breast
> Where the wretch was safe prest!
> Do you see? Just my vengeance complete,
> The man sprang to his feet,
> Stood erect, caught at God's skirts, and prayed!
> — So, *I* was afraid!"

XI

It is facts such as these which justify us in our conviction that non-resistance is practicable. Theoretically, as we have just seen, it is the embodiment in human action of two great laws — first, that like produces like; and secondly, that spirit conquers flesh. Practically it is the tried and tested rule of life of those who have had faith to see, courage to dare, and strength to endure.   Of course it goes without saying, that the application of the non-resistant principle to the hundred and one intricate problems of human relationships is not always successful.   It fails only less often than the resort to force as a method of solution of these same problems.   But in the case of the former, as not in the case of the latter, we have a principle which fails not because of its own essential falsity, but because of the weakness, timidity, halfheartedness of those who strive to put it into practice.   Not too frequently can we remind ourselves of the counsel of " Golden-Rule " Jones of Toledo, Ohio.   " Live always by the Golden Rule," was his word.   " When (it) will not work, it is not the fault of the Rule, but because one does not know just how to work it." [1]   Of itself, " love never faileth." Those who live by this law have the unseen on their side. The very stars in their courses fight for them.   God, in his infinite majesty, stands up and makes their cause his own.

" O ye of little faith "— think well ere ye scoff and turn away!   Not yet has all been learned, that " fools " should not appear to confound the great and wise. Would ye not better pray, that faith may yet be yours, to save the world new terrors and old fates?

[1] See Brand Whitlock, in *Forty Years of It,* page 215.
Note: Is there no qualification to this doctrine of practicable non-resistance? — None in itself!   Were men so minded, they could practise it to-morrow with complete success, and to the indescribable joy of the world.   But that they are not so minded, is evident.   " Of course, all that I have been saying," writes Mr. Bertrand Russell, in a plea for non-resistance in his *Justice in*

War Time, "is fantastic, degrading, and out of touch with reality.
I have been assuming that men are to some extent guided by
reason, that their actions are directed to ends such as 'life,
liberty, and the pursuit of happiness.' This is not the case." [1]
In other words, it is an unescapable fact that men have never
been, and are not yet, ready to practise the precepts of "love
to God and man" which they profess. They persist, in the last
extremity, in reliance upon force for the gaining of their ends.
They will not see, they do not welcome, the gospel here laid down.
Therefore, in pursuit of this unqualified ideal of good, must
qualification in practice be recognised as the condition of ultimate
fulfilment — qualification, it should be said, not on the part of the
single man, who must be wholly faithful, but on the part of groups
of men organised into social entities. In relations between individuals, this qualification is found in the police system, which
takes from the hands of the private citizen all agencies of force,
and restricts their possession to a picked group of men, charged
to use them for the benefit not of themselves but of the community. A disarmed citizenry leads gradually to a disarmed
police; the disarmed police, to a gradual substitution in government of the rule of consent for the rule of force; and the rule of
consent to a gradual establishment of the non-resistant ideal in
social action. Similar, I believe, must be the course of evolution
toward the unqualified non-resistant ideal in relations between
states. Not by preparations for war, not by alliances offensive
and defensive, not by balances of power, not by leagues to enforce peace, will the way to peace be found. Rather must the
arms of separate states be transferred completely to an international police force, charged by an international tribunal of ex-
ecutive administration to employ these arms not for the benefit
of itself, or of any nation or group of nations, but for the better
ordering of mankind. What has been accomplished in the United
States, in relations between states, must be accomplished in the
world at large, in relations between nations. By such a method
of compromise, shameful and yet necessary, will the area within
which force can be operated be ever more and more narrowly
confined, until at last, without as already within enlightened
communities of our own time, it will disappear altogether before
the universal reign of reason and goodwill. Mr. Russell, in the
essay to which I have referred, names one condition as a justification of the use of force. It is just this condition which I
would rather define as the one qualification of our non-resistant
ideal, necessitated by the imperfect spiritual development of men.
"The use of force is justifiable," he says, "when it is ordered
in accordance with law by a neutral authority in the general
interest." [2]

[1] See page 52.
[2] See *Justice in War Time*, page 41.

CHAPTER VIII

IS WAR EVER JUSTIFIABLE?

"The notion of a right to go to war cannot be properly conceived as an element in the law of nations. For it would be equivalent to a right to determine what is just, not by universal external laws limiting the freedom of every individual alike, but through one-sided maxims that operate by means of force. If such a right be conceived at all it would amount, in fact, to this: that in the case of men who are so disposed it is quite right for them to destroy and devour each other, and thus to find perpetual peace only in the wide grave which is to cover all the abomination of the deeds of violence and their authors!"— Immanuel Kant, in *Eternal Peace.*

CHAPTER VIII

IS WAR EVER JUSTIFIABLE?

THE acceptance of non-resistance as a working principle of life, and the belief in its entire practicability, still leave unanswered certain phases of the question of international war. On general principles, of course, the non-resistant can have nothing to do with armed conflict of any kind. But as there are exceptions to all rules, may there not be an exception to this rule? Is not war, in other words, sometimes inevitable and therefore justifiable even for the non-resistant, just to the extent that relations between nations, unlike relations between individuals, have not yet been ordered and moralised? Does not the undeniable assertion of General Bernhardi, in his *Germany and the Next War*, that the absence of centralised and supreme authority in the world at large, leaves to each nation the high task of defending its own integrity and finding its own " place in the sun," point to a situation which makes war at times a duty as stern as it is terrible? What about the Northern states after the firing upon Sumter? What about Belgium in August, 1914? What about America, if Germany had defied President Wilson after the sinking of the *Lusitania?* Do not occasional conditions such as these make war not only justifiable but honourable? To the discussion of this question we now turn.

I

War between the nations of the earth is on the defensive to-day as it has never been before. There was a time, not so very long ago, when war was glorified quite apart from any of the particular circumstances of its precipitation, and the warrior extolled as among the bravest and noblest of mankind. But now all this is changed. War to-day is almost universally regarded as a degradation, and the maker of war an enemy of the race. So at least we discovered when the Great War burst upon the affrighted world. Here for the first time was a war for which nobody was willing to assume responsibility —" a foundling," to use the striking phrase of David Starr Jordan, to which no one of the nations involved would give refuge. Here was a war which was hailed from one end of the earth to the other, not with shouts of exultation, but with the curses of men and the tears of women. Here was a war which brought down upon the heads of those who are rightly or wrongly charged with responsibility, such a tide of hatred and execration as has come upon no individual, or group of individuals, since the passing of Bonaparte and his marshals. Nothing could be more remarkable, and at the same time more encouraging, than the expressions of detestation and horror which everywhere appeared when it was first realised what had come upon the world. Newspaper cartoons and editorials, magazine articles, sermons and addresses, all joined in denouncing the conflict as an unspeakable outrage and in calling upon those in places of authority to secure peace. Especially significant were the utterances of the poets, who sounded not songs of battle, but almost without exception the sad refrains of dirges and lamentations. Rudyard Kipling's famous lines, as hard as the " steel and stone " of which he chanted, and John Masefield's elegy, as pathetic as that written in an earlier age in a country churchyard, are regarded not without good reason as the typical expressions of the hour.

While it is true, however, that war in general is condemned in our time as it has never before been condemned in human history, it is to be noted, on the other hand, that war in the case of each particular nation is justified to-day in exactly the same way that it has always been justified in the past. The defence is not quite so jubilant as formerly, but it is a defence all the same. Englishmen of course hate war in general as much as Germans, and Germans as much as Frenchmen. Mr. Asquith regards this particular war as inexcusable and unnecessary as does the Crown Prince of the German Empire or the Czar of all the Russias. But England is as certain that Germany and Austria are to blame for the struggle as the Teuton states are certain that England and her allies are to blame; and the individual Englishman is as eager to fight for the banner of St. George as the individual German for the Prussian Eagle. War is undoubtedly wrong, but this particular war is undoubtedly right for Englishmen, or Frenchmen, or Germans, or Belgians, as the

case may be.   Only in the United States has there been
a condemnation of the business which is specific as well
as general, but this is only because we are altogether
outside of the area of battle.   Professor John Erskine,
of Columbia University, is perfectly right, as events
since the *Lusitania* outrage abundantly attest, when he
points out, in reference to this fact, that " there can be
little question that if the United States were actually
in the conflict this . . . attitude would largely disappear."   That is to say, we condemn war " for the other
fellow," but we justify it so soon as we ourselves are
challenged to take up arms !

Now it is this extraordinary fact that war is universally abhorred and denounced to-day, so long as it
is regarded by itself and is thus judged strictly upon
its own merits, but speedily wins the approval of the
citizens of any one state so soon as it becomes involved
in any way with the interests or honour of that state,
which justifies the searching question as to whether war
is ever justifiable.   It is all well and good to condemn
war in the abstract as " the sum of all villainy," but
what avails it if war straightway becomes the sum of all
virtue just the moment it becomes our war as contrasted with some one else's war?   It is profitable, no
doubt, for the peacemaker to work for peace when
" wars and rumours of wars," are far removed from the
bounds of possibility, but what becomes of the profit if
the peacemaker abandons his cause the very moment
that war becomes a contingency for the nation to which
he belongs and in which alone he has any influence?

It is admirable to denounce war in general, but how much " forwarder " are we if denunciation of war in general can be changed into approval of this particular war the very instant that this particular war is imminent? Somewhere there is a fundamental fallacy. War, like slavery, cannot be wrong in one place and right in another place. War, like religious persecution, cannot be justifiable for Englishmen and unjustifiable for Germans. One and the same thing cannot be right and wrong, just and unjust, at one and the same time. Here in the fact of war do we have a perfectly simple and well-understood social phenomenon. It has presented the same general characteristics and followed the same processes of action from the ancient day of clubs and stones to the modern day of Zeppelins and super-dreadnaughts. Those who engage in it, on one side or the other, engage in identically the same work of plunder, pillage, destruction, and murder. Now is this thing right, or is it wrong? Is it justifiable or is it unjustifiable? Study it from any standpoint — judge it on its own merits — put aside all the ambitions, prejudices, and fears of national feeling — and what must the verdict be!

II

Before getting to the real issue which is involved in this inquiry, it will first be necessary to clear away some perplexing and enticing illusions which have complicated this question of the justifiability of war more or less from the beginning. Only as we dissipate these

illusions, and thus set the mind free from the entangle-
ments of self-deception, can we see things as they must
be seen, with an eye that is " single " and therefore full
of light.

In the first place, let us note that war cannot be
justified on the ground that it generates within the
human heart the heroic virtues.   I am not one of those
who are inclined to extol the moral influences of war.
I recognise the heroism of the sentinel who keeps guard
in the filthy trenches, of the sailor who watches nightly
on the frozen deck of the battleship, of the woman who
waits in agony of spirit in the lonely home for news,
good or bad, of her beloved.   But I recognise, also,
that for every one heart that is stirred by pure and
noble emotion of this kind, there are a hundred hearts
that are stirred by the blackest passions to which the
human breast is heir.   War turns men not into angels
but into devils!   The path of war is strewn not with
the flowers of love but with the ashes of hate!   Cæsar
bestrides the battlefield, and not Christ!   Nevertheless,
even if it were true that war developed the heroic virtues in exactly the way described by the rapturous
eulogists of war, still would it be true that this would
offer no adequate justification of this horror.   A great
fire in New York would undoubtedly produce prodigies
of valour, but this fact would not justify the Fire Department in not doing its utmost to extinguish it.   A
plague of cholera would generate such devotion and self-
sacrifice on the part of physicians and nurses as
would baffle adequate description, but the Health De-

partment would not feel justified for this reason in
starting and maintaining an epidemic. Most of the
noblest deeds in human history are to be found in the
annals of martyrdom — we would not willingly surrender the record of these deeds! — and yet this does
not tempt us to justify the persecution which produced
the martyrs. There is no plainer witness to the essential divinity of the human spirit than its unfaltering
courage in the face of disaster, and its abiding faith
in the midst of evil. But disaster still remains disaster,
and evil evil, even though the soul can make itself triumphant over both. To look at the great memorial
in Boston to Robert Gould Shaw and his Negro regi-
ment is to feel one's pulse quicken and one's heart
refreshed. But these soldiers marching away to heroic
death no more justify the Civil War than " the noble
army of martyrs " perishing in the Roman arena justifies the persecutions of Nero.

In the second place, war cannot be justified by the
sincere motives, generous impulses and high ideals which
oftentimes lie behind it. Again and again we are persuaded to characterise a certain war as " true and
righteous altogether " because the men who went into
it, on the side in which we happen to be interested, were
moved by the noblest sentiments and were serving the
best interests of humanity. Thus we justify the Civil
Wars in England because Cromwell and his Roundheads
represent one of the most remarkable moral movements
in modern history. We justify the American Revolution because the colonists were battling unselfishly for

the great principle of political and social liberty. We justify the American Civil War because the " boys in blue " laid down their lives for the holy purpose of saving the Republic and emancipating the slave. And so, at the present moment, most Americans are justifying the war now being fought by the Allies on the ground that England, France, and Russia are protecting civilisation from the menace of German militarism. In all of these instances, undoubtedly, we have wars fought from the noblest motives and with the most unselfish desires. But how far this comes from justifying war in itself is shown by the fact that we find exactly these same motives and desires present in the hearts of those against whom our chosen heroes were fighting. The Cavaliers of Charles were every whit as sincere as the Roundheads of Oliver Cromwell. Lord North and the English Tories fought the American colonists in the honest conviction that these colonists were traitors to the king and enemies therefore of the British realm. The " boys in gray " died as gallantly as the " boys in blue " for a cause which was to them as precious. And in the war now being fought in Europe there is nothing finer than the absolute devotion of a united people to what they regard as the sacred cause of the Fatherland. The fact of the matter is that motives apply to persons and not at all to events. No mistake is more frequent, and yet no mistake should be more obvious, than that of carrying over the question of motive from the actor to the action, and thus of confusing the intrinsic merits of the former with the intrinsic merits of the latter. No social phenomenon, least of all one which involves the happiness and lives of millions of human beings, can be justified by the motives of the participants therein. Human sacrifice was for centuries practised by men and women as a religious rite and therefore in the noblest spirit of devotion. Persecution has again and again been visited upon helpless victims by men whose motives were as unselfish and idealistic as those which animated the breast of Marcus Aurelius, when he drew his sword against the Christians. Most of the enormities which have characterised the present-day struggle between capital and labour have been committed on both sides by men who were sincerely convinced that they were serving the best interests of humanity. The motives involved in these dreadful acts may justify the persons performing them, as I have said, but they have nothing to do with the justifiability of the acts themselves. The present war, like human sacrifice or religious persecution, must be justified, if at all, for reasons quite apart from the motives of Englishmen, Frenchmen, Belgians, Austrians, Germans, which are in all cases, I have no doubt, equally fine. And what is true of this war is true of every war that has ever been fought.

In the third place, it is important to note that war cannot be justified by the beneficent results which it may achieve. That great good, both for nations and individuals, has at times been the consequence of war, is beyond question. Marathon repelled the barbaric hordes of Asia from the shores of Greece; Charles Martel saved Christianity from being overwhelmed by Mohammedanism at the battle of Tours; the Crusades brought light out of darkness and made possible the Protestant Reformation; the wars of the Netherlands destroyed the tyranny of Spain and led the way to the great achievement of religious liberty; the American Revolution is a landmark in the history of political democracy; and a by-product of the American Civil War was the emancipation of the slaves. Facts like these inevitably tempt us to believe that, however it may be with wars in general, these particular wars at least stand justified by their results. A little careful thought, however, will quickly show how impossible is such a conclusion. The " Black Death," which destroyed one-half of the population of Europe in a single year, brought to the surviving workers the indubitable boon of high wages and abundant labour; the Great Fire of London wiped out the last vestiges of the Great Plague; the Reign of Terror sealed the fate of the *Ancien Régime* and marks the opening chapter of the history of European liberty; the Chicago Fire turned a shabby frontier town into a modern municipality; the sinking of the *Titanic* made ocean travel for the first time reasonably secure; but who of us would argue, on this basis of results, that these dreadful disasters are therefore justified? Who of us would be willing to have them repeated for the sake of securing further beneficent results of the same kind? These events undoubtedly prove that good is stronger than all ill — that this universe is so divinely constituted

that, in the long run, bane can work nothing but blessing — that " there is a power not ourselves " which
brings righteousness out of evil, security out of disaster, life out of death — that God can make the ignorance, the folly, even the wrath of men, to praise him!
But they do not prove that evil is in itself anything
but evil, or crime in itself anything but crime.   If war
sometimes works good, it is not because it is itself ever
good, but rather because God lives to confound the
fury of men, and men live to prove themselves better
than their own weaknesses and sins!

III

Having cleared away these two or three illusions by which the minds of men have ever been beset
in their discussion of this problem of the justifiability
of war, we are now ready, perhaps, to consider the immediate issue which is before us.   War, as we have just
seen, cannot be justified by the heroic virtues which it
may generate in the hearts of men — by the noble motives of which it may be the consecrated expression —
or by the beneficent results which upon occasion it may
unquestionably produce in society at large.   No one
of these considerations comes anywhere near to what
may be called the real heart of the problem.   For if
the phenomenon of war is to be justified at all, it must
be justified, in the last analysis, like every other social
phenomenon, simply and solely by its relation to the
great fact of life — by the contribution which it makes,
or does not make, to the wholeness of man's existence

upon the earth. "I come that they might have life, and have it more abundantly," said Jesus, defining the standard by which he wanted his career to be measured. "Die when I may," said Abraham Lincoln, to his friend, Joshua Speed, "I want it said of me by those who know me best, that I always plucked a thistle and planted a flower where I thought a flower would grow."

> "Give me the power to labour for mankind,
>   Make me the mouth for such as cannot speak;
>   Eyes let me be to groping men and blind;
>   A conscience to the base; and to the weak
> Let me be hands and feet; and to the foolish, mind;
>   And lead still further on such as thy kingdom seek."

said Theodore Parker, in his sonnet, entitled *Aspiration*. Here are different, and yet very similar, expressions of that one permanent idea, which is as applicable to social institutions and processes as to individual human beings, that the test of life is nothing other than life — that life is itself the end and aim of life — that the justification of one life is the service of another! Does this particular man bring richer, fuller, more abundant life to other men — planting two blades of grass, perhaps, where only one grew before? Then is he "a good and faithful servant," however humble his name or lowly his station. Does this particular institution — the state, the church, the school, the corporation, the labour union — foster, enlarge, liberate, ennoble the lives of men? Then does it stand justified, and rightly call for protection and support. Does this social process or plan of social action — monogamous marriage, representative government, manhood suffrage, restricted immigration, public worship — add to the health, happiness, integrity, efficiency, beauty, of human living? Then is it also justified, and entitled therefore to men's favour. But does this man, or institution, or social process, weaken life, enslave it, degrade it, impoverish it, destroy it? Then does it stand condemned, whatever may be its merits from other and different points of view. Life, after all, is the only thing that counts in this world of men — this universe of God. The test of Christ is universal and infallible.

> " 'Tis life of which our nerves are scant;
> O life, not death, for which we pant;
> More life and fuller that we want."

This, as Tennyson has put it so vividly in these lines from *The Two Voices*, is the supreme and perfect aim. Anything which serves this aim is thereby justified and perpetuated. Anything which fails, for any reason, to serve this aim, is thereby condemned, and sooner or later must be

> " cast as rubbish to the void."

Now one only has to define this fundamental standard of justification, in order to see at once what must be our answer to the question as to whether or not war is ever justifiable. War is the exact antithesis of " life more abundantly "— the enemy of everything that makes for life and the friend of everything that makes for death! "What is the net purpose and upshot of war," asks Thomas Carlyle, in an unforgetable passage. "To my own knowledge, for example, there dwell in the British village of Dumdrudge some five hundred souls. From these there are selected, during the French war, say thirty able-bodied men. Dumdrudge at her own expense has suckled and nursed them; she has fed them up to manhood and even trained them to crafts, so that one can weave, another build, another hammer. Nevertheless, amid much weeping and swearing, they are selected, all dressed in red, and shipped away some two thousand miles, or say only to the south of Spain, and fed there till wanted. And now to that same spot in Spain are thirty similar French artisans from a French Dumdrudge in like manner wending; till at length, after infinite effort, the two parties come into actual juxtaposition; and thirty stand fronting thirty, each with a gun in his hand. Straightway the word 'Fire' is given, and they blow the souls out of one another; and in place of sixty brisk, useful craftsmen the world has sixty dead carcasses which it must bury." Multiply this number, now, by a hundred, a thousand, yea a hundred thousand — add the horrors of bayonet charges, mine explosions, artillery bombardments, frozen trenches, and hospitals — and we begin to have a suggestion at least of the meaning of war in its relation to the great reality of life.

And this is only the beginning! For what accompanies this slaughter of one body of men by another?

If the killing of the soldiers were all, we might conceivably become reconciled to war as sometimes inevitable and justifiable. But along with this business of killing those who are set apart for this especial sacrifice, there goes the wasting of harvest fields, the burning of great cities with their busy streets and peaceful homes, the outraging of women and little children, the starving and scattering of unnumbered millions of the young, the aged, the weak, the crippled, whose only crime is that they stand in the pathways of contending armies. Look at the situation in Europe to-day — Belgium wasted from end to end, thousands of her unoffending civilians slaughtered or outlawed, and her people generally only saved from starvation by the kindly intervention of neutral states — Poland, East Prussia, Galicia, Serbia, similarly devastated, in an even worse condition of misery because of their remoteness from sources of possible relief — and now, as the crowning iniquity of all, Germany and England each deliberately setting themselves to the monstrous task of starving an entire population as a legitimate expedient of warfare! Look at such things as these, and then let us ask ourselves where is the justification of war from the single standpoint of life as the aim of life?

Nor is this the end! For thus far we have spoken only of the physical horrors of international conflict. But life certainly is more than bread, or raiment, or the sweet flesh of the body. Life involves also, and more truly, the minds and souls of men — their thoughts, affections, ideals, aspirations, hopes, dreams

and faiths.   And here do we find that war is as ruthless a destroyer as in the lower and more obvious realm
of things material.   War burns the library of Alexandria and the University of Louvain.   War destroys
the fair columns of the Parthenon, and smites the towers of the Rheims cathedral.   War silences music,
paralyses art and literature, and turns " the towers of
learning into new Babels, so that our physicists and
geographers, our economists and biologists and dram-
atists, speak in strange and fearful tongues."   War
strangles truth, destroys righteousness, and makes of
hate a new virtue of the soul.   War makes " were-
wolves of neighbouring peoples in their imaginations of
each other "— sets faithful against faithful, priest
against priest, church against church — turns a world
of friends and neighbours into a world of outlanders,
aliens and foes.   War violates all the finer sensibilities
of the race — weakens the claims of mercy and justice
upon the soul — stamps the growing generations with
barbarism — fosters national prejudices, religious an-
tagonisms, and racial animosities.   War makes destructive and not constructive the work of human
hands — makes hate and not love the proudest possession of human hearts — makes death and not life the
chief end of man.   War destroys the body; but, worse
than this, it mutilates the spirit, so that men, even
though they live, are men no longer, but animals seeking whom they may devour and what they may destroy.

   Nor is this the end!   For the ravages of war cease
not with the laying down of arms.   War destroys not

only the thousands of men who fall and rot upon the field of battle, but the unnumbered thousands as well who would inevitably have sprung from the loins of these men had they been left to walk the ways of peace and propagate their kind in love.   War picks to be its victims the young men who are without blemish — the strong, the healthy, the fair, the noble — as the Minataur of old selected the most beautiful youths and maidens of Athens to feed its maw, and thus leaves the weak, the anæmic, the unfit to be the progenitors of the new race of the future.   " Greece died because the men who made her glory had all passed away and left none of their kin and therefore none of their kind." Rome went the same way, because her slaves and not her warriors bred her children.   The campaigns of Napoleon, we are told, reduced the height of the average Frenchman by three inches.   America has never recovered from the awful losses suffered in the Civil War. And what shall be said of the permanent ravages of war in the realm of the spirit — man's eye accustomed once again to blood-letting, his heart poisoned with lust and hate, his soul prostituted to the works of savagery?   Nation after nation has perished of empire. Civilisation after civilisation has risen into glory only to decline and fall through the death of body, mind and spirit that follows, like the pestilence, in the train of war.   Look at Europe to-day, and what guarantee have we got at this moment that H. G. Wells's prophecy, made in his *Social Forces in England and America,* in anticipation of just such a universal conflict as is now raging, will not come true? "Every modern European state," he says, "is . . . like a cranky, ill-built steamboat in which some idiot has mounted and loaded a monstrous gun with no apparatus to damp its recoil. Whether that gun hits or misses when it is fired, of one thing we may be absolutely certain — it will send the steamboat to the bottom of the sea."

From every point of view, therefore — from the standpoint of things spiritual as well as of things material, from the standpoint of the future as well as of the present — war is the antithesis of life. Its one end is to destroy what has been builded up through many years by the sweat and tears of men. Its one aim is to kill the lives which men have conceived in joy, women born in agony, and both together reared in love. Its one supreme triumph is to turn a busy factory into a pile of wreckage, a fertile field into a desert, a home of joy into an ash-heap of sorrow, a living soul into a rotting carcass. Why, if war could once be carried through to its logical conclusions — if there were not a limit to all strength, and a point of exhaustion for every passion — mankind would long since have annihilated itself and this planet become as tenantless as the silent moon! And yet there are some — yea, there are many! — who are ready to assert that this foul business is sometimes and somewheres justifiable. This I deny without qualification or evasion of any kind. War is never justifiable at any time or under any circumstances. No man is wise enough, no nation is important enough, no human interest is precious

enough, to justify the wholesale destruction and murder which constitute the essence of war. Human life
is alone sacred. The interests of human life are alone
sovereign. War, as we have now seen, is the enemy of
life and all its interests. Therefore, in the name of
life and for the sake of life, do I declare that war must
be condemned universally and unconditionally.

It is with war to-day exactly as with similar abominations yesterday. Plato thought that human slavery
was justifiable, since it enabled the free citizens of his
ideal republic to live the good life. Torquemada
thought persecution justifiable, since it gave protection
to the true faith. The manufacturers of England in
the early decades of the nineteenth century thought
that the degrading labour of women and children in
factories and coal-mines was justifiable, since it gave to
England the industrial leadership of the world. In
the same way we deceive ourselves to-day into believing
that war is justifiable, when it is fought on behalf of
political liberty, we will say, or in defence of the integrity of a nation. But some day men will awaken
from this illusion and see that war is never justifiable.
It will be with war as it was long since with human sacrifice. This hideous practice, like the equally hideous
practice of war, was bound up with the most solemn
customs and the most desperate fears of men. It
seemed as sacred and as necessary to the ancients as a
war of liberty does to us to-day. But there came a
time when men and women, out of sheer regard for the
sanctity of human life, revolted against this practice.

In face of persecution and ridicule, they pointed out that, in sacrificing one little child upon the altars of the gods, a wrong was wrought upon their kind so terrible that it could not be justified by any good achieved or any evil forefended. Better that men perished altogether than that one life should be thus destroyed! And little by little men came to agree with these pioneers, and human sacrifice was abolished.

So will it be with war. A few men have always seen, and more men are in our time beginning to see, that nothing can justify the human sacrifice of a soldier upon the field of battle, and therefore that war must go, at whatever cost. War is hate, and hate has no place within the human heart. War is death, and death has no place within the realms of life. War is hell, and hell has no more place in the human order than in the divine. Walt Whitman, in language as forceful as it is inelegant, summed up the whole matter when he said, " O God! this whole damned war business is about nine hundred and ninety-nine parts diarrhœa to one part glory. . . . Wars are hellish business — all wars. . . . Any honest man says so — hates war, fighting, blood-letting. I was in the midst of it all — saw war where war was worst — not on the battlefields, no — in the hospitals: there war is worst: there I mixed with it, and now I say God damn the wars — all wars: God damn every war: God damn 'em! God damn 'em! "

IV

To many persons this indictment of war will undoubtedly seem in the main to be just, but in certain particular cases at least to be unjust. The average war, you say, is without any question indefensible. But are there not some wars in the past which have been justifiable on the very grounds which you have laid down, and is it not likely that there may be some wars in the future, in which our own nation may become engaged, which may be similarly justifiable? Are there not two kinds of war at least which must be excepted from even the most sweeping indictment — on the one hand, the war which is fought on behalf of some great principle, of which the Civil War is a good example; and on the other hand, the war which is fought in the defence of nationality, of which Belgium's present war against Germany may be taken as an illustration?

Taking the war on behalf of principle for our first consideration, let me point out in the beginning that this so-called "moral justification of war" is nearly always the flimsiest kind of a pretext. The real cause even of those wars which are placed on the highest moral plane is national jealousy, commercial rivalry, industrial selfishness, imperialistic ambition, diplomatic misunderstanding, rather than any truly genuine principle of idealism. It is a poor king or chancellor or president who cannot find high moral grounds for going to war with a neighbouring state when there are economic or political conditions which make such a war

desirable. Take the present conflict in Europe, for
example. The striking fact about this most horrible
of all wars is that every nation is pretending to fight for
reasons which are absolutely unselfish and beneficent.
England as well as Germany, Austria as well as France,
was forced into the struggle wholly against her will,
that civilisation might be maintained, that a pledged
word might be fulfilled, that the interests of humanity
might be safeguarded against violation and destruction!
In the face of such a unanimous profession of national
virtue, unexampled in this hitherto imperfect world, we
are all tempted to believe that some nation or group
of nations is a liar. And those who have no particular
interests or prejudices at stake, are pretty well convinced by this time that all of them together are unworthy of confidence. Let there be no mistake about
this! Nations go to war to-day, as they did yesterday,
for reasons which are selfish and therefore immoral.
There are foreign markets to be won, surplus capital to
be invested and thereafter protected in alien lands, concessions to be gained and held at any cost in undevel-
oped continents, rich profits to be accumulated from
the exploitation of savage peoples, vast power to be
wielded in colonial empire — and all such goals to be
won at the expense of other nations striving for the
same or greater ends! It is for these reasons, partly
political, mostly economic, that armaments are builded
and wars declared. Wars for ideals, liberties, civilisations — these are illusions behind which are hidden the
hideous struggle for industrial supremacy. Real wars,

at least in our time, are simply so many moves in the
great game for profits.   They are made behind closed
doors, by a few men, for an ignoble materialistic end.
Reduced to its lowest terms, for instance, this present
struggle is simply and solely a battle not between the
Kingdom of Darkness and the Kingdom of Light, but
between industrial England and industrial Germany for
the industrial mastery of the world!

But surely there have been some wars which were
fought for a high and noble purpose.   What about the
American Civil War, for example?

To this plea I make answer that there undoubtedly
have been a few wars of this kind, and that the Civil
War is most surely one of them.   If any war in the
history of the world was ever fought unselfishly, this
is the one.   The pathetic face of Abraham Lincoln,
and the noble figure of Robert E. Lee, tell the whole
story.   But to this plea I would also make the answer,
offered by Prof. Durant Drake, of Wesleyan University, in his recent book on *The Problems of Conduct*
— a moralist, it may be pointed out, who does not regard war as an unmitigated evil! — that " nearly always (in such cases) the good aimed at could have been
attained without the evils of war.   If the American
colonies," he continues, referring to the Revolution,
" had had a little more patience, they could have won
the liberty they craved without war and separation
from the mother country — as Canada and Australia
have done.   If the United States had had a little more
patience and tact and diplomacy, it is probable that

Cuba could have been saved from the intolerable oppression of Spain without war." And the same thing
is true of the Great Rebellion! This fight has been
described as "an irreconcilable conflict." But it was
irreconcilable, not because of any elements in the problem itself, but because of the compromises, the stupidi-
ties and the blind passions of men on both sides of
Mason and Dixon's line. Slaves had been freed before
'61 without disrupting a nation and precipitating a
civil conflict. And yet I am told that because statesmen in this country did not have the skill, the tact, the
patience, the courage, of statesmen in other countries,
men must shoulder their muskets and enter upon the
business of mutual slaughter! I do not believe it. I
cannot believe it. There is always a better way in all
of these disputes. And our failure to find this better way can never justify our taking the way of
evil.

But what about a war fought in self-defence? Must
not this at least be an exception to our rule of universal condemnation? Is there anybody who would not
justify Belgium for her battle against Germany?

Remembering that at the present moment, every one
of the thirteen nations, from Germany on the one side
to Russia upon the other, is fighting a defensive war, I
am tempted to put this whole plea out of court by declaring that there is no such thing as defensive war.
Granting, however, for the sake of the argument, that,
as in the case of Belgium, there are wars which are
purely defensive, I venture to lay down, in accordance

with the true doctrine of non-resistance, two safe principles which some day are going to be apprehended and accepted by the souls of men, even though they be not so apprehended and accepted at the present moment.

In the first place, no defence of a nation is a real defence unless it be a defence of the spirit, and against a defence of this kind the arms of the flesh are ineffectual. It is possible for the soldiers of one nation to occupy the territory of another nation — seize her ports, capture her cities, occupy her strongholds, levy tribute on her citizens — but what avails such a victory of arms? The legions of Rome overran the peninsula of Greece, destroyed her cities, laid waste her shrines, and enslaved her people — but the light of Greece was not and could not be extinguished. The barbarians from the forest fastnesses across the Rhine and Danube invaded, captured and sacked Rome, not once but many times — but the *Æneid* of Virgil, the *Odes* of Horace, and the Laws of Justinian are still with us. The armies of Napoleon conquered Germany from end to end in 1806 and 1807, but Goethe still reigned supreme in Weimar, Fichte still taught in Berlin, and the spirit of Martin Luther and Immanuel Kant still brooded in the hearts of conquered men — and the culture which these men embodied and set forth lives on to-day a hundred years after the empire of Napoleon crashed to ruin. And so to-day the armies of the Allies may march from west to east to the city of Berlin, and hurl a proud people prostrate in the dust, but neither Cossack nor Zouave will weaken, much less destroy, the world dominion of all that is good in German culture. Or, reversing the picture, the legions of Germany may ravage France from Ostend to Marseilles, leave England a desert island in a wintry sea, conquer Russia and add it to the empire of the Kaiser, but Coligny, Molière, Hugo, Berlioz, Rodin, will still survive; the language spoken by Shakespeare and the science taught by Darwin will still illume the minds of men, and Tolstoi will still rebuke from his grave the pride of kings. Not territory but learning, not wealth but vision, not political headship but spiritual leadership — this constitutes a nation. And this it is which needs no defence of battleships and forts. Let Germany come here to America to-day as she came to Belgium yesterday — what of it? The Declaration of Independence would defy her sword, the Constitution resist her 42-centimetre guns, the memory of Lincoln shame her panoply of arms. Let her come, and we will not only prove unconquerable, but we will ourselves conquer our conquerors, as Greece conquered her Roman masters, and as Rome in turn conquered her Ostrogoth and Visigoth invaders.

The spirit, therefore, is the essential thing — and this, if it be true, can survive all accidents of arms. And yet, is it possible to disregard so completely all geographical and political consideration? Must we not love our country, as we love our homes — and must we not be prepared to defend our country, as we would our homes, when the enemy comes against it? Is not patriotism a true and noble instinct — and must we not, like the Belgians, be faithful to this instinct even unto death?

This brings us to the second principle which must be offered in answer to the plea of self-defence. Patriotism, assuredly, is one of the strongest and purest instincts of the soul. That man has indeed a dead soul, as Sir Walter Scott has told us,

> "Who never to himself hath said,
> This is my own, my native land."

Noble as it is, however, patriotism cannot be regarded as a complete and perfect virtue in itself, but only one step onward in the development of that final virtue, which is the sentiment not of country but of humanity. There was a time, in ages long gone by, when man's noblest passion found expression in the defence of nothing larger than his hole in the rocks or his bower in the tree. Later on village life developed, and patriotism took the form of defending a single community against the men of the next community. Later still, came the canton or state — and then, as in ancient Greece, or mediæval Italy, or in America only fifty years ago, man's highest duty was to defend his state in preference even to the nation. Now we are in the nationalistic stage of evolution, where no higher conception of human relationships is generally apparent than that of a country such as England, Germany, or America. And to many a devoted soul, this marks the end of progress. But not so, if vision is at all clear. Beyond the nation is the world, and beyond the people of one country the great circle of humanity. And as sure as we are living at this moment, so surely, in the distant future, the day will come when we shall recognise that our first and highest duty is to mankind as a whole, and not to any single section of mankind. I love America. I cherish her history, revere her heroes, admire her people, hail her destiny. But not yet do I love her enough to seek, in the name of that love, to injure or destroy any other people on this earth. If I must hate Germany, in order to love America, I will not love her. If I must take up arms against the English, in order to defend America, then I will not defend her. If I must sacrifice my membership in the human family, in order to keep my citizenship in America, then I will not keep that citizenship. There was a time, not so long ago, when men in this country had to choose between loyalty to Virginia and loyalty to America, and we believe that those chose rightly who chose America. So even now is there come the time when we must choose between loyalty to America and loyalty to the world, and I believe that those will choose rightly who choose the world. Not to America or Germany or England but to that one blood of which God hath made all nations of men — not to Americans or Germans or Englishmen but to " the brethren " everywhere — not to king or kaiser or president, but to God the universal Father — must we pledge our first allegiance. " Let not a man glory in this, that he loves his country," says Baha o'llah, in one of the

noblest statements which has ever fallen, like sweet
music, upon the human heart, "let him rather glory in
this, that he loves his kind."

V

Here, then, is our answer to the question, Is War
Ever Justifiable?   No — war is never justifiable under
any circumstances.   And this means what, in practical
terms, to-day?   It means not only that war in general
is unjustifiable in general, but that this English war
to-day is unjustifiable for Englishmen, and this German war unjustifiable for Germans.   It means that this
war which may, in the folly of men, come to America
to-morrow, is unjustifiable for Americans.   It means
that sometime, somewhere, somehow, war, like famine,
disease, cannibalism, infanticide, human sacrifice, will
be utterly abolished, and permanent and universal peace
established on the earth.   Then shall we see at last that
every argument for war is sophistry and every act in
war a crime.

CHAPTER IX

IS PERMANENT AND UNIVERSAL PEACE
TO BE DESIRED?

" 'Twas said, 'When roll of drum and battle's roar
Shall cease upon the earth, oh, then no more
The deed, the race, the heroes in the land.'
But scarce that word was breathed when one small hand
Lifted victorious o'er a giant wrong,
That had its victims crushed through ages long;
Some woman set her pale and quivering face
Firm as a rock against a man's disgrace;
Some quiet scholar flung his gauntlet down,
And risked in Truth's great name the Synod's frown;
A civic hero, in the calm realm of laws,
Did that which suddenly drew a world's applause;
And one to the pest his lithe young body gave,
That he a thousand thousand lives might save."

— Richard Watson Gilder.

CHAPTER IX

IS PERMANENT AND UNIVERSAL PEACE TO BE DESIRED?

THE mention of the certain coming of a day when war will be abolished and peace secured, raises at this point the further question as to whether permanent and universal peace is really a desirable state of affairs. Most men without doubt cherish this hope as one of the most beautiful and beneficent visions of the human spirit. The present war, for example, is saved from being an absolutely unmitigated horror by the prospect that it may take its place in history, to quote Mr. Wells again, as " the war that ended war."

Just how this longed-for end is going to be achieved, no one, not even Mr. Wells, ventures to say. Some dream of the establishment of an International Court of Arbitration which shall be backed by a degree of political authority which will enable it to enforce its decrees upon the wayward wills of men. Some believe that out of this stupendous struggle will come a new and permanent alliance of all the leading nations of the world, which will have for its purpose not the maintenance of a so-called balance of power, but rather the enforcement of the rule of peace upon all less advanced and more barbarous peoples. Others like to think that out of this war will come a United States of

Europe, as out of the Revolution of 1776 there came a United States of America, which will enable all the countries of the continent to live together in harmony, after the example of the forty-eight states of our great Republic. A few men even hark back to the essay of Immanuel Kant, written in 1795, on *Eternal Peace*, and contemplate again the conception that arose in the mind of this greatest of all modern philosophers, of the establishment throughout Europe of those republican forms of government which must, from their very nature, guarantee the reign of peace.

But however we may differ in our hopes and prophecies as to the means which may be employed for the attainment of this great end, we are certainly agreed as regards the end itself. The establishment of permanent and universal peace upon the earth is the one adequate compensation for the hideous slaughter and exhaustion of this world-wide cataclysm. The very determination of the nations which now seems so ruthless; and which, more than anything else, is making the struggle so terrific, is the one thing which gives the surest guarantee of the ultimate attainment of this goal. For when the tide of war has swept on to the last bloody and shattered trench, when the nations engaged in the awful struggle at last lay down their arms from sheer inability to hold and wield them longer, will not these same nations be ready to see, as never before, the futility of it all, and in their very weakness band themselves together not merely for mutual support, but for the higher aim of establishing that condition of universal brotherhood which has for so long been regarded as but the dream of poets and prophets? This, certainly, is the thing for which we hope! Some day far hence when our children or children's children look back upon this awful struggle, as we look back upon the civil struggle in America, may they be able to say, what we have long since learned to say of the great Rebellion, that, as James Russell Lowell put it, this battle was " the great corrector of enormous times "!

I

It is a mistake, however, to cherish the illusion that this desire for permanent and universal peace is a unanimous sentiment. For there are many men in the world to-day, as there have always been such men in other days, who believe that war is in its essence beneficent, and that the establishment therefore of permanent and universal peace would constitute a genuine disaster. Some of these men, of course, have extraneous motives for regarding peace as a curse and war as a blessing. Thus, army officers and navy officers, for example, whose trade is war, naturally desire that this trade should prosper. Editors of irresponsible newspapers inevitably welcome scenes of war as a more liberal and constant provider of sensation than the quiet ways of peace. Manufacturers of rifles and ammunition see clearly enough that the battlefields are the best markets that can be secured for the disposal of their goods. These men have good reason for believing that the establishment of permanent and universal peace would be disastrous; but these reasons are so obviously founded upon selfish considerations that they can of course play no part in a serious discussion of the general problem.

Along with these men, however, are certain other men — statesmen, poets, prophets, thinkers — who hold exactly the same opinions in regard to the essentially beneficent character of war, but whose motives are as disinterested as their ideas are clear and emphatic. These men recognise that war involves evil as well as good; but they assert that the same contradiction is to be found in peace also. And when they come to compare the evil and the good of the one with the evil and the good of the other, they do not hesitate to declare that the balance of good is to be found most decidedly on the side of war. Peace is undoubtedly to be accepted as embodying the normal condition of affairs; an uninterrupted state of armed conflict would be intolerable and in the end suicidal. But the abolition of war as a recurring condition of human relationships would likewise be disastrous; for without those qualities which " war alone," in the phrase of Theodore Roosevelt, can develop, man will " rot and decay." If the race is to survive, to say nothing of advancing, man must ever be fundamentally militaristic — which means that war must be safeguarded as a perpetual contingency and an occasional reality.

II

This point of view is to many of us so strange and perhaps unconvincing, that it may be well to consider in some detail the arguments on behalf of war that have been formulated and maintained by some of the master minds of past and present.

For our first example we may turn to the great Athenian scientist and philosopher, Aristotle, who is commonly regarded as the most wonderful thinker of the ancient world, and has more than once been described, as by John Fiske for example, as " the greatest intellect " that the human race has produced. Now Aristotle, it is interesting to note, believed that war was not only a good thing but, from the moral standpoint, indispensable; and therefore he taught that its abolition in favour of permanent and universal peace would be a calamity. In the pages of his treatise on *Ethics*, we find a careful and persuasive statement of the reasons which led him to this conclusion, which seems more surprising to our age, undoubtedly, than to his own. In this book he discusses the various virtues of human life, and endeavours to arrange them in a scale of values, just as James Martineau attempted to do in much more elaborate fashion in his *Types of Ethical Theory*. As the highest of the virtues, Aristotle names courage; and, as the highest of different forms of courage, he places the courage displayed by the soldier upon the field of battle. All courage, he says, is at bottom an expression of contempt for mere physical

existence. It is a willingness to treat life not as something to be enjoyed in itself but as something to be
used for the higher and nobler interests of the spirit.
The coward is fundamentally the one who would preserve his life at any spiritual cost, the hero is the one
who would gladly fling away his life, as a worthless
encumbrance, if thereby he might win the " prize " of
some " high calling."

Now there are many contingencies, continues Aristotle, where the choice has to be made between the rôle
of cowardice and the rôle of courage as thus defined.
A man is stricken with some dread disease, and is
forced to contemplate the imminent prospect of its
fatal termination. Or he stands upon the deck of a
sinking vessel, waiting to begin the battle for life in
the icy waves. Or he finds himself looking into a
blazing building, whence come agonizing cries for the
help that he alone can give. Here in each and every
case is the test of virtue, in the Greek or Aristotelian
sense of that word. But not the supreme test! For
in all of these contingencies, as the philosopher points
out, the choice between cowardice and courage is in-
voluntary. The challenge has been met by accident,
and not sought out by deliberation. In one contingency only is there a free choice of the hazard of life
and death — and that is the contingency of battle.
The soldier purposely puts himself into the situation
where the sacrifice of his physical existence may become an immediate necessity. He deliberately pursues,
until he finds it, the perfect test of courage, which, as

we have seen, is to be rated as the highest of all moral qualities. Therefore do we have in the soldier, who marches away to the field of battle, the supreme manifestation of human virtue; and in the battle itself the indispensable condition of this manifestation. What would it mean to humanity if this ultimate challenge to the soul were permanently abolished, and man never forced to meet the final test of facing death in its most sudden and dreadful form in the clash of deadly weapons? Is it not obvious, says Aristotle, that if peace were permanently and universally established, and the hazard of battle thus permanently and universally removed, the noblest type of human virtue would disappear, and mankind enter a slow but sure period of disintegration? " The brave man," in the exact words of this teacher of ancient Greece, " has to do with terrible things. But death is the most terrible of all things. . . . And yet the brave man does not appear to have to do with death in every form, as at sea or in disease, but only with the most honourable kinds of death. . . . And those that occur in war are of this kind, for in war the danger is the greatest and the most honourable."

A second example of this viewpoint is John Ruskin, who would seem to be the last person in the world to find excuse for such a social abomination as international conflict. In his *Notes on the Political Economy of Prussia*, published in his volume entitled *The Crown of Wild Olive*, however, he confesses to having had always the most contradictory opinions upon this subject. " It is impossible," he says, " for me to write consistently of war, for the group of facts which I have gathered about it lead me to two precisely opposite conclusions. . . . The conviction on which I act is, that it causes an incalculable amount of avoidable human suffering, and that it ought to cease among Christian nations; and if therefore any of my boy-friends desire to be soldiers, I try my utmost to bring them into what I conceive to be a better mind. But, on the other hand, I know certainly that the most beautiful characters yet developed among men have been formed in war — that all great nations have been warrior nations, and that the only kinds of peace which we are likely to get in the present age are ruinous alike to the intellect and the heart."

Enlarging upon this statement of the case in his lecture on *War*, Ruskin lays down the categorical propositions that " all the pure and noble arts of peace are founded on war," and that indeed " no great art ever rose on earth, but among a nation of soldiers." He buttresses this astonishing assertion by detailed references to the history of Egypt, Greece, and the Middle Ages, showing that art is in each case the expression of " the faculties of men at their fulness," this " fulness " in turn being the direct consequence of war; and that when war subsides and peace is established, art immediately " declines " and in some cases disappears altogether. " War is the foundation of all the arts," says Ruskin, and by this he means fundamentally that " it is the foundation of all the high virtues and faculties of men." " It was very strange to me to discover

this," he continues, " and very dreadful — but I saw it
to be quite an undeniable fact. . . . We talk of peace
and learning, and of peace and plenty, and of peace
and civilisation; but I found that those were not the
words which the Muse of History coupled together:
that, on her lips, the words were — peace and sensual-
ity, peace and selfishness, peace and corruption, peace
and death. I found, in brief, that all great nations
learned their truth of word, and strength of thought,
in war; that they were nourished in war, and wasted by
peace; taught by war, and deceived by peace; trained
by war, and betrayed by peace — in a word, that they
were born in war, and expired in peace."

From this astounding interpretation of the problem,
John Ruskin goes on in his lecture from qualification
to reservation, until little seems to be left of this sweeping assertion with which he started. Again and again
he gets entangled in hopeless contradictions, as for
example in his closing appeal to women, where he prays
them to use their influence to bring wars to an end and
shows them that if this influence were used aright, " no
war would last a week." It is evident that every essential instinct of his nature cries out against what he
calls, in a passionate and unguarded outburst, " the
poverty, misery, and rage of battle," and that if he
followed the spontaneous impulses of his heart, he
would end war at once and forever. But his intellect
leads him to a different verdict. Therefore, while his
whole soul is plainly agonising, does he plead for the
continuance of warfare, and directs his entire lecture

on the subject to the specific end of strengthening the trust of young soldiers " in the virtue of their profession." In all this there is no consistency, as he himself admits. And yet, out of all the jumble of confusion and contradiction, there comes the emphatic declaration that war is necessary to the health of nations, and that the establishment of permanent and universal peace would therefore be a calamity.

A third illustration of this point of view is furnished by the late Professor Cramb, of Cambridge University, England, in his book on *Germany and England*. The lectures gathered together in this fascinating volume have been strangely enough described as constituting an " answer to Bernhardi " and the other more or less familiar militaristic writers of modern Germany. Never was there a more hideous misnomer. It is true that Professor Cramb, like every other cultured man of our time, recognises the appalling cost of war and is anything but indifferent to its attendant horrors. But quite in the spirit of Bernhardi and his school, he affirms the superiority of war to peace as a condition of individual and social virtue, deplores the agitation for the abolishment of war as wholly pernicious, and again and again summons his countrymen, as Demosthenes summoned the Athenians, to take up arms, as not only the wisest but also the noblest thing that they can do. " Rouse yourselves from your lethargy ! " is his word of counsel. " Arm and stand in the ranks ! " In pages which are fairly reeking with sarcasm and irony, he emphasises the futility " from the beginning of the world."

of all man's dreams of peace. He shows how these dreams have been conceived and proclaimed by the seers and saints of all the ages gone — that no century has passed without its poetic and prophetic champions of human concord. And he points out with almost exult-ant satisfaction that we are as far away from the prac-tical fulfilment of this dream to-day as ever. All his other dreams, man has realised sooner or later. " To-wards other ideals," he says, " man has progressed — in his war against disease, for instance, and in his war against nature, the forest, the sea, the vicissitudes of season and of climate." But here he has encountered nothing but failure. " Toward this ideal alone he has made no progress." Which means not that man has not the power to abolish war, as he has every other abomi-nation which has stirred his hate, but simply and solely that he has not, in the innermost parts of his con-sciousness, any real desire to abolish war! He may de-nounce its cost and deplore its miseries. He may turn his fancies toward the coming of the day of peace. But in his heart of hearts, he knows that war in its essence is a good thing, that it is well worth its stupen-dous cost, that its material horrors are more than com-pensated for by its heroisms, sacrifices, and sorrows.

In order to show just what he means by this eulogy of war, Professor Cramb tells in truly eloquent phrase the thrilling and touching story of Captain Scott and the four comrades who perished with him in the frozen wastes of the Antarctic. Why did these men under-take, in defiance of every consideration of practical reason, this hazardous trip to the South Pole? What could they bring back which would in any. way counterbalance the deprivations, miseries, and perils which their venture involved? Are not their useless deaths in the whirling snow the crowning indictment of their folly, and the final proof that the world of men suffered nothing but total loss in this foolhardy expedition? So it might seem to the sober judgment of the mind. But not so has this experience touched the hearts of humankind. The world has already enrolled these noble five among the heroes of all time. Everywhere do men applaud not merely their courage but their wisdom. Even in the face of ultimate and complete disaster, under the most painful circumstances possible, do we declare that the undertaking was well worth while, and the five not to have died in vain. What would become of the race if men were not ready to take supreme hazards of this kind, and did not ever find opportunity for such hazards? What were Englishmen if this were not the type and symbol of what they all would do, had they all the coveted chance? " Here surely," says our author, " we have a kind of heroism which it would daunt the courage of any . . . *doctrinaire* to explain by the profit-and-loss theory or to analyse by the ordinary processes of reason at all."

Now what is true here of " Captain Scott's last trip," says Professor Cramb, is true in an even more perfect and sublime way of war. " There is something in war, after all, that is analogous to this heroism in the Antarctic zone, something that transcends reason." The same idea that led Scott and his comrades into the frozen regions of the Antarctic leads thousands of men on to the field of battle; and the same ideal that justifies the death of the explorer in the snowy hut, justifies the death of the soldier in the bloody trench. In both cases, we have life redeemed from all that is selfish, sordid and profane, and thus lifted, as it were by some divine transcendence, to the highest degree of nobility and honour. Why talk, in such a presence, of loss or pain? Why measure cost, or pity suffering? What even is death, in the glory of such a life? " In war and the right of war man has a possession which he values above religion, above industry and above social comforts; in war man values the power which it affords to life of rising above life, the power which the spirit of man possesses to pursue the Ideal. In all life at its height, in thought, art, and action, there is a tendency to become transcendental; and if we examine the wars of England and of Germany in the past we find governing these wars throughout this higher power of heroism, or of Something, at least, which transcends reason."

Here, now, are some of the arguments which have persuaded good men and true to justify war and view with apprehension the possible establishment of permanent and universal peace upon the earth. These arguments of course have received their extreme expression in our time in the writings of such men as Treitschke, Steinmetz, and Bernhardi, whose teachings so largely explain the militaristic ideals of modern Germany. To these men war is no longer a mere occasion for the ex-

pression of virtue, as with Aristotle and Cramb, or a
mere condition of the development of human genius, as
with Ruskin; but is itself become synonymous with all
of virtue and of genius. From their point of view, the
individual lives primarily in order to fight, and society
is organised primarily for the better functioning of warfare. Military efficiency is the coefficient of individual
and social virtue.

But we do not have to go to any such extravagant
lengths as this to understand what is in essence involved
in this whole attitude toward the problem of war and
peace. At bottom, of course, is the feeling that peace
sooner or later means the degeneracy of the individual
and the corruption of the state. In times of peace men
find security, and security brings with it ease, selfishness, cowardice, luxury. The body grows soft, the
mind sluggish, the spirit feeble. Hazards are no
longer sought, nor perils courted. The "transcendental," to quote Professor Cramb's word, disappears
altogether, and the dryrot of routine, surfeit, pleasure,
mild content, usurps its place. With the inevitable result of slow decay — final death! It is from this ignoble and disgusting fall that war enables men and nations to escape. War means courage, sacrifice, suffering, consecration to a great ideal and love of a noble
cause. It means the striving of the deepest impulses
of the soul. In war a man is fronted with reality both
inside and outside. His body is toughened, his heart
cleansed, his spirit challenged. Now or never must he
prove his manhood. Now or never must he be his own

best self.   Now or never must he live — and die! War,
in other words, is the great agent of moral redemption.
It purifies and ennobles men, and by uniting men into
one supreme and all-absorbing adventure of divine faith,
lifts nations to the farthest pinnacles of purity and
honour.   Theodore Roosevelt sums up this entire
gospel, in his *The Strenuous Life,* where, on the one
hand, he deplores peace on the ground that it trains a
nation " to a career of unwarlike and isolated ease "
and thus dooms it " to go down in the end before other
nations which have not lost the manly and adventurous
qualities "; and, on the other hand, applauds war on
the ground that " by war alone can (men) acquire those
virile qualities necessary to win in the stern strife of
actual life."

III

What, now, is to be said in answer to this plea on
behalf of war?   Can these considerations, which we have
just been interpreting, be regarded as sound?   If so,
what becomes of humanity's long-cherished dream of
peace on earth, goodwill toward men?   And if not so,
why not so?   Where stands to-day, in short, this whole
problem of the desirability of permanent and universal
peace?

First of all, it must be seen that this whole argument on behalf of war is based upon a fundamental
misconception of the character of war and its effect
upon the life of the individual and of the state.   That
there is much of the heroic and the sublime in the spec-

tacle of an entire people putting aside the quiet pur-
suits and comfortable pleasures of peace and entering
steadfastly and unafraid upon the awful perils and
miseries of armed conflict, goes without saying. Doctor Rainsford was not wholly wrong when he described
the present situation in Europe as a supreme justification of the everlasting reality of religion, in the best
sense of that word, since in it we see the glad sacrifice,
on the part of millions of men and women, of " the best
they have to the best they know." But to argue, from
this unquestioned fact, that war ennobles human nature
and dignifies the life of nations, is certainly a gross ex-
aggeration. Nay, more, it is an untruth! War, in
the last analysis, as we have seen, is a reversion to savagery; and its advent marks the awakening from slum-
ber of all that is beastly in the human heart. Man is
at best a complex of the animal and the human. On the
one hand are the primitive passions of the flesh, tamed
and rigidly controlled by the customs, habits, and regulations of ordinary social intercourse. On the other
hand, are the attributes of the spirit — intelligence,
sympathy, generosity, mercy, faith, love — which mark
a man distinctly as a man and which constitute the very
basis of his relationship with his fellows. War is in
essence chaos and not order, discord and not concord,
hatred and not goodwill. It brings liberation to the
lowest and suppression to the highest that man knows.
Let the passion of war sweep widely through a nation,
and instantly the beast, that is lurking in every human
heart, is freed from its social bonds and the spiritual

being which is his best self is instantly imprisoned or destroyed. Courage remains, but it is the courage of the frenzied beast and not of the patient martyr. Sacrifice appears, but it is the sacrifice of madness and not of calm deliberation. And in all and through all and over all are lust, brutality, vengeance, hatred, blood.

This present conflict has brought us amazing evidences of this terrific psychological phenomenon. See, for example, the experiences of Dr. Frederick Lynch, as narrated in his little book, *Through Europe on the Eve of War!* On one day, as he tells us, he saw merchants, clerks, farmers, peasants, husbands, fathers, brothers in France and Germany, going quietly about their business. On the next day had come the declaration of war, and instantly these men were transformed into beasts. "We saw great crowds drunk with brandy, and howling 'To hell with Germany!' or 'To hell with France!' We saw French soldiers try to pull a German out of a train window, while he clung to his two little babies that he was trying to get into Switzerland. We saw Germans yank a Russian and his wife out of a train, and so frighten the wife that her little baby could not nurse for two days. . . . At one station, I saw three young men, flushed with drink, leap from a car standing on a side-track, and try to pull three young girls into the car on to the straw. . . . The thousands of men we saw howling in all the cities of Europe were not men any longer. They had become beasts. . . . They howled for only three things — drink, women, and blood of their brothers." The same

kind of testimony was brought to me personally by a
famous theological teacher of this country, who chanced
to be travelling from Belfort to Paris on the first night
of French mobilisation.   His train was packed with excited reservists hastening to the colours — fresh, eager
young men who had only the day before been living
peacefully and gently in their homes.   This night,
however, they were animals.   Language of the vilest
description was shouted through the cars.   Acts of
indescribable indecency were openly and boastfully perpetrated.   Men were tortured, women insulted, children
terrified.   "Only one word can describe those fifteen
hours with those young soldiers," said my friend, " and
that is 'hell!'"   And all this before the fighting had
begun, or a single drop of blood had been shed!   The
mere call to arms had liberated " the ape and tiger," and
the mad orgy of lust and fury was on.   Talk about war
purifying, ennobling, strengthening men!   Talk about
war instilling patience, sacrifice, heroism in the human
heart!   War is the corrupter of virtue, the despoiler
of purity, the murderer of courage, honour, and chivalry.   Some men of imagination and self-control it lifts
and glorifies.   But the average man it degrades to the
base level of the brute.   Doctor Lynch is perfectly right
when he speaks of "the beast which such a crisis as
this [war] reveals as only slumbering."

And if this be true of the individual, it is no less true
also of the nation.   John Ruskin has spoken eloquently
of the awakening of genius under the stimulus of the
deep emotion stirred by war.   Cramb bears testimony

to the transcendental quality that enters into the soul
of a people under the unifying idealism of nationalistic
adventure.   These phenomena have again and again
appeared, of course.   But they are momentary, and
pass almost as rapidly as they appear, to be succeeded
by fatigue, indifference, cynicism, and finally out-and-
out corruption.   Not the state of a nation at the outbreak of war or during the continuance of war, but after
the war is over — this is the test of the spiritual consequences which have really been engendered.   We only
have to consider the death of the Athenian democracy
after the age of Pericles, the spiritual as well as the
material prostration of Germany after the Thirty
Years' War, the unspeakable political and business corruption rife in America in the decades following the true
idealism of the Civil War, to understand what war does
to a nation.   Felix Adler tells the whole story in a
trenchant observation contained in a recent sermon on
war and peace.[1]   " I happened to be in Berlin," he said,
" during and after the Franco-Prussian War, and I
remember well the kind of vertigo that seized upon the
people after the payment of the French indemnity.
The defeat for France was no less a defeat for what was
best in the German soul."

The case against war as a source of human misery
and degradation would seem to be decisive.   Not on this
ground alone, however, are our militaristic friends to be
converted to the acceptance of the prospect of perma-

[1] See the December 1914 number of *The Standard*, published by
the Ethical Culture Society.

nent and universal peace. Granted that all you say about war, they argue, is true. Still is it also true that war cultivates certain qualities of soul, both individual and social, which are indispensable, as you yourself admit, and which cannot be obtained in any other way. Bad as war undoubtedly is, therefore, it still would be a calamity to abolish it altogether and thus lose these essential elements of the highest type of life. Supreme sacrifice, perfect heroism, purest honour — these are inseparably related to war, and without war would vanish altogether.

This brings us to the second point which must be made in answer to the militaristic plea on behalf of war. I refer to the fact that all the virtues which can by any possibility be ascribed to war must be regarded as by-products, and that no by-product has ever yet been accepted by the conscience of mankind as adequate justification for the continuance of a recognised abomination.[1] I suppose, as a matter of fact, that there has never been any single ill that flesh is heir to which has not brought along with it some incidental good as a kind of by-product of its essential evil. Take gambling, for example. There can be no question that this pernicious habit has the indirect result, upon the individuals addicted to its practice, of fostering undubitable and worthy virtues in their hearts. There are qualities in the typical gambler that win the admiration and affection of us all. He has self-control, patience, easy mas-

[1] See Dr. Adler's elucidation of this point in the address just referred to.

tery of his emotions; he can be calm in moments of
tense excitement, and is " a good sport " in the sense
that he can face misfortune without complaint; he is
care-free, easy-going, optimistic, as delightfully irresponsible as a little child; especially is he generous, sympathetic, as quick to give money to a friend as he is to
win it from an opponent at the table. The gambler is
not all bad, by any means. But these virtues, such as
they are, are all incidental, by-the-way. At bottom,
gambling is a disease which eats away the fundamentals
of character as surely as cancer eats away the vitals of a
physical organism. The experience of unnumbered generations demonstrates the fact that this vice is essentially disintegrative of all those higher qualities of mind
and conscience which go to the making of manhood in
the right sense of that great word. Therefore is it universally agreed that gambling must be fought to the
death, whatever the incidental losses to be suffered in
the destruction of its incidental by-products of good.

Another and different kind of illustration is furnished
us by the great political and military institution of
feudalism. Here was an order of society which fulfilled
a vital and indispensable function in the development of
European life, and which introduced many admirable
and even beautiful social features. One has only to call
to mind all that is suggested by the single word " chivalry " to understand something of the good that can be
said of this mediæval system of society. The history
of mankind has nothing finer to show us than the perfect knight, Sir Galahad, with his purity, his honour,

his courage, his blameless service of the poor and weak, his stainless reverence for womanhood. Since chivalry disappeared, the world has produced no type of manhood comparable to that which was the glory of the feudalism of the Middle Ages. And yet chivalry had to go, since it was the by-product of a social order which, in the course of centuries, had become the citadel of ignorance, despotism, and oppression. Humanity could not afford to sacrifice the life and happiness of the masses of mankind, in order that a few chosen knights might manifest and enjoy the unsullied privileges of an Arthurian Round Table.

And so the illustrations might be multiplied, all pointing to the conclusion that no evil can be fostered merely because of the by-product of good which may attend it. We do not burn down our cities, because the San Francisco fire gave to the citizens of that community the chance to build a healthier and more beautiful city than would have otherwise been possible. We do not argue against the extinction of disease, because leprosy gave us Father Damien and tuberculosis Doctor Trudeau. We do not plead for the continuance of religious persecution, on the ground that saints and martyrs are the certain result of the sword, the faggot, and the gibbet. And why is not exactly the same thing true about our attitude toward war? What could be more absurd, or more cruel, than to eulogise war and argue for its occasional perpetration, on the ground that it never fails to produce a few heroes and to stir momentarily the noblest passions of national life! Let us admit the truth of all that the most enthusiastic of militarists can say on behalf of the service rendered by international conflict to the cause of individual and social virtue. Let us agree with Aristotle that the highest type of courage is impossible without war — let us endorse the suggestion of Professor Cramb that war does for millions of men what the perils of the Antarctic did for Scott and his four comrades — let us endorse the verdict of Ruskin that no deep feeling, and therefore no great art, has ever been inspired by times of peace! Still, is it not true that these things are by-products, and in themselves not vital enough to outweigh the abominations which comprise the very essence of this hideous business? Look at Europe to-day — its slaughtered men, its weeping women, its homeless children — its wounded, sick, and imprisoned — its devastated fields and ruined cities — its lost faiths, shattered hopes, debased ideals — its new hatreds, lusts, and barbarisms — and who can say that war brings us anything that can compensate for such as these? War is at bottom evil; and, whatever its incidental goods, it must, like other evils, be abolished!

IV

Not yet, however, have we answered the contentions of those who sincerely deplore the prospect of the passing of war and the coming of peace; for it is just these men who will argue, in answer to our questions, that war does bring compensations even for such horrors as are this very day before our face and eyes. Nay, they.even go so far as to reverse the situation, and declare that it is the horrors which are the real incidentals or by-products of war, and it is the strengthening of hearts and stirring of ideals which constitute the essentials. It is just here, on this matter of relative viewpoint, that the militarist and pacifist usually fail to find a common ground for discussion; and just here, therefore, that the latter usually fails to make any impression upon the former. After this advocate of peace has said all that can be said in regard to the abomination of armed conflict, the Bernhardis and the Crambs still support the position that these features of war, while of course regrettable, are comparatively unimportant, and are overshadowed by these other things which are absolutely dependable upon the continuance, at intervals at least, of battles, sieges, and campaigns. This is the attitude, strange as it may seem, even of a man like Prof. William James. "One cannot meet [these considerations]," he says in his essay on *The Moral Equivalent of War*, "by mere counter-insistency on war's expensiveness and horror. The horror makes the thrill; and when the question is of getting the extremest and supremest out of human nature, talk of expense sounds ignominious. The weakness of so much negative criticism is evident. . . . The military party denies neither the bestiality, nor the horror, nor the expense; it only says that these things tell but half the story. It only says that war is *worth* them; that, taking human nature as a whole, its wars are its best protection against its weaker and more cowardly self, and that mankind cannot afford to adopt a peace-economy."

In considering this final point, it is necessary to emphasise at once the apparently irreconcilable dilemma which is always presented by the militarist, as he argues this important point. Always does he present the two extremes of war on the one hand, and of dull, cowardly, materialistic, degenerate peace upon the other. Always does he assume that the virtues inherent in war can be obtained under no other conditions and purchased at no other price, than those provided by the slaughter and devastation of armed conflict. Not even with Aristotle is there any golden mean in this case. It is one thing or the other — either war with its glorified heroes and redeemed nations, or peace with its corruption and decay.

Now we may perhaps be pardoned for saying at this point that this kind of rigid alternative irresistibly reminds us of the familiar Elian essay of Charles Lamb, entitled *A Dissertation upon Roast Pig*. This is the highly amusing story of how a Chinaman came home one day and found to his dismay that his house had been destroyed by fire. While poking round in the smoking ruins of the little building, he chanced to come upon the body of a pig that had been caught in the flames and burned to death. At once he noticed that the roasted flesh gave off an exceedingly fragrant smell. Then, touching the meat with his finger and applying the finger to his mouth, he found that it had a taste which was delicious beyond belief. Devouring the animal with in-

finite satisfaction, he forthwith proceeded to tell the
good news to his neighbours.   Whereupon every man of
them proceeded to put his pig in his house, and then
burn the house to the ground, in order that he too
might enjoy a feast of roast pork.

It is of course unnecessary to point out the ridiculous
side of this story to those who know full well that it is
possible to roast a pig without destroying homes by
fire.   But wherein is it any more absurd for the Chinaman to argue that you must burn your house in order
to obtain a toothsome dinner, than it is for the militarist to argue that you must destroy your civilisation
by the ravaging of fire and sword, in order to obtain the
priceless treasures of martial virtue in individual and
nation?   It is perfectly possible to roast a pig and still
preserve your house from destruction; and in exactly
the same way it is possible to develop every virtue inherent in the mad struggle of international war, and
still preserve the lives of men from slaughter and the
material structure of society from ruin.   Turn to that
very book by Professor Cramb wherein war is described
as an indispensable condition of the development of
those transcendental aspects of life, which defy all
standards of rational expediency.   When Professor
Cramb wants to tell us what he means by these transcendental aspects of life, what does he do?   Does he cite
examples of courage and endurance from the field of
battle?   Does he tell stories of heroic daring and sublime sacrifice in time of war?   Not at all!   On the contrary, he leaves the smoke and flame of battle far be-

hind, takes us away to the wastes of the Antarctic,
and points us to Oates walking out into the storm to
his certain death, and to Captain Scott dying patiently
and bravely in his snow-hut. Where is the war which
was indispensable to the virtue of these men? Wherein
was the period of profound peace, in which they set
forth upon their immortal quest, incompatible with
sacrifice, heroism, and manly love? This whole tale is
a part of the annals of peace, is it not? — and yet it is
this which Professor Cramb cites most naturally as the
illustration of that which war alone can accomplish.

Inconsistency could seem to go no farther, unless it is
in Professor Cramb's further statement of the great
victories that man has achieved, in days gone by, in
pursuit of his ideals. He speaks here of the success
which man has won in his " war against disease, war
against nature, the forest, the sea, the vicissitudes of
season and of climate." War, not against other men,
but against nature and natural evil! War, in time of
peace! War, under conditions of peace! What,
pray, can Professor Cramb mean by pleading for the
everlasting continuance of war with swords and
guns against our fellows, when here is war right to our
hand against things which it is beneficent to overcome and destroy! Peace, by Professor Cramb's
own testimony, is not wholly incompatible with struggle,
and fight, and triumph. Peace, if this be true, is not
necessarily a condition of stagnation, cowardice, dull
content, and easy pleasure. If armed conflict between
international bodies of men has any virtue at all, it is

only because it gives to the human heart a foe to challenge, a goal to achieve, a victory to win. And lo! here do we find that peace hath its foes and goals and victories, no less renowned than war — that peace can foster martial heroism and high idealism as well as war — that everything that war can give can be given equally by peace, and without any of the horrors which make war an intolerable disaster!

It is this idea which William James puts forth so impressively in his essay on *The Moral Equivalent of War*. He points out the foes of disease, national cataclysms, social corruptions, etc., which are waiting to be fought and overcome. He shows us the perilous work at sea, in mines, on steel buildings, which is ever waiting to be done. And he calls upon men to organise themselves to fight these battles of peace, just as now they organise themselves for war against their neighbours. " In the future toward which mankind seems drifting, we must still subject ourselves collectively," he says, " to those severities which answer to our real position upon this only partly hospitable globe. We must make new energies and hardihoods continue the manliness to which the military mind so faithfully clings." And then he illustrates his " idea more concretely," by conceiving " instead of military conscription, a conscription of the whole youthful population to form for a certain number of years a part of the army enlisted against nature. . . . To coal and iron mines, to freight trains, to fishing fleets, to road-build-

ing and trench-making . . . would our youths be
drafted off . . . to get the childishness knocked out of
them, and to come back into society with healthier sym-
pathies and sobered ideas. . . . Such a conscription
. . . would preserve in the midst of a pacific civilisation the manly virtues which the military party is so
afraid of seeing disappear in peace."

v

Here, now, is the full and final answer to the militarist. First, the virtues of war are grossly exaggerated. Secondly, these virtues, whatever they are, are
mere by-products, and as such cannot be regarded as
adequate justification for the continuance of an institution essentially evil. Thirdly, these virtues are not
in themselves dependent upon war, but can be fostered
in peace organised for strife against nature and her
ills. Permanent and universal peace, if not now desirable, *can be made desirable!*

The whole lesson can be summed up in this single
word — that our task is not the perpetuation of war
for this or any other purpose, but the redemption of
peace from ease, sloth, and corruption. *The first condition of such a redemption of peace is the total and
permanent abolition of war!* For so long as war continues to recur at intervals, man will remain convinced
that there is nothing to fight against except his brother;
and so long as peace is only a recurring interval from
strife, man will remain convinced that this is but a time

of repose and idle enjoyment.   Away, therefore, with
war, that worthy peace may come!   Speed the night,
that morn at last may break!

> "It is the Dawn! The Dawn! The nations
> From East to West now hear the cry!
> Though all earth's blood-red generations
> By hate and slaughter climbed thus high,
> Here, on this height, still to aspire,
> One only path remains untrod,
> One path of love and peace climbs higher.
> Make straight that highway for our God." [1]

[1] Alfred Noyes, in *The Wine-Press.*

CHAPTER X

THE DUTY AND OPPORTUNITY OF AMERICA TO-DAY

" It is a beautiful picture in Grecian story that there was at least one spot, the small island of Delos, dedicated to the gods and kept at all times sacred from War. No hostile foot ever pressed this kindly soil, and citizens of all countries met here beneath the ægis of invincible Peace. So let us dedicate our beloved country. . . . The Temple of Honour shall be enclosed by the Temple of Concord, that it may never more be entered through any portal of War; the horn of Abundance shall overflow at its gates; the angel of Religion shall be the guide over its steps of flashing adamant; while within its happy courts, purged of Violence and Wrong, Justice shall rear her serene and majestic front. . . .

" And while seeking these fruitful glories for ourselves, let us strive for their extension to other lands. Let the bugles sound the Truce of God to the whole world forever. Not to one people, but to every people, let the glad tidings go. . . . History dwells with fondness on the reverent homage bestowed by massacring soldiers upon the spot occupied by the sepulchre of the Lord. Vain man! why confine regard to a few feet of sacred mould? The whole earth is the sepulchre of the Lord; nor can any righteous man profane any part thereof."— Charles Sumner, in *The True Grandeur of Nations.*

CHAPTER X

THE crisis now facing Europe is apparent. The probabilities of destruction, blood-letting, exhaustion, reversion, are fast becoming realities before our eyes. What we are not seeing so clearly is the fact that this crisis involves not merely the nations which are directly concerned as belligerents in the conflict, but the neutral countries as well; and first of all, among these, the United States. Not only the destinies of Germany, France, Russia, England, Austria, Italy, are hanging in the balance, but also the destiny of America, even though the Republic continues to hold aloof from actual hostilities and thus does not in any way become involved in the armed struggle of life and death.

I

The occasion of this stupendous crisis for America is of course the amazing discovery that war in its most hideous form can burst upon the world without warning, and sweep down not merely upon those nations which have interests to serve upon the field of battle, but also upon those nations which are least prepared for, and certainly least desirous of, its coming. This has given us, for the first time in our history, a feeling of insecurity which is amounting almost to panic. And

329

this feeling is presenting us with a problem of national policy which is new to our political and social life. Already the problem has crystallised into a definite dilemma. Are we to continue to remain faithful to the pacifist ideals which have made America unique among modern nations; or shall we follow the rest of the world in building up huge armaments and joining questionable political alliances? Are we to continue to rely upon the international policy of "with malice toward none, with charity for all" as the sole protection of the state; or must we, however reluctantly, arm ourselves adequately in preparation for anticipated conflicts? Can we still believe, as we have hitherto believed, that "Salvation shall be (our) walls and bulwarks, and (our) gates Praise," or must we for the first time seek refuge behind the guns of battleships and the walls of fortresses?

II

How these questions are answered, by a large number of American citizens, has been made perfectly plain by the vigorous and widespread agitation in this country, during the last few months, for the indefinite and rapid increase of our armaments. Some of the men who advocate this line of action are unscrupulous politicians and professional soldiers who have personal interests to serve and are therefore not to be trusted. More of these men, however, are scholars, educators, publishers, lawyers, bankers, business men, who are absolutely unselfish, and have no other desire than that of

the sincere and honourable service of the best interests
of the Republic.   The position of these men is easily
stated.

We all of us unite, they say, in deprecating war and
loving peace.   There is nobody in America who would
be guilty of such a crime as that of advocating a policy
which would make the avoidance of war and the maintenance of peace, on the part of our country, more difficult or uncertain.   This present war in Europe, however, has taught us many things which we never knew
before, or perhaps had forgotten or neglected.   And
first of all among these lessons is the fact that we are
still living in a world which is disorganised, undisci-
plined, and to a very large extent barbaric, and therefore a world which is liable to suffer from an outbreak
of war at any time.   After the fate of Belgium and
France in the opening days of the Great War, no
nation can regard itself as any longer safe from hostile
invasion.   The best intentions, the most peaceful policies, the most modern treaties, the firmest reliance upon
righteousness and goodwill, cannot be counted upon to
preserve a country from attack.   The peril is imminent,
for America as for every other people.   Therefore is
it the part of prudence, to say nothing of patriotism,
to prepare the nation for what may at any moment become the inevitable.   As we insure our lives against
accident and death, our houses against fire, our property against burglary, so must we insure our country
against war.   And the only known way of doing this
to-day, is that of building up an army and a navy

which shall be strong enough to repel the attack of any enemy which may undertake to come against us. Therefore must we build more battleships, double our standing army, strengthen our fortifications, perfect our state militia, organise a trained reserve, drill our school-boys and college students. Such activity does not spell militarism, or involve aggression, or overthrow our traditional policy of having the military authorities strictly subordinate to the civil. It simply means a commonsense recognition of the conditions prevailing in the modern world, and a commonsense endeavour to meet these conditions.

III

Without attempting to criticise this position which is being taken to-day by many of our most sincere and enlightened citizens, it may be well to analyse, with some care, the state of mind of which it may be regarded as the reflection.

First of all, there is behind this idea of military preparedness the primitive psychological phenomenon of *fear*. The advocates of great armaments are frankly afraid of the terrible things which might happen in this country if some foreign foe should assail us and find us incapable of defence. Seeing a curious kind of parallel between Belgium, which has for so long been " the cockpit of Europe," is about the size of Maryland, and has some seven millions of inhabitants, and the United States with its geographical remoteness, enormous extent of territory, and one hundred million population, they draw hair-raising pictures of the bombardment of New York by a battle fleet, and the ravaging of our seacoast and interior by an invading army. One of the most eminent scientists in America, for example, declared some months ago in my presence that we might wake up at any moment to find the enemy at our gates, prepared to visit upon us just such indignities, outrages, and injuries as have lately been endured by the unhappy Belgians. Which one of the great nations is thus thirsting for the blood of America, is not said. Which one, so thirsting, is in a position at this moment to undertake the conquest of our country, we are not told. But in answer to our natural inquiry for a bill of specifications, it is triumphantly asserted that such a bill could not have been rendered to Serbia, Belgium, or France, on the first day of July, 1914. The danger, uncertain as it is, is most surely present, and one cannot safely wait until it discloses itself, to make ready to encounter it.

Behind this feeling of fear, there lies, as a second factor in the situation, a deep-rooted distrust of the character and purposes of all the other civilised nations of the world. It is argued, with a good deal of force, that relations beween nations have never been moralised, and that therefore it is folly to rely for security upon pretensions of friendship or pledges of goodwill. The policy of every modern people, like that of every ancient people, is determined by selfish considerations of national aggrandisement and glory. Every nation, whether it confesses it or not, is engaged in the great enterprise of world-empire; and anything which will help on this enterprise, whether moral or immoral, friendly or unfriendly to a neighbouring state, will be done, whenever circumstances are propitious. The present war is an impressive illustration of the ethics of international relationships. To what extent have morality, decency, goodwill, controlled the conduct of any one of the nations involved in this unseemly quarrel? Which one has respected the rights and privileges of its neighbours? Which one has held to its plighted word? Which one has risen to obedience of any higher law than that of necessity, self-preservation, or self-aggrandisement? What a nation wants, it takes — what is in its way, it destroys — what it finds defenceless, it outrages and defies. America may well be cautious about taking its place in a company of international freebooters without being carefully and fully armed. Our nation is one which might well be coveted by every crowned head of the world. South of us are fair dominions, which more than one country of Europe has lusted after, but which we have solemnly sworn to defend against assault. Our world-wide commerce, our possessions in Hawaii and the Philippines, our valuable and strategic property in the Panama Canal, are treasures which must be guarded against spoliation. Treaties are no protection. Friendship may be but the mask of brigandage. To " speak softly and carry a big stick " is the only wise policy in a world wherein the hand of every nation is against that of every other!

In the third place, as a final complication of the situa-

tion, there is what we may call a purely materialistic
conception of the significance of national life.   Our
patriotism here in America, in other words, is as sordid
and unspiritual as our business, our art, or our religion.   This is shown clearly enough in the very language which we use to symbolise our country.   Thus
we speak of our flag, which must never be hauled down
from its proud position " on high "; we talk of our soil,
which must never be profaned by the footsteps of an
invader; we refer to our blood, which must never be
shed by a hostile hand.   America, to nine people out of
ten, is simply a territory which can be over-run and
conquered — a group of cities which can be bombarded
and laid under tribute — a certain amount of trade,
commerce, and natural wealth which can be seized — a
certain number of millions of men, women, and children,
whose bodies can be outraged and destroyed.   To
speak of " the soul of America," as Dr. Stanton Coit
has done in his recent book of that title — a " soul "
which can be corrupted by a depraved spirit, but is impregnable to attacks of sword and spear — is to leave
us mystified and disturbed.   Such language at once
takes us into a realm where can be found, perhaps, the
ideas of God, immortality, and the soul of man, but certainly not the idea of country.   " My country " means
a great stretch of territory reaching from the Atlantic
to the Pacific, and from the Great Lakes to the Gulf
of Mexico.   It means an aggregation of millions of people who live within the borders of this territory.   It
means a vast machinery of government, which has its

main plant in a place called the District of Columbia. It means a group of cities like New York, Chicago, St. Louis, and San Francisco — a group of states like Massachusetts, Ohio, Louisiana, and California. It means stupendous business interests, running all the way from the mining interests of the West to the manufacturing interests of the East. It means a hundred and one things, all of which can be seen, touched, handled, counted — and lost. And this being our conception of country, it naturally follows, does it not, that our love of country means a love of these more or less material things and a determination to preserve them and glorify them at any price? And this means, in turn, that true love of country must find its inevitable expression in a clamorous demand for armaments, that territory, people, government, and wealth may not fall into the hands of the enemy. We must have the weapons of the flesh, in other words, to protect the things of the flesh. So long as a country means to us so much soil and not so much soul, so many people and not so many ideas, so much wealth and not so much holy spirit, then indeed must we rely not upon God, but upon chariots and horsemen — and this for the very good reason pointed out by Isaiah, that chariots are " many " and horsemen are " strong "!

IV

In these three things which have just been enumerated — fear of the calamitous uncertainties of the future, distrust of the faith and honour of other peo-

ples, and a materialistic conception of the meaning of
America and its place in the family of nations — do
we find what I have called the state of mind of those who
believe that we should forthwith proceed to arm ourselves to the limit of endurance, in view of the hazard
of war now forced upon our attention by events across
the seas. Without attempting to submit this state of
mind to any critical examination, let us consider at once
another and very different state of mind in which certain
people in this country are at this moment endeavouring
to meet the moral crisis of the hour. This state of
mind, as will be seen, presents factors which in each
and every case are diametrically opposite to those involved in the first and more belligerent state of mind.

In the first place, we find that this second group of
people refuse to cherish any fears as to the dangers
which threaten this country to-day or may threaten it
in the future. They listen to the hideous stories of
captured cities, invaded shores and slaughtered citizens, with indifference, amusement, or out-and-out contempt. Looking at the matter from no higher standpoint than that of the military problem involved, they
assert with assurance that the invasion of a country,
removed from any hostile base of operations by three
thousand and more miles of open and tempestuous sea,
is as impossible a feat of arms, under modern conditions of warfare, as would be the conquest of a country stretching three thousand miles east and west
and fifteen hundred miles north and south, and in-
habited by a population of one hundred million. These

people find their position laid down with perfect precision by Prof. Roland G. Usher, in his much-read book on *Pan-Germanism*. " The United States," he says, in the tenth chapter, " is beyond question invulnerable to the assaults of foreign fleets and armies. It has been pointed out that the Japanese might successfully land an army upon the Pacific coast, or the Germans land an army in New York or Boston, practically without opposition. *Sed cui bono?* The strategical and geographical conditions of the country on either coast are such that a foreign army would occupy the ground it stood on, and no more. The British discovered in the Revolutionary War that the occupation of New York, Boston, and Philadelphia put them no nearer the military possession of the continent than they were before, and that marching through provinces was not subduing them. However seriously the capture of New York might cripple our commercial and railway interests, the difficulty, even at its worst, could be easily overcome by shifting the centre of business for the time being to Chicago, and the possession of New York would certainly not permit a foreign army to conquer the country, even if it were possible for any nation to maintain an army so far from its real base of supplies in Europe. The possibility of invasion is made of no consequence by the simple fact that no foreign nation possesses any inducement for attempting so eminently hazardous an enterprise." Such a statement of the actual facts of the situation is like a breath of fresh air, blowing into the fever-laden atmosphere of a plague-house. It is

like the light of morning breaking upon the spectre-
haunted shadows of the night.   There is no more reason,
as a matter of fact, to be afraid of a successful or even
attempted invasion of our country than there is to fear
an invasion of our planet from flaming Mars.   In the
one case as in the other, " strategical and geographical
conditions " are our all-sufficient safeguard against attack.

But these people, of whom we are now speaking, do
not stop here.   They not only decline to give way
to fears regarding the threatened invasion of America
from abroad, but they decline also to give way to unworthy suspicions regarding the intentions and purposes of other nations.   They recognise, to be sure,
that the history of international relationships is a continued story of falsehoods, deceits, betrayals, broken
pledges, and violated treaties.   They agree that the
diplomatic record of this present conflict is one long
series of outrages, from Germany's indefensible invasion of Belgium in violation of the treaty of neutrality, to England's equally indefensible blockade of Germany's shores in violation of the Declaration of Paris.
Well may one seem to be justified in asking to-day,
What nation of the earth can be trusted to act toward
other nations as one gentleman would act toward other
gentlemen?   But to this plea the answer is inevitable,
that the dishonour of one nation is only the fruit which
has been grown by a universal system of dishonour.
Nations are treated by one another, in other words,
just exactly as they deserve to be treated.   They reap

only what they have long since sown. With what measure they have meted, it is measured unto them. Diplomacy has long been an evil plot, but it is a plot in which all the nations of the world are conspirators together. What is needed to untangle the Gordian knot of treason, and thus to bring honour among nations as among gentlemen, is only the honourable example of one great power. And it is just this honourable example that America has given to the world, in the few isolated cases in which she has been dragged into the game of international diplomacy. With the result that never yet has any country played her false! In other words, the sure way of maintaining relations of friendship and honour with other nations, is not to suspect them and deceive them, to try to outwit them and always arm to the teeth against them. On the contrary, the only sure way is to trust them, play them fair, and approach them with hands not clenched and armed in hate, but open in confidence and affection. " The only way to have a friend," says Emerson in his essay on *Friendship*, " is to be one "— an affirmation which is as true of nations as it is of individuals! If we distrust the nations, they will justify that distrust by intrigue and betrayal. If we act as though we expected them to attack us at any moment, they will justify that expectation by attacking us, lest we shall attack them first. Russia distrusted Germany in July, 1914, and mobilised her army as though she expected Germany to attack her — and Germany did attack her! On the other hand, Germany distrusted France at the same moment, and invaded Belgium as though she expected France to move against her — and France did move against her! Suspicion begets suspicion, attack precipitates attack, preparation for war hastens war. The only road to friendship is friendship. The only way to protect one nation from attack is to have confidence that no other nation will assail her without cause. The only way to secure peace is to walk steadfastly in the ways of peace. Let this Republic, said Carl Schurz, " stand as the gentleman *par excellence* among nations — a gentleman scorning the rôle of swashbuckler whose hip-pockets bulge with loaded six-shooters and who flashes big diamonds on his fingers and shirt-front; a gentleman modest in the consciousness of strength, and carrying justice, forbearance and conciliation on his tongue and benevolence in his hand, rather than a chip on his shoulder "— and lo! she " shall be far from terror, for it shall not come nigh (her)"!

More important, however, than such considerations as these is the conception of nationality which constitutes the distinctive state of mind of those who are opposed to all agitation for armaments at this or any other time. To such persons, a nation appears not as a stretch of territory, or a group of people, or a mass of wealth — not at all as a " great power," in the political sense of that term — but simply and solely as an idea, or group of ideas. Greece means not a peninsula, but an idea of beauty which is still the delight and despair of men. Rome means not a city nor an empire, but an idea of law which has slowly moulded our

western world from chaos into order. Englartd means
not an island, but an idea of liberty — Germany not a
political group of Teutonic states, but an idea of culture — and so on with all the peoples of the earth that
have a life which is in any sense distinctly national.

What is true now, of such countries as these, is true
to an altogether remarkable degree of America. Who
thinks, when this magic word is mentioned, of a particular geographical locality, a particular breed of
men, or even of a particular kind of government?
Immediately are we transported into the realm of ideas,
and there brought face to face with certain great conceptions of the spirit. "Four score and seven years
ago," said Lincoln at Gettysburg, "our fathers brought
forth upon this continent a new nation conceived in liberty and dedicated to the proposition that all men are
created equal." In such a declaration as this, do we
find a definition of what America really means. Not in
the things of the flesh, but in the things of the spirit did
we have our origin; not in population or wealth, but in
ideas do we have our empire; not in the conquest of
territory, but in the winning of souls do we find our
destiny! "America," says Dr. David Starr Jordan,
"stands, has always stood, for two ideals from which
she cannot escape, for they are fundamental in her
origin and her growth."

First of all is the idea of internationalism or brother-
hood. America's first citizens were colonists from
England, and her last have just this day landed at
Ellis Island from the shores of Europe, Asia, and Aus-

tralia. Thirteen millions of Americans at this moment are foreign born of foreign parents; eighteen millions more are native born of foreign parents; and the rest, who boast of being true Americans, must all trace back their parentage of a few generations ago to some country far across the seas. In the larger sense of the word, that is, we are all of us immigrants from some Fatherland to this, which has been well-called " the beloved Brotherland." America is the gathering place of all the tribes of earth — the melting-pot, as Zangwill has put it, into which the ingredients of every race, religion and nationality have been freely poured. And out of it has come not a new nation, but a new idea — the idea of brotherhood. Here all national antipathies, hereditary hatreds, race prejudices disappear, as though bred out of the stock by some miracle of intercrossing. Englishman lives side by side with German, Catholic with Protestant, Gentile with Jew. At the very moment when England, Germany, France, Russia and Austria are fighting one another to the death, their children in this land are living, working and playing together without enmity or friction. The average American is a cosmopolitan — a true human if there ever was one. "This is the land where all hate dies," said a certain man quoted by Dr. Jordan in his book on *America's Conquest of Europe*, "My father was a German, my mother French. What do I care for all that? I am an American. The old hatreds and rivalries are nothing to me." It is true, of course, that America has not always been true to this idea of brotherhood. Every one of her foreign wars has been an infidelity, and all preparation for such wars a serious lapse. But, on the whole, this great idea has never been lost sight of — a wonderful reality in the present and a prophecy of mighty promise for the future.

If the first ideal of American life is international brotherhood, the second, of course, is none other than democracy — that idea which finds its noblest expression in Lincoln's description of a government which is " of the people, for the people, and by the people." Here is the land where social distinctions of every kind are definitely eliminated, where nothing counts but simple manhood and womanhood — the strong hand, the valiant heart, the seeing soul. Democracy had its beginning here on the frontier, where every man fought and hewed his way to independence by the sweat of his own brow and the cunning of his own mind. " These pioneers," said John Hay, " looked on no one as their superiors, and on none as their inferiors. They knew no want they could not satisfy themselves." And it is just this pioneer idea which has now been carried over into every department of American life. Equality of economic opportunity, equality before the law, equality in access to the land, to education, to legislation — here is the idea of democracy, now working itself out into the conception of a state which is an organisation of " mutual adjustment for collective benefit." It is needless to point out how often America has failed to fulfil her own ideal of democracy. It is needless to specify the menaces to American democ-

racy which are involved in the social and industrial
developments of our own day and generation. But
even in the darkest days of slavery, it was not forgotten that " all men are created free and equal." And
now when social snobbery, industrial tyranny and law-
less wealth are apparently all-powerful, the conscience
of the nation remains as sound and whole as ever. The
battle for democracy has in many ways just begun —
but that it has gone far enough to indicate that it is to
be fought through to a successful finish, however long
delayed, is apparent.

In these two great ideas of brotherhood and democracy, is the essence of American life. This is what
America means to-day, as Greece yesterday meant
beauty and Rome law. And just here in this spiritual
idea of nationality, do we find the supreme and unanswerable vindication of the men who would save America at this time from militarism and the huge armaments which militarism would build. Of course, if you
have no higher conception of America than a stretch of
land, comprising forty-eight states, three-and-a-half
million square miles of territory, one hundred millions
of inhabitants, and no higher conception of patriotism
than a frenzied passion to make the inhabitants of this
particular political division of the earth's surface the
dominant people of the world, then you had better
build as many dreadnaughts and train as many soldiers as you can, for these weapons can alone avail you
anything in this realm of sheer materialism. But if
you look upon America as a great ideal of the spirit,

independent of territory and population and wealth, then all such things as armies and navies become matters of supreme indifference. For the spirit is impregnable to all the attacks that the hand of man can bring against it. What if the soldiers of another nation should occupy our territory, seize our ports, capture our cities, occupy our strongholds, levy tribute upon our citizens? What if Germany came here to-day as she came to Belgium yesterday! Would she not find it as impossible to conquer "the soul of America" as she has already found it impossible to conquer the soul of Belgium? No conqueror that ever lived could destroy the sense of brotherhood that is at the heart of our American life; no sword that was ever forged could smite the love of democracy which is the impulse of our civilisation. A free people would still be free, even though in chains — and a valiant spirit still survive, even the hour of death. Nay, we will not only not be conquered, but we will ourselves be conquerors in this higher realm of the spirit. Let our enemies come against us with sword and shield and trumpet, and we will meet them with our faith in brotherhood and democracy. And, behold, in the very process of this conquest, they will themselves be conquered! America will conquer the thousands who come in arms against her, as she has already conquered the millions who have sought her shores in peace!

To all such attacks as these, the soul of America is impregnable. But there is another kind of attack, which may well be feared by all those who love this

nation not for what she has, but for what she is. I
refer to the attack not upon her soil but upon her soul
— an attack which is now being conducted all along
the line by those who, for the reasons which I have described, would have America abandon her priceless
ideals of brotherhood and democracy, and follow the
melancholy example of the great empires of history.
Why worry about the enemies who may be lying in
wait against our country on some far horizon of the
sea, when enemies much more serious are lying in wait
against her right here within her borders? Why worry
about the armies and dreadnaughts that may be marshalled against her territory in Germany or Japan,
when lies and deceits are even now being marshalled
against her soul in Washington and on Governor's
Island? Our real foes are of our own household —
those men who, from motives however worthy, would
lead America out of the trodden paths of fraternity
and peace, into the treacherous ways of blood and iron.
Once let the policy of armaments get fastened upon
this Republic, and our mission as a nation is at an end.
No longer shall we be a people of ideas. On the contrary, we shall be a people of wealth, power, dominion,
glory — a people who measure their greatness by the
territory they occupy or the trade they own, and not
by the ideals of the spirit which they serve. In becoming an empire we shall lose that brotherhood which has
long been the hope of a disordered world. In becoming
a " great power " we shall sacrifice that democracy
which long has been the open door of opportunity to

mankind. In gaining the whole world, we shall lose
our own soul — die as Athens died, Rome died, Spain
died! Here is a conquest to be feared in very earnest
— a conquest beside which the bombardment of cities
and the ravaging of territory are as nothing. If I had
to choose between having America's soil over-run from
end to end by the triumphant legions of Von Hinden-
burg, and having her soil untouched by the foot of the
invader, but her soul at the same time surrendered to
the gospel of Treitschke and Bernhardi, I would unhesitatingly choose the former fate. For nothing is
lost, if the soul is safe; and nothing is safe, if the soul
is lost. And it is just because our militarists, on the
specious plea of saving our shores from invasion, are
doing nothing more nor less than opening the soul of
America to a peril of conquest of this kind, that, in
spite of their sincerity, they are to be so greatly feared.

v

To keep America faithful to her ideals — to help
her at this crisis of temptation, to preserve her soul
inviolate — this is the highest duty of the present hour.
And this duty has a purpose which far transcends the
selfish interests of the American people themselves.
For why is it the duty of America to preserve her
ideals, if not that she may transmit these ideals to the
world? "America," said the great Belgian statesman,
Henri LaFontaine, in an address at Baltimore in 1911,
"has to liberate Europe from its burdens, its prejudices, its hatreds. It is your duty, it is your highest

duty, to reconcile outside your borders the people you
have reconciled within your borders. For indeed the
American people . . . is the elect people which can
alone transform all of the peoples of the earth into a
family of nations, a brotherhood of men."

In such a conception as this do we see what is the
duty of America — to " conquer Europe," as President
Jordan has put it, not by force of arms, but by force
of ideas! And when was there such an opportunity to
fulfil this duty as at this hour of world agony? When
did America's ideas of brotherhood and democracy
ever appear more lovely than they do to-day? And
when will the people of the earth be more ready to accept them than at the moment when they lay down their
blood-stained arms and seek the ways of peace? It
seems as though this war were a kind of terrible purg-
ing of the ancient world, in preparation for the coming of the modern world. And yet there are those who
would fling away this God-given opportunity for fear
that some material disaster may come upon this nation! Not thus, we may be sure, will America be destroyed. Let her put her trust not in arms, but in the
ideals which are the peculiar possession of her people,
and she will live forever, like " the tree of life " whose
" leaves are for the healing of the nations." But let
her abandon those ideals, and seek security not in love
but in power, and verily her days, like the days of
every empire, will be numbered.

" How long, Good Angel, O how long? " asks the
poet, Sidney Lanier, in his *Centennial Cantata*. How

long shall beloved America endure? List how the
Angel speaks!

> "Long as thine Art shall love true love,
> Long as thy Science truth shall know,
> Long as thine Eagle harms no Dove,
> Long as thy Law by law shall grow,
> Long as thy God is God above,
> Thy brother every man below,
> So long, dear land of all my love,
> Thy name shall shine, thy fame shall grow."

APPENDIX

I

THE one supreme text book of non-resistance is the *Bible*. In scattered narratives in *Genesis, Samuel, Kings,* in the prophecies of Isaiah, Jeremiah, and Micah, in the four *Gospels,* the Pauline *Epistles,* and certain of the Catholic *Epistles,* are to be found a rich treasury of non-resistance ideas and ideals.

Other so-called sacred literatures are likewise to be noted, especially those of Tao-ism and Buddhism. A useful collection of important passages can be found in Moncure D. Conway's *Sacred Anthology*.

To these ancient religious writings must be added the literature associated with Bahaism. Few nobler utterances on peace have been produced in any age than those which may be found in the *Tablets* of Baha o'llah and Abdul Baha.

II

Certain of the more important books and essays bearing on the subject of non-resistance, or the more radical ideas of peace, are as follows:

Angell, Norman — *America and the New World State.*
Angell, Norman — *Arms and Industry.*
Angell, Norman — *The Great Illusion.*

Anonymous — *How Diplomats Make War.*

Babson, R. W.— *The Future of World Peace.*

Ballou, Adin — *Christian Non-Resistance.*

Brailsford, H. N.— *The War of Steel and Gold.*

Burritt, Elihu — *Thoughts and Things at Home and Abroad.*

Buxton, C. R., et al.— *Towards a Lasting Settlement.*

Child, Lydia Maria — *Letters.*

Conway, Moncure D.— *Essays and Addresses.*

Crane, Frank — *War and World Government.*

Crile, George W.— *A Mechanistic View of War and Peace.*

Crosby, Ernest — *Garrison the Non-Resistant.*

Darrow, Clarence — *Non-Resistance.*

Emerson, Ralph Waldo — *Lecture on War.*

Erasmus — *The Plea of Reason, Religion, and Humanity Against War.*

Fiske, John — *The Destiny of Man.*

Fox, George — *Journals.*

Garrison, William Lloyd — *Life*, by his children.

Gulick, S. L.— *The Fight for Peace.*

Hobson, J. A.— *Towards International Government.*

Howe, Frederic C.— *Why War?*

Hull, William I.— *Preparedness.*

Hunter, Robert — *Violence and the Labour Movement.*

James, William — *The Moral Equivalent of War.*

Jefferson, Charles E.— *Christianity and International Peace.*

Jordan, David Starr — *America's Conquest of Europe.*

Jordan, David Starr — *The Human Harvest.*

Jordan, David Starr — *War's Aftermath.*

Kant, Immanuel — *Eternal Peace.*

Lynch, Frederick — *The Last War.*

Lynch, Frederick — *The Peace Problem.*

Lynch, Frederick— *Through Europe on the Eve of War.*

MacKaye, Percy — *A Substitute for War.*

Marshall, H. R.— *War and the Ideal of Peace.*

Mitchell, P. C.— *Evolution and the War.*

Nasmyth, G. W.— *Social Progress and the Darwinian Theory.*

Perris, G. W.— *War and Peace.*

Rolland, Romain — *Above the Battle.*

Ruskin, John — *War.*

Russell, Bertrand — *Justice in War Time.*

Spencer, Herbert — *Principles of Sociology.*

Sumner, Charles — *The True Grandeur of Nations.*

Tolstoi, Leo — *Bethink Yourselves!*

Tolstoi, Leo — *Confessions.*

Tolstoi, Leo — *My Religion.*

Walling, William E.— *Socialists and the War.*

Wilson, William E.— *Christ and War.*

III

In recent years a remarkable series of imaginative works on the subject of non-resistance have been produced. Some of these are as follows:

Brownell, Atherton — *The Unseen Empire.*

Copley, Frank — *The Impeachment of President Israels.*

Crosby, Ernest — *Swords and Ploughshares.*

Dix, Beulah Marie — *Moloch.*

Galsworthy, John — *The Mob.*

Kennedy, Charles Rann — *The Terrible Meek.*

Newton, W. D.— *War.*

Noyes, Alfred — *A Belgian Christmas Eve.*

Noyes, Alfred — *Rada* (the above in its original form).

Noyes, Alfred — *The Wine-Press.*

Trask, Katrina — *In the Vanguard.*

Von Ende, Amelia — *The Wages of War.*

Wentworth, Marion C.— *War Brides.*

Zangwill, Israel — *The War God.*

INDEX

A

Abdul Baha, 247, 248, 351
Acts, quoted, 177
Adams, John Quincy, 102, 253;
 letter to Pres. Monroe on
 preparedness, 102
Adams, Samuel, 133
Adler, Felix, 316; quoted, 315
Agamemnon, 115
Ahaz, 107, 156, 214
Albert, King, 134
Alexander VI, Pope, 61, 214
Alexander the Great, 20, 107
Alexandria, library of, burned,
 280
Alfred, King, 190
Alliances, relation to problem
 of security, 14
Allies, the, 289
America (United States), 49,
 216, 219, 246, 254, 265, 287,
 290, 291, 292, 329, 331, 334;
 unprotected boundary line
 between, and Canada, 253;
 true defence of, 290, 346;
 and patriotism, 292; duty
 and opportunity of, to-day,
 327–350; crisis facing, 329;
 lessons taught to, by Great
 War, 331; Belgium con-
 trasted with, 332; and preparedness, 332–342; im-
 pregnable to attack, 338;
 two ideals of, internationalism, 342, and democracy,
 344; real foes of, inside instead of outside, 347; destiny of, 348; conquest of
 Europe by, 349; "How
 long, Good Angel, O, how
 long," 350

Anarchy, the logic of force, 54
Ancien Régime, 274
Angell, Norman, 11; quoted,
 105.
Antediluvian monsters, extinc-
 tion of, 75
Anthony, Susan B., 215
Anti-slavery struggle, 133, 203,
 288
Antoninus Pius, 57
Antwerp, 104
Armenians, persecutions of,
 245
Aristotle, 301, 310, 319; de-
 fence of war by, 301-303
Arnold, Sir Edwin, quoted,
 153 (note)
Arnold, Matthew, quoted, 146
Asquith, Mr., 267
Assyria, 99, 103; war against
 Ahaz, 158
Athenian democracy, death of,
 through war, 315
Athens, 109, 255, 281; after
 Persian Wars, 109
Aurelius, Marcus, 10, 60, 62,
 273; character of, 56; work
 of, as emperor, 56; wars
 of, 57; persecution of
 Christians by, 58; explana-
 tion of, 59; illustration of
 dangers involved in use of
 force, 61
Australia, 91, 287, 343; part of,
 in Great War, 91
Austria, 63, 100, 267, 286, 329

B

Bab, the, 247
Babylonia, 103
Bach, 108